THE INNOVATOR'S COMPASS

Make Innovation Measurable with ROI²

Yann Rousselot-Pailley

The Innovator's Compass: Make Innovation Measurable with ROI²

First edition, 2026.

Published by RPA
30 N Gould St Ste N, Sheridan, WY 82801, United States
https://rpa.group
ISBN: 979-8-9963941-1-1

In memory of Virginie, and the wonder of her unconditional love

Table of Contents

Introduction: The St. Lawrence Equation

A good skipper is just a bad skipper who survived.

The first thing you notice is the cold. Not the polite autumn chill of a city park, but the deep, muscular cold that rises off a river two kilometres wide—a cold that smells of iron and salt and the memory of glaciers. Standing at the edge of the St. Lawrence in October, you feel it in your sternum before your mind catches up, a primal reminder that nature does not negotiate, that you are looking at something genuinely enormous.

On the far bank, the Laurentian escarpment catches the last light, its rock face the rust-orange of old iron. Between you and that far shore, the river does not simply flow—it moves in layers, old water and new water pressing against each other, beluga pods surfacing and disappearing in the grey chop, cargo ships sitting so low in the water that they seem to be part of the river itself. A vessel the length of a city block passes in near silence; a kilometre away, it looks manageable. Right here, at the railing of the ferry terminal, the hull is a wall of painted steel that makes you revise every sense of scale you thought you possessed.

I first came to know this river as a commuter. But that day was different. I wasn't behind the wheel of a car; I was hundreds of nautical miles from Montreal, Canada, somewhere in the middle of this giant river, aboard a sailboat. I was a student of sailing—a trainee earning my place on the water, one seasick lesson at a time.

My instructor was adamant that essential knowledge was key to becoming a good skipper, including knowing how to calculate my position without a GPS. He had me inside the cabin of the training sailboat, battling seasickness and struggling to keep a paper chart still. He had me using a compass, a parallel ruler, and a divider. I painstakingly drew lines from landmarks I could glimpse through the porthole—a lighthouse, a buoy, the edge of a headland. Each line required corrections for magnetic variation and the relentless drift of the current. When enough lines intersected, they formed a small triangle, and within that triangle, supposedly, was our position. It was a fragile geometry, my fate seemingly dependent on the neatness of my pencil marks, which inevitably smeared every time the boat lurched. My instructor watched from the companionway, arms folded, with the patient disgust of a man who had done this calculation a thousand times in conditions I could not imagine. He did not help. That was the point. By the time I finished, the ship had already drifted. The river, it seemed, had little respect for my careful drawings.

This entire ritual, an initiation into the ancient art of seamanship, felt anachronistic and imprecise. It made me wish I were anywhere but in that cabin. Yet, despite its inefficiency, there was a profound comfort in knowing that I could do it. That fundamental knowledge, though rarely needed, is tucked away in my back pocket like a trusted insurance policy. It's a reassurance, a quiet confidence that if all sophisticated technology were to fail—if screens went dark, signals vanished, and the world plunged into digital silence—I wouldn't be entirely lost. I would still possess the primal skill, the understanding of the stars and the sea, to find my way home.

For people living in Montreal, the St. Lawrence River is integral to their lives. Most of them will cross the river daily, not by boat but on one of the bridges. From one of those bridges, commuters can observe the vessels transiting from the Atlantic Ocean to the Great Lakes on the St. Lawrence Seaway. The Seaway Management Corporation requires licensed river pilots to navigate the Seaway. These professionals carry decades of invisible data in their heads: where the November ice forms first, which currents run counter to the wind, the precise depth where a keel will catch gravel, and the best way to pass a specific lock. None of this is written in a manual. It lives almost entirely in their memory.

I watched a river pilot board a container ship one November morning from the deck of a tugboat. He climbed the rope ladder as if gravity were optional, carrying nothing visible—no charts, no instruments, no briefcase. Everything he needed was in his head: not just his own decades of crossings, but the accumulated memory of a Corporation that has been navigating this river since the seventeenth century—transmitted from pilot to pilot across generations, each one inheriting what the previous had learned, tested, and corrected. He carried more data than any dashboard I have ever built.

Innovation, I had been arguing for most of my professional life, works exactly this way. Not like a pipeline, where you push things in one end and products fall out the other, but like a river estuary—layered, tidal, alive with invisible currents, and absolutely dependent on the accumulated knowledge of those who have navigated it before. The tragedy is that most organizations treat their innovation history the way a casual tourist treats the St. Lawrence: they admire the surface, take a photograph, and move on. They do not know about the pilots. They do not know what the pilots know.

This book is about that knowing—the memory a pilot carries in his head, and that most organizations throw away the day the person who held it retires. Its argument fits in a single line: an organization can measure its innovation only to the degree that it remembers it. Everything that follows is built to make that possible.

For thirty years, I was that intermediary, not on a river, but in R&D departments, innovation teams, and boardrooms across two continents. My most useful instrument was never a framework or a diagnostic tool. It was time spent after work with the people who actually knew how the system functioned—the engineers who had found workarounds that their managers had no idea existed, the technicians who had solved problems that the official process said were unsolvable, the researchers who had quietly abandoned a compound that a different team was about to spend months rediscovering. They spoke openly because I was not their boss. I listened because I understood that what they were telling me—off the record, with the particular candour of people who have stopped performing—was the real innovation portfolio of their organization. Not the one in the dashboard. The one that actually existed.

I used to tell my team that those after-work conversations gave me more usable intelligence than all the structured interviews, workshops, and formal consultations combined. The knowledge was always there. What was missing was a trusted channel through which it could travel without political cost.

I cannot be everywhere. Neither can you. But this is precisely what a well-designed AI system, embedded in the fabric of an organization's daily work, can now do at scale.

Innovation methodologies suffer from the same illusion as my early navigation rituals. Generative AI and the economic shift in the world order are drastically changing how innovation projects are born, grow, die, or are considered successful.

Conference rooms adorned with sticky notes, towers built from plastic blocks, large posters of business canvases, and design-thinking chants echoing through workshop halls—these rituals feel good. They give executives the comforting sense that "innovation is happening." But much like my seasick calculations on the St. Lawrence, they are no longer enough to move the boat.

The tide of real-world challenges is stronger than any ritual. And when economic crises hit, the truth becomes starkly clear: these rituals, often presented as preparation for the future, didn't build true resilience. The moment conditions worsen, they are unmasked for what they truly are—reassuring theatre without real impact—and are quickly reclassified as unnecessary overhead, easy to cut when survival is at stake.

The performance has a name. Innovation Theatre is what an organization stages when it must show innovation in progress but cannot show what that innovation is worth: the ritual without the instrument. Eric Ries gave its scoreboard a name of its own—vanity metrics, the numbers that rise reassuringly whether or not anything of value is being built. I will use his term throughout this book, because nobody has coined a better one since. But it is worth saying now what the rest of these pages will demonstrate: nobody stages this theatre out of stupidity. Organizations perform because the honest alternative—measuring what innovation actually builds—has been, until very recently, out of reach. When the real number cannot be computed, an impressive one is staged in its place. The play runs as long as the audit is impossible.

We saw it in 2008, when innovation labs were shuttered the moment the financial crisis hit, and again in 2020, when the pandemic forced organizations to cut what they suddenly called "non-essential." The structures built to prepare for disruption became its first casualties.

Innovation isn't just about ideation management software, methods, or frameworks. Innovation management is an economic discipline; it relies on data and, as such, must have measurable outcomes. For a long time, practitioners believed innovation was not measurable—because it is erratic and alive, influenced not only by fundamentals but also by moods, expectations, and stories. But the stock market is the same, and we still measure it.

This book is an argument for organizational memory as the precondition of measurable innovation. Not memory as nostalgia, not memory as archive—but memory as the living infrastructure that allows an organization to know what it has tried, what it has learned, and what it is genuinely capable of doing next. Academics have given it many names—absorptive capacity, the organizational retention bin. I call it the Compass.

What follows is the argument for why that matters and the framework for addressing it. We will move through three territories: what we have been measuring wrong (Part I: The Wrong Map), what we should be measuring instead (Part II: The Missing Species), and how to build the instruments to do it (Part III: The Pilot's Knowledge). By the end, the navigator in the room will be you.

I won't hand you the entire map right now; that would spoil the voyage. But I can promise you this: by the end of this book, you'll carry a new compass that won't make you immune to storms but will give you the courage to sail through them.

The river is still there. The pilots still cross. But every morning, somewhere in a boardroom not far from this railing, an executive is being shown an innovation dashboard that has forgotten everything the organization ever tried. The numbers look confident. The dashboards glow green. But the pilots have left the building, and the storm is just arriving. To survive it, we must first understand the map that has been leading us into the rocks for fifty years.

A compass does not tell you where to go. It tells you where you are. And knowing where you are, honestly and precisely, is the rarest skill in the whole field of innovation management.

PART I — THE WRONG MAP

In the winter of 1714, the British Parliament did something unprecedented. It offered a prize of twenty thousand pounds—the equivalent of several million dollars today—to anyone who could solve what navigators called the Longitude Problem.

Ships were crossing oceans with increasing frequency. They could calculate their latitude with reasonable precision by measuring the angle of the sun. But longitude—their east-west position—remained a mystery. Without it, captains knew how far north or south they were, but not where they were in the world.

The scientific establishment of the time was certain that the answer lay in astronomy. They would map the stars with enough precision to use the sky as a clock. Isaac Newton agreed. Edmond Halley agreed. The greatest minds of the age looked upward.

John Harrison looked at his workbench.

Harrison was a carpenter from Lincolnshire with no formal scientific training. He had spent years building wooden clocks of extraordinary precision—clocks that used no oil, required no lubrication, and were barely affected by changes in humidity or temperature. He understood something the astronomers did not: the Longitude Problem was not a problem of observation. It was a problem of time. If you knew exactly what time it was in London while you were at sea, and you compared that to the local time measured by the sun, the difference told you your longitude precisely. You needed a clock accurate enough to survive a sea voyage.

The challenge was that metal expands and contracts with temperature. A clock that kept perfect time in a London workshop would run fast in the tropics and slow in the North Atlantic. This simple physics defeated every existing clock.

Harrison's solution was counterintuitive. Instead of fighting the expansion of metal, he layered different metals—brass and steel—whose thermal expansion rates offset each other. When heat made one metal expand and push the clock mechanism one way, the other metal expanded at a different rate and compensated. The errors cancelled each other out. The result was a clock that kept nearly perfect time across temperature ranges that would have destroyed any single-metal chronograph.

He called his fourth prototype H4. It was the size of a large pocket watch. On a voyage to Jamaica in 1761, it lost less than five seconds over eighty-one days at sea. It was accurate enough to locate a ship's position to within half a mile after a transatlantic crossing.

The longitude problem, which had defeated the greatest scientific minds of Europe for a century, was solved not by better observation of the universe. It was solved by understanding that a single material cannot compensate for its own distortions—and that only a composition of different elements, each correcting the other's error, produces reliable measurement in an unstable environment.

We have been trying to measure innovation with instruments made of a single metal.

Chapter 1: The Post-it Illusion

The dashboard on the wall glowed green. Every metric pointed upward. The Chief Innovation Officer smiled at the quarterly review, confident the numbers told a story of progress. Three months later, a competitor launched the product her team had been discussing for two years. The dashboard had never flickered.

That green dashboard is the most dangerous artifact in modern business. It creates a comforting illusion of forward motion while the organization drifts sideways. And it is far more common than anyone admits.

Every organization claims innovation is essential.
Every strategic plan references it.
Every leadership team insists on it.

Yet very few organizations can answer a simple question:

"What value did innovation create last year?"

Most respond with activities:

- number of workshops
- number of ideas submitted
- number of prototypes
- number of digital experiments

Some point proudly to successful products or revenue spikes. But almost no one provides a coherent, multi-dimensional answer.

Innovation is treated as both sacred and mysterious—a necessary engine for growth, but one that resists traditional measurement.

The truth is, innovation is not impossible to measure.
The truth is that **we have been measuring the wrong things.**

What is innovation?

Innovation is the result of the introduction of a novelty in an economic system that produces or extracts a new value that the system didn't generate before.

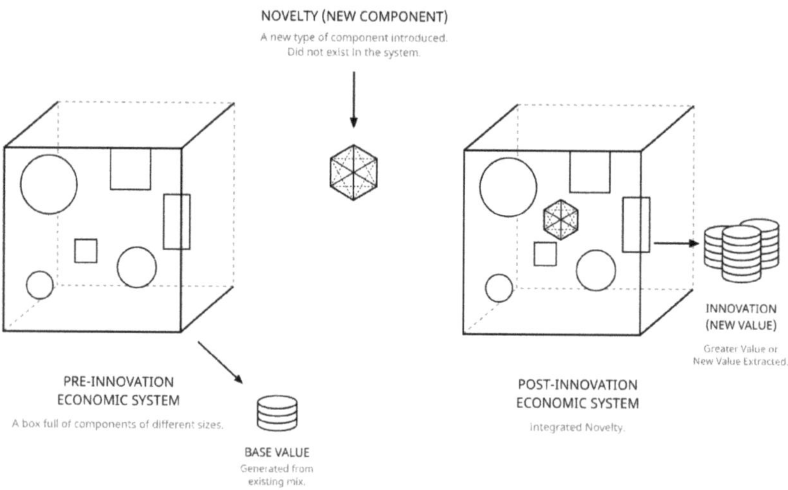

According to the economist Joseph Schumpeter, it is often associated with the destruction of existing elements of the economic system. It is called creative destruction, a phenomenon we have often observed since then.

Many companies track innovation using simple metrics such as the number of patents filed or the amount of money invested in research and development (R&D). While these metrics might seem like straightforward indicators of innovative activity, they often create a misleading picture. A high patent count doesn't necessarily equate to market-disrupting products or services, nor does it guarantee that these patents will ever be commercialized.

Similarly, a hefty R&D budget can be misspent on projects that lack clear strategic alignment or fail to address genuine customer needs. The perception of innovation, built upon these superficial indicators, quickly crumbles when one examines the actual impact on revenue, market share, or customer satisfaction.

This disconnect between perceived and actual innovations underscores the critical need for more nuance and outcome-oriented approaches to measuring creativity and progress within an organization.

A word before the cases that follow: they are illustrations, not proof. Each is the kind of account an industry tells about itself once the outcome is already known—useful for naming a pattern, not for establishing it.

- **Google X.** Insiders admitted that breakthroughs didn't come from sticky-note storms but from small engineering teams rapidly prototyping and killing ideas. The balloon-based internet project, Loon, only moved forward after engineers proved it could survive stratospheric winds—not because a wall of Post-its said: "connect the world."
- **US Federal Government (2008 crisis).** Many "innovation hubs" launched inside agencies were defunded during the financial crisis. They were seen as expendable because few had linked experiments to measurable service outcomes. What was billed as resilience was cut the moment resilience was needed.
- **Nordea Bank's Innovation Garage (2019).** Launched with fanfare but later closed after leadership concluded it was not delivering business impact. The problem wasn't talent—it was

isolation. The lab's projects rarely reached frontline banking operations, and staff began to see it as branding.
- **Airbnb's hackathons.** Famous for company-wide hackathons, but founders admitted most projects "died in the demo." They started to see sustained value when they shifted to running hackathon ideas into small, market-tested pilots.

That distinction—between an illustration and a proof—is not a quibble. It is the whole subject of this book. The evidence does not live in stories of this kind, however apt; it lives in the method that follows, where every claim is meant to be traced from a raw figure to a measured outcome. Hold the four cases above as what they are: a way of seeing the problem, not a demonstration that it is real.

Two Types of Metrics

Years ago, after fourteen months of preparation, I crossed the Atlantic on a 65-foot racing sailboat. It was a journey through storms, silence, exhaustion, and awe—and a masterclass in navigating uncertainty.

At sea, survival—and performance—depend on two completely different families of indicators.

A. Operational Metrics—Are we sailing correctly?

These metrics guide the everyday functioning of the vessel:

- wind angle
- sail trim
- boat speed
- hull stress
- balance and heel
- crew coordination

- responsiveness of the helm

They tell you how the boat behaves **in the present moment**.

But operational metrics cannot tell you whether you are advancing toward your destination.

A boat can be perfectly trimmed—and heading the wrong way.

B. Navigational Metrics—Are we making meaningful progress?

These indicators look beyond the present:

- distance to destination
- storm trajectories
- long-term wind patterns
- energy reserves
- route optimization
- competitive positioning

These metrics reveal the **strategic value** of each decision.

But navigational metrics alone cannot help you adjust a sail or react to sudden gusts.

Innovation works the same way.

Organizations often measure operational activity:

- number of ideas
- prototypes built
- workshops held
- hackathons organized
- experiments run

It is equivalent to excelling at trimming sails and measuring only the nautical miles completed: necessary but not sufficient.

Companies claim to generate "value," but they almost always measure only:

- Revenue from successful initiatives
- cost savings
- adoption numbers
- ROI from the few projects that made it to market

In doing so, they ignore the most important part of innovation: The value is created when the journey improves the next journey.

Just as experienced sailors use each race to improve their next boat, their next regatta, their next technique, their next strategy, organizations accumulate:

- knowledge
- skills
- partnerships
- new capabilities
- better decision-making
- strategic positioning
- resilience
- intangible but compounding assets and expertise

This is the real backbone of innovation value—and almost none of it is measured.

What we Measure—and What we Ignore

When organizations claim to measure the value of innovation, they typically report financial returns from successful projects, revenue generated, and cost savings achieved. These are legitimate numbers. They are also, at best, a quarter of the picture—and they are all *growth* numbers.

What these dashboards ignore is everything that makes the next cycle of innovation possible: the cost of learning, the know-how accumulated along the way, the capabilities developed in teams that may have failed commercially but succeeded educationally. They ignore the expanded organizational memory, the networks created, the partnerships established, the new technical expertise acquired, the refined processes and design methods, the improved speed of execution, the better risk management, and the increased readiness for future opportunities. These elements—the readiness elements—rarely appear in any dashboard. Yet they determine innovation success far more reliably than financial outcomes alone. Innovation produces value in every voyage, not just the ones that reach a profitable port.

The distinction that will run through this entire book is between **growth**—the measurable expansion of revenue, market share, and competitive position—and **readiness**—the accumulated capability that makes the next voyage faster, smarter, and less likely to run aground.

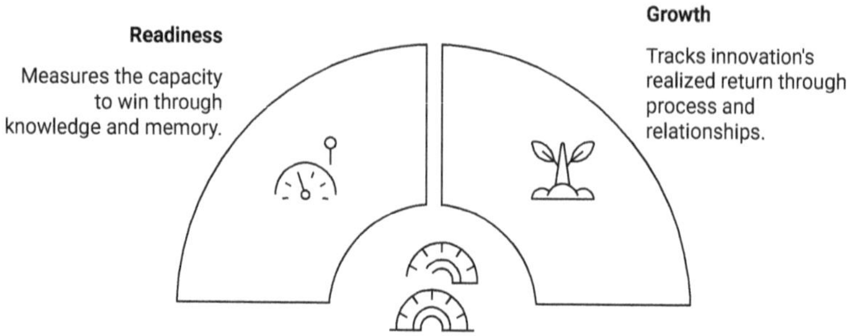

Most organizations measure growth in terms of R&D and Innovation—few measure readiness. The result is a systematic misevaluation of what innovation has already delivered and a systematic blindness to what it has made possible.

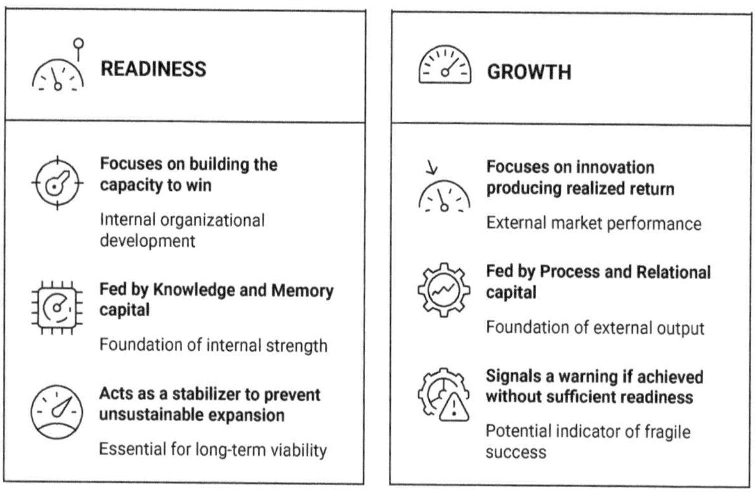

The Innovation Measurement Paradox

As a result, organizations fall into two traps—both of which are traps of incompleteness.

The first trap is measuring only operational activity: workshops held, ideas submitted, prototypes built. This creates the illusion of movement without evidence of progress. Teams are busy. Dashboards glow green. But nothing connects the activity to either growth or readiness. The organization is sailing, but no one is checking the compass.

The second trap is measuring only the financial outcomes of the projects that made it to market. This destroys long-term resilience. It ignores the learning, the failed experiments, the organizational muscle—everything the organization needs to innovate again. It measures growth and assumes readiness will take care of itself. It will not.

The paradox is simple: organizations reward what is visible, not what is valuable. Financial returns are visible. Operational metrics are visible. The readiness that makes the next innovation cycle possible—the accumulated knowledge, the sharpened processes, the deeper relationships—is invisible. And what remains invisible remains unmanaged.

Innovation creates four types of value, but companies traditionally measure only one.

Financial value: Revenue, margins, cost savings.

Strategic value: Positioning, potential options, future market access.

Intangible value: Knowledge, IP, partnerships, brand equity, human capital.

Learning value: Skills, validated insights, new competencies, and capability building.

This is exactly like sailing:

- Financial value is the distance travelled
- Strategic value is the route chosen
- Intangible value is the readiness of the vessel and crew
- Learning value is the skill upgrades that make every next crossing easier

No single metric can capture innovation. It is inherently multi-dimensional.

Innovation Value Accumulates Invisibly

→ Innovation value is cumulative.

Each experiment, each failed prototype, each insight adds a new layer of intangible capital that determines whether the next innovation cycle will succeed.

But because this capital is intangible, traditional measurement methods ignore it entirely.

This is why innovation feels risky, unpredictable, and unaccountable—it is not the nature of innovation that creates the mystery, but the inadequacy of the measurement.

Why a New Measure Is Necessary

To solve this, innovation needs two things it has never had.

The first is **a way to measure growth**—the value that innovation creates in the present. Revenue from new products. Cost savings from process improvements. Market share gained through strategic positioning. These are the numbers that boards already demand, and they are legitimate. The problem is not that organizations measure growth. The problem is that they measure only growth.

The second is **a way to measure readiness**—the value that innovation creates for the future. Organizational memory prevents the next team from repeating the previous team's mistakes. The technical capability that turns a three-month experiment into a three-week one. The relational capital that gives the organization access to external knowledge before competitors can reach it. Readiness is the accumulated capability that makes the next innovation cycle faster, cheaper, and more likely to succeed.

The Invisible Innovation Tax

Every organization pays an invisible innovation tax. This tax is not a line item in any budget. It does not appear in any financial statement. It is the cumulative cost of innovation waste—duplicated research, repeated failures, abandoned insights, and lost institutional knowledge—that arises when the organization lacks an effective innovation measurement and memory system.

The innovation tax has four components, each corresponding to a failure:

- **The Duplication Tax (Knowledge failure).** Teams that solve problems that have already been solved elsewhere in the organization. The precise cost is difficult to quantify because duplicate work is rarely labelled as such—it appears simply as project spend. But the pattern is consistent: in every organization I have worked with where we mapped active projects against the existing knowledge base, we found meaningful overlap between current initiatives and prior work that teams were unaware existed. The waste is real, structural, and compounds with organizational size.
- **The Coordination Tax (Relational failure).** Innovation projects that fail or stall because the right people were not connected—because the team in Munich did not know that the team in Singapore had already developed a solution, or because the supplier with the needed capability was not in the innovation network—the coordination tax increases exponentially with organizational size and geographic distribution.
- **The Decision Tax (Process failure).** Slow, bureaucratic, or politically compromised decision-making delays innovation projects, allows market windows to close, and demoralizes innovation teams. The decision tax is often invisible because delayed decisions are not recorded as costs. Still, the opportunity cost of a six-month delay in a competitive market can exceed the entire project budget.

- **The Amnesia Tax (Memory failure).** The most insidious of the four: the cost of forgetting. Projects that repeat mistakes made three years earlier. Customer insights that are discovered, documented, and then lost. Technical approaches that are abandoned and then rediscovered, at full cost, by a different team. The amnesia tax is the compound interest on unmeasured knowledge loss.

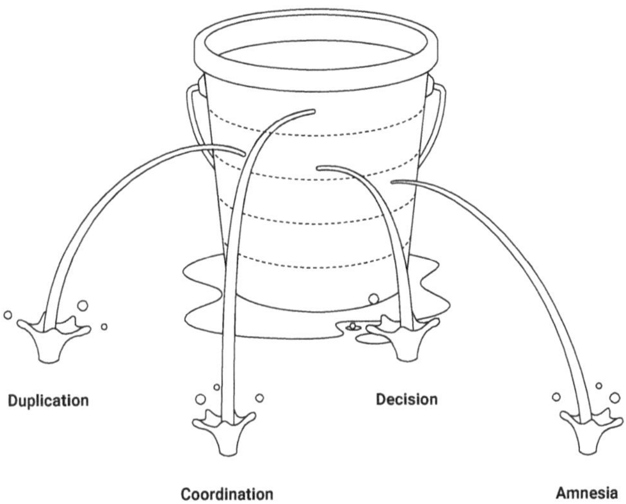

I have collected these taxes in person. During a project-inventory engagement at a telecommunications company—my mandate was modest: interview the teams and catalogue what existed—I met an innovation team whose flagship project had been stalled for months by a single technical wall. In another interview, days later, I met a second team that had already solved that exact problem and, having no idea anyone needed it, was hunting for a practical use case solid enough to defend its next round of funding. Two teams, one company, each holding the other's missing piece; neither knew the other existed. The introduction that unblocked the first project and funded the second required neither a platform nor a budget. It required an outsider with a list. I have watched the same scene since, under different logos, in Canada, in France, in Vietnam, in Saudi Arabia—and it surfaced, unprompted, in every interview of my doctoral research. This is not an anecdote. It is a condition.

Most organizations have never calculated their total innovation tax. Not from negligence: the calculation requires reading a memory most of them have never kept. The theatre continues, in other words, because the audit that would end it has never been possible.

The Duplication Tax is quantified by tracking the overlap between current projects and prior knowledge (the inverse of the Reuse Rate). The Coordination Tax is quantified by measuring the density of cross-boundary collaboration. The Decision Tax is quantified by measuring decision latency. The Amnesia Tax is quantified by tracking the Memory Fracture Risk score.

What does the tax look like once it's finally computed? Take a representative mid-sized organization—the figures are illustrative, the method is not: $60 million of annual innovation and R&D spend, forty-five active initiatives, three hundred and fifty technical staff. The knowledge audit surfaces the four components one by one. Duplication: four initiatives are substantially re-solving problems the organization has already solved, at an average of $700,000 spent before anyone noticed, and nine more are re-buying knowledge that already existed internally—$4.2 million. Coordination: six initiatives stalled an average of three and a half months waiting for expertise that was on the payroll all along, burning $120,000 a month each—$2.5 million. Decision: thirty go/no-go decisions a year, each arriving seven weeks later than the four-week governance benchmark, holding teams in partial idle at roughly $9,000 a week—$1.9 million. Amnesia: seven senior departures whose knowledge left with them, plus two failures repeating mistakes documented three years earlier—$3.6 million. Total: $12.2 million a year, against $60 million of spend—one dollar in five, paying for the absence of memory.

> **→This book proposes a new framework called S4IL—a layered system of mechanisms that enables the measurement, including the reduction of the innovation tax.**

When the Head of Innovation can stand before the board and say, *'Our current innovation tax is approximately twelve million dollars per year, and implementing a governance and management system will reduce it by forty percent within eighteen months,'* the business case for innovation measurement becomes irrefutable. (The specific numbers will vary; the diagnostic method for calculating them is described in Chapter 11)

Why Innovation Teams Often Sail Blind

Most innovation teams operate in a data desert. They have access to operational data (sales figures, production metrics, customer satisfaction scores) and financial data (budgets, expenditures, revenue forecasts). What they lack is innovation-specific data—evidence about the health of the innovation process itself.

The data desert exists because innovative data is harder to collect than operational data. Operational data is generated automatically by the systems that run the business—every transaction, every shipment, every customer interaction produces data. Innovation data, by contrast, must be deliberately captured. The insight that emerged during a brainstorming session, the reason a prototype failed, the customer reaction to an early concept—none of these generate data unless someone takes the time to record them.

This book will introduce you to the **S4IL framework**, a set of mechanisms to transform the data desert into a decision-making support system by defining what innovation data should be captured (the curated indicator set), when it should be captured (the governance rhythm), how it should be stored (the AI-enabled organizational memory), and who should use it (the measurement cascade). The framework does not require perfect data—it requires sufficient data, collected consistently, analyzed regularly, and connected to decisions.

The minimum viable measurement set for an organization starting this journey requires capturing four data points per innovation initiative per month: one Input indicator (knowledge or resources invested), one Throughput indicator (process health), one Output indicator (deliverables produced), and one Outcome indicator (value created or learned). Four data points, twelve per quarter, forty-eight per year. This is not burdensome. It is the minimum navigational information needed to steer the innovation ship.

> **→ Data-driven initiatives are essential to the success of innovation.**

The Innovation Kabuki

Picture this: a conference room on the fourteenth floor. Twenty-three people sit in ergonomic chairs arranged in a horseshoe. A facilitator in a black turtleneck distributes pads of fluorescent Post-it notes and fat-tipped markers. "No bad ideas!" she announces with practised enthusiasm. For the next ninety minutes, the group generates 147 sticky notes, photographs them with a phone, and pastes the images into a slide deck labelled "Innovation Pipeline Q3." By Thursday, the slide deck will sit in a shared drive that no one will open again—the facilitator invoices for her day rate. The 147 ideas dissolve like sugar in rain.

This is Innovation Kabuki: elaborate performance art that satisfies the organizational need to appear innovative without producing measurable value. It is not malicious. The people in that room genuinely believe they are doing important work. The facilitator has a certificate to prove her competence. The problem is structural, not personal.

The room has been booked since Tuesday. Fourteen people sit around a conference table that was clearly designed for twelve, the extra chairs sourced from the corridor, creating a slight asymmetry that no one mentions. The windows overlook a car park. Someone has put a bowl of individually wrapped mints in the centre of the table, and by ten-fifteen, they are nearly gone.

The facilitator—brought in at a day rate that would have funded a small product sprint—is drawing a double diamond on the flip chart. The participants watch with the careful, patient attention of people who have seen this particular diagram before, possibly many times. In the back row, a product manager is composing an email on her phone under the table. A finance director has arranged his notepad so that the blank side faces up; he will not take notes today.

On the whiteboard at the side of the room, someone has already laid out five dozen Post-it notes from the pre-work exercise. They are colour-coded: yellow for problems, pink for ideas, green for solutions. Nobody has quite figured out the difference between a problem and a solution in this taxonomy, resulting in some notes that belong in at least two categories. The facilitator has not mentioned this yet. He will work around it.

By eleven o'clock, a theme has emerged: 'the customer journey.' By eleven-thirty, it has been refined to 'the end-to-end customer journey.' By noon, the room has produced a journey map on butcher paper that stretches across one entire wall, contains forty-seven touchpoints, and has been photographed by three people on their phones. The photograph will live in a Slack channel called #ion-workshop-nov for approximately four months before the channel is archived.

This scene—and its near-infinite variations across industries, continents, and organization sizes—is what I think of as innovation kabuki: a performance so stylized, so carefully observed, and so completely divorced from organizational reality that its primary function is not to produce innovation but to produce the appearance of innovation. The Post-it note is the instrument. The double diamond is the score. The facilitator is the conductor. And the audience, in the boardroom upstairs, is reassured that the orchestra is playing.

I am not making fun of Post-it notes. The technology—pressure-sensitive adhesive, repositionable, the perfect physical token for a provisional idea—is genuinely elegant, and in my humble opinion, would be a better icon of innovation than the light bulb.

I am not making fun of journey maps, design sprints, or any of the other tools that fill the innovation practitioner's kit bag.

Most of these tools work under the right conditions and with the right inputs when connected to real organizational knowledge.

The problem is not the hammer. The problem is that the organization keeps forgetting where it put the nails.

The Measurement Maturity Gap

Between 2015 and 2025, innovation investment grew substantially across the private sector. Chief Innovation Officers became standard fixtures in large organizations. Design thinking workshops became ubiquitous. Innovation labs proliferated. Yet the fundamental measurement problem remained essentially unchanged: most organizations still cannot tell their boards, with credible evidence, whether their innovation investments are producing returns.

This is the **Measurement Maturity Gap**—the distance between the sophistication of an organization's innovation activities and the sophistication of its innovation measurement. Organizations that have invested heavily in design thinking, agile methodologies, lean startup processes, and AI-enabled tools are still measuring their innovation performance with the same tools they used a decade ago: project milestone tracking, patent counts, and annual revenue from new products.

A lack of available metrics does not cause the gap. The opposite is true—there are hundreds of innovation metrics available in the literature, from idea velocity to time-to-market to innovation premium. A lack of integration causes the gap. Individual metrics exist in isolation. They measure specific activities without connecting those activities to a coherent picture of innovation health.

Imagine a ship's captain who has a speedometer but no compass. She knows how fast the ship is moving, but not whether it is heading toward or away from the destination. Now imagine a captain who has both a speedometer and a compass, plus a depth sounder, a wind gauge, and a radar display—but a different company manufactures each instrument, uses a different coordinate system, different scales, and cannot communicate with the others. The vessel produces data in abundance. What the captain lacks is a navigational system.

This is the state of innovation measurement in most organizations today. The instruments exist. The navigational system does not. The framework is that navigational system.

Most Innovation Programs Stall After Eighteen Months

There is a pattern that innovation consultants see repeatedly but rarely discuss in public: the eighteen-month stall. An organization launches an innovation program with executive sponsorship, dedicated budget, and genuine enthusiasm. The first six months produce a burst of activity—workshops, ideation sessions, prototype sprints, pilot projects. The next six months see the first projects reach decision points—some succeed, some fail, some pivot. Then, around the eighteen-month mark, something shifts.

The executive sponsor asks a reasonable question: *'What have we gotten for our investment?'* The innovation team produces a report full of activity metrics: the number of ideas generated, the number of prototypes built, and the number of workshops conducted. The executive looks at the report and sees effort, not results. Budget discussions become difficult. The innovation team loses political capital. A reorganization moves the program under a different executive who has less patience and more pressing priorities. The program does not die—it slowly starves.

The eighteen-month stall is almost always caused by a measurement failure, not an innovation failure. The innovation team was doing good work. They were generating real value. But they could not demonstrate that value in terms the boardroom understood. They were reporting on how hard they were sailing, not on where they were sailing or why the journey mattered.

The framework is designed specifically to prevent the eighteen-month stall. By establishing a measurement system from Day One—one that tracks not just activity but impact across four capitals—the innovation team builds the evidence base that sustains executive support through the inevitable period when investments have been made, but returns are still materializing. ROI^2 provides the language. The Four Compass Readings provide the evidence. The dashboard provides visibility. The eighteen-month stall happens when the innovation team cannot answer the boardroom's question. The framework ensures they always can.

The quarterly budget review began as it always does: with a question no one wanted to answer. The CFO, a tall woman with reading glasses perched on her forehead, flipped to slide fourteen. "What have we gotten for eleven million dollars?" she asked. Not hostile. Curious. The innovation director opened his mouth, closed it, and reached for the water glass. He had activity metrics. He had participation rates. He had a beautiful funnel diagram showing 340 ideas narrowing to 12 pilots. What he did not have was a number that connected any of it to business value.

That silence is the reason S4IL exists. The Four Compass Readings are designed to ensure no innovation leader ever faces that question without an answer.

The Amnesia Problem

Eighteen months after the workshop described above, I interviewed the product manager who had been composing emails in the back row. She had moved to a new role—still in the same organization, but in a different division. I asked her what had come of the workshop's outputs.

"We ran a pilot," she said. "It had some interesting results. Then the sponsor got moved to another project, and the team disbanded." She paused. "I think there's a report somewhere. I don't know where. The person who ran it left six months ago."

This is not a story about organizational dysfunction. This is a story about organizational normality.

Organizational knowledge decays over time unless it is actively maintained, and that decay accelerates with organizational size, personnel turnover, and the absence of structured retrieval infrastructure. In practice, the window between a project's completion and the effective disappearance of its institutional memory is shorter than most leaders assume. The knowledge does not vanish all at once—it diffuses. The champion moves on. The documentation migrates to an archive folder. The colleagues who remember the pilot are reassigned to other priorities. And then, two years later, a new team discovers what they believe to be an unexplored opportunity, assembles in a conference room, and puts Post-it notes on a whiteboard.

The tools are not the problem. The memory is the problem. And the failure to diagnose memory as the core problem is why innovation, in most organizations, remains episodic—a sequence of discrete performances that do not accumulate, do not compound, and do not build toward anything resembling systematic capability.

What a Compass Actually Does

Before GPS, navigators used a compass in conjunction with a chart, a clock, and a log. The compass told you your heading—the direction you were pointing. The chart told you the terrain. The clock told you how long you had been travelling. The log told you your speed. Together, these four instruments let you calculate your position through what navigators called dead reckoning: not a live fix, not perfect certainty, but a continuously updated estimate of where you were based on everything you knew about where you had been.

A good innovation measurement system works exactly this way. It does not provide a live satellite fix of your innovation position. It gives you the tools to calculate where you are based on your organizational history—your past investments, accumulated knowledge, lessons from failed experiments, and absorptive capacity. Heading: What direction is your innovation effort pointing? Chart: What does your competitive landscape look like? Clock: How long have you been investing in this capability? Log: what have you actually produced, and at what rate?

The Innovator's Compass is not a magic metric. No single number captures the totality of your organization's innovative capacity. What it is—and what this book will build, piece by piece—is a framework for connecting the things your organization already knows into a coherent navigation instrument. The Post-it notes can stay. The workshops can stay. What has to change is the relationship among today's workshop, last year's pilot, and the institutional knowledge that existed before either.

The Post-it note on the whiteboard is not the enemy. The enemy is the organizational system that produces the Post-it note as its primary output—and then forgets what was on it. To understand why that system persists and how to replace it with something more durable, we need to go deeper into the measurement problem: not just what organizations measure, but what the instruments they use were designed to see.

The compass exists. The instruments can be built. But first, we need to understand why the instruments that most organizations already use are not just insufficient—they are actively misleading. That story begins with a three-letter acronym that has done more damage to innovation than any competitor, any recession, or any disruption ever could: ROI.

Measuring the right things is only half the battle. The other half is understanding why the instrument you have been using—the one labelled ROI—was designed for a world that no longer exists. And what happens when you try to navigate a living system with a dead instrument?

The Post-it notes are still on the wall. The photographs are in the shared drive. The workshop invoice has been paid. But the question lingers: if none of it produced measurable value, what exactly did the organization buy? The answer lies not in better brainstorms but in understanding what innovation investment actually returns—and why every calculation you have seen so far is probably wrong.

→A compass without a map is just a needle.

There is one tool that has done more damage to innovation measurement than any other. Not because its creators were wrong. Because they were right—for a completely different world.

The Skipper's Log

Position — The green dashboard measures motion, not value. A portfolio can glow while the organization drifts sideways, and no metric on the wall will flicker.

Sighted — The Innovation Kabuki — measurement performed for an audience — and the invisible innovation tax, paid every year in duplicated work that no report ever itemizes.

Charted — The line between activity metrics and value metrics: the first distinction on which every honest measurement system is built.

Course — Take your current dashboard and ask of each metric: what value does this prove? Strike everything that only proves effort. What survives is your real instrument panel — and it will be uncomfortably short.

Chapter 2: The ROI Trap

It always starts with a spreadsheet: the lights dim, the projector hums, and numbers spill across the wall like modern scripture—Return on Investment, Net Present Value, Internal Rate of Return. They look clean and comforting, like control itself. But when applied to innovation, they fail.

Why ROI is not the right compass

Innovation isn't a factory line. It doesn't behave like a predictable cash flow model. It's more like fire prevention than quarterly accounting. Imagine if we judged firefighters by the number of fires they put out each year. Safe cities would look like failures. Worse, firefighters might start lighting fires to meet their targets. It's absurd—but this is exactly how many companies measure innovation: counting patents, prototypes, or launches, instead of asking whether they're ready for the future.

→ Readiness matters.

The real question a measuring tool should answer is "How quickly can our organization respond to disruption?"

Return on Investment was never designed for ideas. It was born in the age of steel and assembly lines. Frederick Taylor gave managers their first illusion of scientific control; Alfred Sloan at General Motors turned budgets into religion. By the mid-20th century, ROI was the language of power. Peter Drucker told us that what gets measured gets managed. Alfred Chandler institutionalized ROI into strategy. And in 1942, Joseph Schumpeter's warnings—that real growth comes from disruptive innovation—were drowned out by the comfort of neat percentages.

In stable markets, ROI made sense. Building a new car plant? Calculations worked. Oil refinery? Predictable demand. But when markets turned unpredictable—when technologies bent the curve—ROI became a blindfold. It could not see the nonlinear leaps of innovation.

Blockbuster dismissed Netflix because the ROI showed that rental stores were still profitable. IBM clung to mainframes as PCs took off. Nokia clung to feature phones. Swiss watchmakers ignored quartz. Each decision looked rational—until it destroyed billions in market value. ROI reassured leaders even as the ground gave way beneath them.

Clayton Christensen explained this dynamic in his influential book *The Innovator's Dilemma* (1997). He observed that incumbents, guided by ROI and profit margins, chase sustaining innovations in safe markets and overlook disruptive ones that start with low margins or small niches. By the time these disruptive innovations mature and reshape industries, it is too late for the incumbents to respond.

These cases show a clear pattern. Instead of endlessly expanding the list, the lesson is simple: ROI blinds leaders to uncertainty, punishes long-term bets, and rewards complacency.

R&D and Innovation: Two Sides of the Same Coin

Many leaders consider R&D and Innovation as two different things. They treat them as separate business flows.

In reality, they are inseparable. Geoff Nicholson, a father of the Post-it at 3M, defined the difference between R&D and Innovation:

> → **"Research turns money into knowledge. Innovation turns knowledge into money."**

R&D fills the reservoir; innovation taps it. Without integration, R&D risks becoming irrelevant, and innovation risks becoming fragile.

Emerging during the Cold War and in the post-war global economy, the OECD "advises governments on how to deliver better policies for better lives". It provides governments with a neutral way to compare themselves across multiple dimensions. OECD created the **Frascati Manual** and the **Oslo Manual** specifically to evaluate R&D and innovation efforts (OECD, 2015; OECD/Eurostat, 2018).

With countries subsidizing R&D, there was a need for "apples-to-apples" comparisons to ensure fairness in trade and policy. These manuals provided standards so that even bodies such as the World Trade Organization (WTO) could evaluate national efforts without bias.

The Frascati codified R&D as investment; the Oslo showed innovation as a system. The two are different disciplines—but without a shared vision, both underperform.

Henry Chesbrough's idea of "Open Innovation" (2003) adds nuance here. He argued that companies often hoard knowledge in silos, missing opportunities because they fail to let ideas flow in and out. This reinforces the limits of ROI, which values only internal, tangible outputs.

Organizations need a tool to push beyond by asking not only "*what knowledge was created?*", but also "*how it was shared, adopted, and spread across ecosystems?*"

This makes it clear that innovation readiness depends on openness and diffusion, not just internal returns.

Introducing ROI²

What S4IL proposes is an entirely different measure. I call it Return on Innovation Investment—ROI², with a superscript that is not merely stylistic.

The term ROI² has been used in the innovation management practitioner literature—notably by Kandybin and Kihn (2004) and Drake (2006)—to denote a straightforward financial ratio comparing new product revenues to total innovation spend. The framework proposed here is architecturally different: a four-capital composite that integrates financial, intangible, strategic, and learning returns, weighted by strategic intent, and grounded in organizational memory as its operating infrastructure. The shared notation reflects a shared conviction that standard ROI is the wrong instrument for innovation; the measurement systems it produces are not the same.

The superscript 2 in the term ROI² indicates that innovation investment generates two entangled layers of return, whereas standard ROI captures only one.

The first layer is familiar: revenue, margin, market share. These matter. They should be measured. The mistake is not in measuring them but in treating them as the complete picture.

The second layer is the return on organizational learning—the accumulation of knowledge, capability, and absorptive capacity that determines what the organization will be able to attempt next.

ROI² is a tool designed for the messy and uncertain world of innovation.

The **Frascati Manual** emphasizes treating R&D as an investment. The **Oslo Manual** stresses that focusing only on easy-to-measure outputs distorts reality. ROI² adds the missing piece: readiness and adoption.

Traditional ROI is a ruler. It's precise, one-dimensional, and blind to uncertainty. ROI² is a compass. It won't give you exact coordinates, but it will point you toward resilience. It helps leaders orient themselves in unknown terrain.

ROI² should not be applied on a project-by-project basis. Innovation is not linear. It's a portfolio game. Out of ten experiments, seven will fail, two will stumble, and one will change everything. That's why ROI² must be viewed at the **portfolio level**, across four strategic cycles of investment:

- **Where to Play** – scanning and choosing opportunity spaces.
- **How to Win** – testing, prototyping, scaling solutions.
- **How to Deliver** – converting validated concepts into deliverable products, services, or processes through development, IP creation, and productization.
- **How to Get Adopted** – commercializing, embedding, and diffusing ideas into practice.

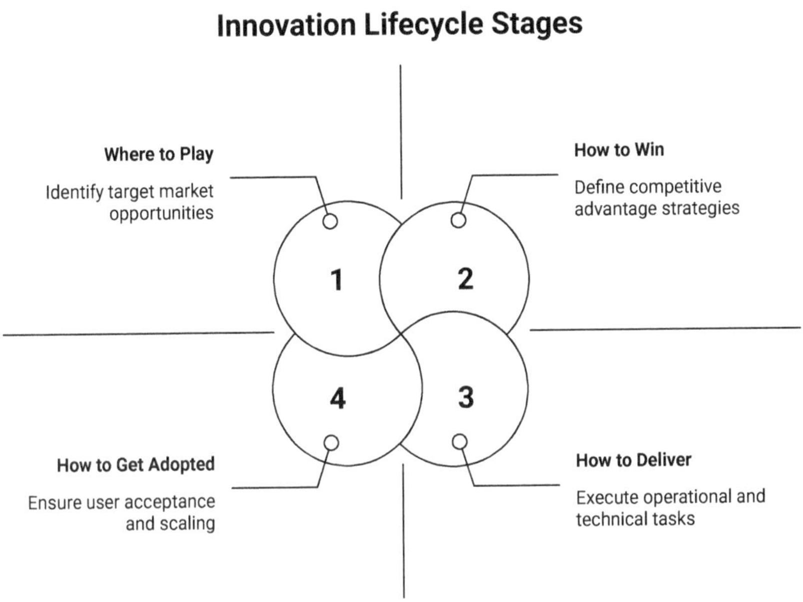

The value comes not from a single project's ROI, but from how the portfolio moves initiatives back and forth through these investment phases.

Consider how leading organizations embrace readiness rather than chasing a 100% success rate. They accept that failure is part of the process—and that it builds capacity for future breakthroughs:

- **DARPA** accepts that most of its projects will fail. That's not a bug—it's the model. The ones that worked gave us the Internet and stealth technology.
- **Pharmaceutical R&D** discards 9,999 molecules to find one blockbuster drug.

- **Germany's early renewable energy programs** appeared inefficient, yet today their adoption has helped drive down global solar costs.
- **Venture capitalists** fund 10 startups, expecting only 1 or 2 unicorns, while the rest serve as learning experiences.
- **Large tech firms like Google** tolerate failed products—Google Glass, Wave, or countless experimental apps—because each builds capability and skills for the next breakthrough.

ROI would call these failures; ROI² would call them deliberate investments in readiness, resilience, and future opportunity.

ROI measures the past. ROI² measures readiness for the future. It asks, *Are we building memory? Are we resilient to shocks? Are we cultivating culture and ecosystems that let ideas stick?*

These are the balance sheets of the future. Without them, companies collapse in storms. With them, they turn storms into opportunities.

The tools exist. The frameworks exist. The missing ingredient is not another framework.

But before we build the alternative, we need to understand precisely how the existing instruments failed—and why organizations that were not foolish, not lazy, and not uninformed kept using them anyway.

The most instructive example is not a story of corporate incompetence. It is the story of an organization that had excellent instruments—and the judgment to see they were built for the wrong problem.

Why You Innovate

In the autumn of 2009, I was discussing with a friend—a brilliant French-Canadian film director. Before becoming my friend, Marc-André was a client I helped to implement an innovation management process for his production company. A film director's entire career depends on making creative bets under uncertainty, which makes them a natural innovator, and Marc-André was no exception to that stereotype.

We were sitting in his Montreal office, talking about how video production and consumption changed over the years, when the conversation drifted to a TED Talk that everyone seemed to be sharing that month.

Simon Sinek had just delivered "Start With Why"—the argument that the most effective leaders and organizations begin not with what they do or how they do it, but with why they do it. The video was spreading through management circles with the particular velocity of an idea that people already feel but have never heard articulated. Marc-André played it on his laptop. I watched it again. And something clicked—not about leadership in general, but about innovation specifically.

Why do you innovate? Not what do you innovate—that is the product. Not how do you innovate—that is the process. Why. The answer, when you strip away the corporate vocabulary and the strategic posturing, is always the same. You innovate for two reasons, and only two.

You innovate to grow. To enter markets that did not exist. To serve needs that customers have not yet articulated. To build products and services that generate new revenue, new margin, new competitive advantage. **Growth is the engine**.

And you innovate to be ready. To build the capabilities, the knowledge, the organizational muscle that will allow you to respond when the world shifts—because it will shift, and the shift will not send an invitation. **Readiness is the hull.**

An engine without a hull sinks. A hull without an engine drifts. Every innovation investment, every experiment, every failed prototype and every successful launch, produces some combination of growth and readiness. The organizations that measure only financial return see only the growth. The organizations that measure only activity see neither.

ROI^2 measures both. At its simplest, ROI^2 asks two questions: how ready is this organization to innovate, and how effectively is it growing through innovation?

This is the why that precedes everything else in this book. Before the formulas, before the indicators, before the governance frameworks and the AI copilots and the ninety-day journey: why are you doing this? You are doing this because your organization needs to grow and it needs to be ready, and no instrument that measures only one of those has ever been sufficient.

Sinek was right. Start with why. In innovation, the why is always the same.

The Chip Apple Didn't Need to Build

For most of the 2010s, somewhere in Cupertino, the numbers said no. Apple was pouring billions into designing its own processors—the A-series chips that powered the iPhone and the iPad. The work was brilliant and the work was expensive: a standing army of microarchitecture engineers, fabrication partnerships, years of iteration on a problem that, for the Mac at least, was already solved. Intel sold

Apple excellent processors off the shelf. Any analyst running a clean return-on-investment case on a Mac chip would have reached the same conclusion, year after year: don't build it. The supplier is competent, the margins do not justify the spend, and the engineering risk is enormous. The spreadsheet was right. And it was pointing in exactly the wrong direction.

Because Apple was not trying to earn a return on a Mac processor. It was accumulating something the spreadsheet had no column for: a decade of compounding expertise in designing chips for its own software, its own thermal envelopes, its own idea of what a computer should feel like in the hand. Every A-series generation deepened that capability. None of it showed up as Mac revenue, because capability under construction does not have a line item—any more than human expertise does, or a patent before it earns its first dollar of licensing.

Then, in 2020, Apple began doing the thing the numbers had argued against for a decade. It dropped Intel and, within three years, moved the entire Mac line to its own silicon—and the first M1 machines did not merely match the ones they replaced. They embarrassed them: a performance-per-watt advantage the rest of the industry could not approach, because the rest of the industry had been buying chips while Apple had spent ten years learning to build them. The switch that would have looked reckless on any single year's ROI sheet was, by the time it came, almost inevitable. The option had been paid for years in advance.

This is the decision a return-on-investment lens cannot make. ROI asks what a project will return this year, or next. It is the right question for a known investment with a measurable payoff. It is the wrong question for the thing innovation actually produces: an option, a capability, a position you cannot buy back later at any price. Apple was not optimizing ROI. It was optimizing what this book calls ROI^2—the return that counts the strategic, the intangible, and the learned alongside the financial.

Reverse the story and you have the more common one—the one practitioners usually tell about Kodak. A company runs the clean ROI case, and the spreadsheet reports honestly that the new thing is expensive and the old thing is profitable. Kodak hesitated over digital photography in part for exactly this reason: its film and chemistry threw off a river of recurring revenue that the digital scenario erased, and the numbers could see the income it stood to lose far more clearly than the franchise it would forfeit by waiting. They were not wrong. They were answering a smaller question than the one that mattered. By the time the larger question announces itself—a supplier that becomes a competitor, a technology that matures faster than anyone expected—the option is gone, and no amount of capital buys back a decade you did not spend.

The ROI trap is not a failure of intelligence. It is a structural feature of how most organizations have been trained to evaluate innovation. Understanding why the trap exists is the first step toward escaping it.

Why ROI Is the Wrong Question

Return on investment is an excellent tool for evaluating decisions where the inputs and outputs are well-defined, the time horizon is known, and the assets involved are already captured on someone's balance sheet. Capital expenditure decisions, production efficiency improvements, real estate acquisitions: these are precisely the kinds of decisions that ROI analysis was designed for. The formula works.

Innovation is none of these things. Innovation by definition involves uncertain inputs, unknown outputs, variable time horizons, and the creation of value in forms that existing accounting systems were not designed to capture. The dominant accounting frameworks in use today were largely codified in the nineteenth and early twentieth centuries, when the primary assets of a successful enterprise were physical: land, buildings, machinery, and inventory. The frameworks are excellent at tracking these things. They are structurally unable to track what economist Baruch Lev identified, in his landmark 2001 work, as intangible assets: knowledge capital, organizational learning, customer relationships, and brand equity.

The result is a systematic accounting for what innovation destroys—existing margins, existing channels, existing workforce competencies—and a systematic blindness to what innovation creates. The spreadsheet was not wrong about the costs. It was simply silent about the assets.

This asymmetry has a compounding effect that is rarely acknowledged. Because ROI models cannot value intangible assets, organizations learn to discount them. Because they learn to discount them, they invest less in maintaining them. Because they invest less in maintaining them, the accumulated knowledge of what works, what doesn't, what was tried and abandoned, and why—degrades. And as the knowledge degrades, the organization becomes progressively less capable of the kind of learning-intensive innovation that would allow it to survive disruption.

The trap is not the spreadsheet. The trap is the assumption that what cannot be measured in the spreadsheet does not exist.

Harrison's insight was not to build a better clock. It was to combine materials whose errors cancelled each other out—brass that expanded where steel contracted, each correcting the other's distortion. ROI^2 works on exactly this principle.

Financial Return and Learning Return are not simply additive. They are complementary. When financial metrics overcount short-term gains, learning metrics correct for the capability being consumed. When learning metrics suggest expanding exploration, financial metrics constrain the portfolio to what the organization can actually sustain. Neither capital can compensate for its own blind spots. Composition is what enables reliable measurement in an unstable environment.

But complementary measures still measure something, and it is worth naming what before naming how. An innovation initiative, whatever else it produces, always produces one or more of four kinds of assets: something tangible the organization can now do more efficiently, something intangible it now knows, a lesson it did not have before, or a partnership it did not have before. Tangible, intangible, lessons, partnerships—these four are the capitals this book keeps returning to: Process, Knowledge, Memory, and Relational. Everything ROI^2 measures is measured on one of these four. The returns that follow are not a second framework bolted onto the first. They are the instrument for reading what the capitals already contain.

The Four Returns of Innovation Investment

The traditional ROI calculation—return divided by investment—assumes that 'return' is a single number, typically expressed in financial terms. ROI^2 challenges this assumption by recognizing four distinct types of return that innovation produces, each valuable, each measurable, and each invisible to the traditional formula.

Financial Return. The first is Financial Return—the revenue, cost savings, and margin improvements that innovation generates directly.

This is the return that traditional ROI measures, and it is real and important. But it is typically the last return to materialize and the easiest to attribute to non-innovation factors. A new product generates revenue, but the sales team claims credit for market positioning, the operations team claims manufacturing efficiency, and the finance team claims pricing strategy. The innovation team's contribution becomes invisible in the attribution battle.

Intangible Return. The second is Intangible Return—the knowledge, capabilities, and relationships that innovation activities create even when individual projects fail. A failed product launch that produces deep customer insight, a new manufacturing capability, and a strengthened supplier relationship has generated real value—but that value appears nowhere in the financial statements. ROI^2 captures Intangible Return through Knowledge Capital indicators.

Strategic Return. The third is Strategic Return—the optionality and competitive positioning that innovation investment creates. Every exploratory innovation project is, in financial terms, a real option: it gives the organization the right, but not the obligation, to pursue a market opportunity in the future. A company that has explored autonomous driving technology, even if it has not yet launched a product, has a strategic option that competitors who have not explored lack. ROI^2 captures Strategic Return through portfolio diversity metrics and Horizon balance indicators.

Learning Return. The fourth is Learning Return—the organization's accumulated ability to innovate more effectively over time. An organization that has run 100 innovation experiments has (or should have) a higher innovation success rate than one that has run 10, not because the individual experiments were better, but because accumulated learning improves the quality of future decisions. ROI^2

captures Learning Return through Memory Capital indicators and the Factorless Income Residual.

- **Financial Return** and **Strategic Return** measure **Growth**.
- **Learning Return** and **Intangible Return** measure **Readiness**.

The compass has two needles because the voyage has two purposes.

This is the mapping promised earlier. Each of the **four returns** is simply how one of the **four capitals** shows up on a balance sheet built to see it—Knowledge Capital, Relational Capital, Process Capital, and Memory Capital.

The four returns correspond to the four capitals, and this is not coincidental—it is architectural. Each capital represents a type of value that innovation creates, and each compass reading measures a dimension of that value.

- **Financial Return** flows from **Process Capital** (efficient operations).
- **Intangible Return** flows from **Knowledge Capital** (new skills, know-how and capabilities).
- **Strategic Return** flows from **Relational Capital** (partnerships and market position).
- **Learning Return** flows from **Memory Capital** (accumulated organizational wisdom on market and technology).

Together, the **Four Capitals** provide the complete picture that ROI alone cannot.

A note on the Financial Return mapping that practitioners sometimes question: why does Financial Return flow from Process Capital rather than from all four capitals simultaneously? The answer lies in what the framework measures and at what level. A single project that reduces costs is a process optimization. A single project that captures a market need is a better process for serving customers. Measured in isolation, both are outputs of individual effort. But the framework forces the organization to consider its innovation initiative as a portfolio managed across an investment season—where multiple projects cross-pollinate, where the learning from one experiment informs the design of the next, and where governance decisions are made based on accumulated evidence rather than individual intuition. In this context, Financial Return becomes the product of a systematic process. It is the portfolio discipline, not the individual project hygiene, that converts innovation activity into compounding financial value. This is why the framework does not rely on the ROI performance indicator, which would measure innovation efficiency on a project-by-project basis. The framework relies on ROI² to measure innovation portfolio efficiency, season by season.

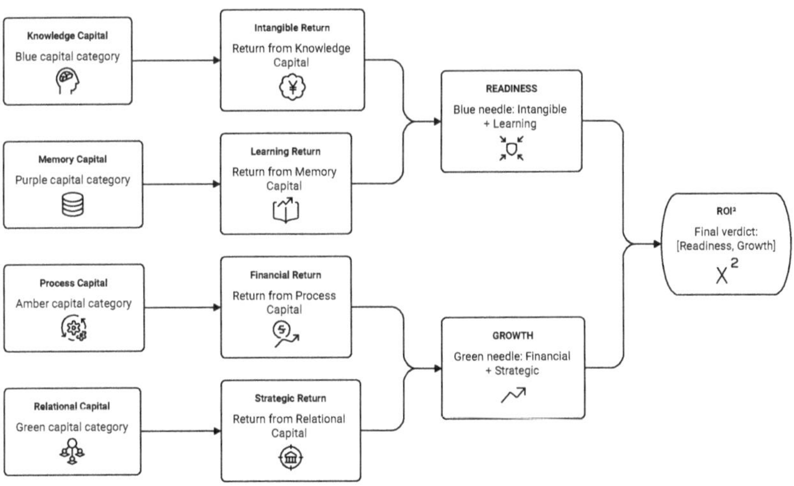

ROI² offers a better formula, and we will return to it in the coming pages.

But applying a better formula to forgotten data yields the same result as applying a worse formula: confident ignorance. The real question is not how to calculate the return on innovation. The real question is why organizations systematically destroy the knowledge that would make any calculation meaningful. The answer, it turns out, is not negligence. It is something far more interesting—and far more dangerous.

The ROI trap is real and expensive. But measuring the wrong things is not the worst of it. There is something far more corrosive lurking beneath the surface of most organizations—a collective forgetting so pervasive that entire product histories vanish within a single employee turnover cycle. It is not ignorance. It is not incompetence. It is systemic amnesia. And it is the subject of the next chapter.

THE SKIPPER'S LOG

Position — ROI is an excellent answer to a question innovation does not ask. Forcing it produces confident ignorance — a worse error than no number at all.

Sighted — Innovation pays in four currencies — Financial, Intangible, Strategic, Learning — and conventional accounting reads only the first.

Charted — ROI^2, a composite that reads all four returns against the cost of the season. Introduced here as a concept; computed, step by step, in Chapter 8.

Course — Stop asking what the ROI of innovation is. List, however roughly, the four returns your portfolio produced last season. The blank lines are the diagnosis.

Chapter 3: The Amnesia Epidemic

In the autumn of 2003, a project manager at a mid-sized European pharmaceutical company sat down to write a post-mortem for a failed clinical trial. She had done this before. She wrote it carefully, filed it on the shared drive under the project number, and moved on.

Three years later, a different team in the same company began a strikingly similar trial. They encountered the same failure mode—a subtlety in the assay protocol that the first team had identified, documented, and filed. No one on the new team knew it existed. The shared drive had seventeen thousand folders.

That gap—between knowledge that exists and knowledge that works—is the most expensive in modern business. It does not appear in any balance sheet. It is not measured by the Frascati Manual, which tracks R&D spending. It is not captured by the Oslo Manual, which surveys innovation outputs. It lives in the space between what an organization has learned and what it can actually use the next morning.

Every attempt to fix innovation measurement—Frascati, Oslo, ROI2 (without a superscript 2)—ran into the same wall. Not a methodological wall. An organizational one.

Practitioners in the field knew this intuitively. Doctoral research on enterprises in emerging markets has consistently revealed that firms often adopt superficial innovation practices without ever embedding them into their organizational fabric. The result was repetition of the same mistakes, shallow cycles of novelty, and no lasting transformation.

In other words, organizations failed not because they lacked ideas or resources but because they lacked memory.

Michel Godet, the French master of Strategic Foresight—what the French call Prospective—used to warn against the tyranny of clichés in strategic thinking. He urged innovation management practitioners to be rigorous, to question assumptions, to avoid the trap of repeating empty managerial formulas. Yet when faced with uncertainty, most organizations reached for "best practices" rather than their forgotten experiments. They ignored the treasure buried in their own archives of trials, errors, and tacit learning. Innovation became amnesia with a glossy cover.

The truth, as we can see now, is that the missing piece in every attempt to measure innovation has nothing to do with the quality of the frameworks. Frascati was rigorous. Oslo was comprehensive. The missing ingredient is not an accounting methodology. It is not an innovation management platform. It is not another "Design Something" Lego-Post-it based set of workshops.

It is something every organization already has—in fragments, in silos, in the heads of people who are about to retire or resign.

It is **Organizational Memory**.

The question is not why organizations forget. The question is why they keep building systems that lead to it.

Two Faces of Amnesia

Xerox PARC in the 1970s pioneered the graphical user interface, Ethernet, and the computer mouse. Yet Xerox itself failed to capitalize. The inventions were real, but they languished as the organization forgot how to connect laboratory breakthroughs with its commercial identity. This was technical amnesia: the memory existed in prototypes but was lost at the level of strategy.

Nokia, by contrast, illustrates narrative amnesia. A company that had once reinvented itself repeatedly—from pulp to electronics to mobile phones—forgot its own story of adaptability when smartphones emerged. It clung to the safety of its feature phones, overlooking how reinvention had always been its strength. Forgetting its narrative of transformation proved more fatal than any technological shortfall.

- **Technical Amnesia** occurs when inventions and prototypes are forgotten or fail to be linked to strategy. Kodak's digital camera and Xerox PARC's GUI, Ethernet, and mouse languished because leadership ignored them.
- **Narrative Amnesia** occurs when firms forget their own story of adaptation. Polaroid, once the champion of instant adoption, failed to remember its own lesson when digital arrived. Nokia, once a master of reinvention, clung to feature phones, forgetting its past identity as an agile transformer.

Together, these forms explain why traditional measurement has failed. Input and output metrics overlook the role of memory in shaping resilience and renewal.

What follows in this chapter is deliberately thorough—and deliberately long. Corporate amnesia is not a simple problem with a simple diagnosis. It is an ecosystem of pathologies, each reinforcing the others, each with its own mechanism and its own remedy. The journey through this chapter maps those pathologies in sequence. First, the paradox that memory itself can become a cage—the Kodak problem, where remembering the wrong things is as dangerous as forgetting the right ones. Then, the knowledge management systems that were supposed to solve the problem and did not. After that, the deeper pathology: the reasons people actively hide, hoard, and distort knowledge inside organizations—not out of malice, but out of rational self-interest in systems that reward the wrong behaviours. Finally, the diagnostic instruments that allow a Head of Innovation to assess which of these pathologies is at work in their own organization, and the measurement framework that makes the cost of amnesia visible for the first time.

The rocks, reefs, and even the safe harbours and deep passages in shallow waters that no one captured in the chart—these are the organizational equivalents of the knowledge that was never documented, the failure that was hidden, the expert who left without transferring what she knew. Against all logic of navigation, hundreds of organizations sail these waters every year without a map. This chapter builds the map.

→ But Memory can become a cage.

There is a paradox buried inside the argument for organizational memory—one that the literature documents carefully and that practitioners discover painfully. Memory not only enables organizations. It can constrain them just as powerfully.

Kodak did not fail because it forgot. It failed because it remembered, too well and too faithfully, what it meant to be a film company. Its organizational memory—the incentive structures, the project approval templates, the career paths, the vocabulary of success—was exquisitely tuned to a world that was disappearing. When digital arrived, the memory system worked exactly as designed: it filtered out the new signal as noise.

Nokia is the same story. Not amnesia. Calcification. The organization's memory of what had made it successful—hardware design, carrier relationships, a particular idea of what a phone was—became the lens through which every new development was evaluated. It passed. Smartphones did not.

The organizations that get into trouble are not the ones that forgot. They are the ones who could not forget when it became necessary.

For a Head of Innovation, this creates a practical responsibility that most memory frameworks ignore: the obligation to curate which memories the organization keeps and which it actively retires. A memory system without a deprecation policy is an archive that grows heavier with each passing year, eventually pulling the organization backward under its own accumulated weight.

What Strategic Forgetting Looks Like in Practice

Strategic forgetting is not about erasing what happened. The historical record should stay intact. It is about removing the normative power of outdated assumptions—the "this is how we do things" framing that gets attached to past successes. Three categories of stored knowledge require periodic review:

- **Outdated technology assumptions.** Any knowledge artifact that assumes a specific technology architecture should be tagged with an expiry review. A five-year-old assessment of what AI can do for your innovation process is not a memory asset. It is a liability.
- **Superseded market hypotheses.** Customer behaviour, competitive dynamics, and regulatory environments shift. A market analysis that shaped a strategy three years ago should not automatically shape today's portfolio decisions. Flag it. Review it. Retire it if it no longer holds.

Contextually obsolete failure lessons that no longer apply. *"We tried that, and it didn't work"* is only useful if the conditions that caused the failure still exist. Many organizations carry institutional scars from failures in a world that has since changed.

A simple discipline: every knowledge artifact in your memory system must carry "properties" such as "review by" date to establish a pattern detection mechanism able to flag when a stored lesson is being cited in contexts that no longer match the conditions under which it was generated.

Why Knowledge Management Fell Short

In the 1990s and 2000s, organizations poured resources into knowledge management platforms—intranets, databases, case repositories, and SharePoint sites. These systems promised to preserve lessons learned.

Yet they often became graveyards of static documents. Employees rarely uploaded their failures, and when they did, the context was stripped away. No one volunteered to memorialize mistakes that could reflect badly on careers. The most valuable data—the near-misses, the informal warnings, the painful missteps—never entered these repositories. Human reluctance made systematic capture impossible.

The most vivid case of this is not corporate at all. When NASA looked into building a new heavy-lift rocket, it turned back to the F-1 engine that had carried Apollo to the Moon—the most powerful single-chamber engine the country ever flew. The blueprints had survived. Every drawing, every specification, filed and intact. And they were not enough. Each F-1 had been built largely by hand, and the engineers who built them carried the decisive knowledge in their heads and on scraps of paper long since gone: the undocumented welding techniques, the manual adjustments, the reasons behind a particular tolerance. When a team revisited the engine in 2013, they did not rebuild it from the 1960s drawings; they reverse-engineered a surviving museum unit with modern scanning and manufacturing. The documentation had been preserved perfectly. The knowledge had not. Storage is not memory.

However, the culture of innovation spread during the 2020s. More people started to recognize that failure has a value. The concept of Knowledge Management came back with a different name: platforms. For instance, initiatives in the banking sector have shown how an organizational memory can be deliberately cultivated.

- Citi prevents technical amnesia by documenting every pilot and startup engagement, enabling rapid pivots when opportunities reappear.
- Morgan Stanley prevents narrative amnesia by embedding inclusion into its Multicultural Innovation Lab, remembering what venture capital often forgets.
- Wells Fargo balances both, preserving technical lessons from failed fintech pilots and narratives from evolving sectors.

The Frascati and Oslo manuals revealed the limits of measurement. Case studies revealed the cost of forgetting. AI now provides the means to restore what was missing all along: memory. With ROI^2, we can finally connect technical and narrative threads, turning organizational memory into a measurable, strategic asset.

Innovation has never been only about ideas, budgets, or patents. It has always been about what organizations choose to remember—and what they allow themselves to forget.

This is also why AI marks a turning point: where knowledge management platforms failed to capture failures and hard lessons, AI can automatically collect and contextualize them. By integrating both victories and mistakes into a shared memory, AI succeeds where knowledge management stalled, creating a living foundation on which ROI^2 can finally be built.

One powerful anecdote comes from the pharmaceutical industry. A mid-sized European lab once abandoned a compound after a failed round of testing. Traditionally, that story would have been buried, filed away as a failure no one wished to recall. Years later, during the COVID-19 pandemic, AI-driven pattern recognition flagged the same compound as a potential antiviral. Because the abandoned data and negative results had been preserved, researchers could quickly repurpose the compound, shaving months off the development timeline. What had once been dismissed as useless failure became a vital stepping stone. This is the promise of organizational memory made visible: mistakes reframed as assets, waiting for the right context to reveal their value.

→ The innovation management lifecycle enables the management of innovation as a portfolio.

Innovation Management has long lived in two different worlds. Research and Development (R&D) is built for exploration—eyes on uncertainty, hands in experiments, ears tuned to faint signals at the edge of what's known. Innovation management is built for adoption—bringing ideas to market, changing behaviours, and making things work at scale.

For years, we've treated these worlds like neighbouring rooms with different furniture and different rules. In practice, they share the same roof. The weather rolls from one room into the other. A single, fragile plank crosses the distance between discovery and adoption:

Organizational Memory—the habit of keeping the logbook as we go so the next watch doesn't sail blind.

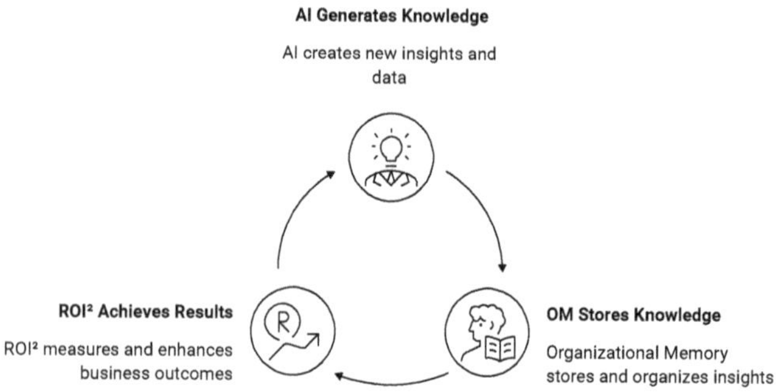

This chapter is about that plank. Not as software. Not as a capital-P Program. As a working style: light, persistent, and honest enough to preserve headwinds as well as horizons. When memory holds, yesterday's false starts fertilize tomorrow's successes. When it cracks, even good teams pay twice for the same lesson.

Two stories illustrate what this looks like in practice—one from a pharmaceutical laboratory in Europe, and one from four hundred million kilometres away. Both are about the same failure: a system that stored knowledge but could not retrieve it when it was needed most.

A team solves a problem that once looked impossible: a sensor finally hears a signal through the noise. There's a graph and a grin. Weeks later, someone asks why *that* threshold, at *that* tolerance. The answer exists—somewhere—split across a notebook, a late-night message, and a code commit helpfully named "final_final." The person who remembers is on another project. The story hesitates, and momentum drains. The bridge between R&D and innovation is not theoretical. It's where incomplete stories go to slow down.

Organizational Memory keeps the story whole. Not polished—whole. It preserves the doubt, the try-and-fail, the detour that saved the day. It leaves enough breadcrumbs for the next step to follow the path more quickly.

Common Misunderstandings

"R&D = innovation."
R&D is an input. Innovation is an implemented change. Innovation Management embraces both.

"Incremental doesn't count."
It counts if implemented and scaled. Oslo says so; your customers confirm it.

"Standards make us slow."
Heavy process makes you slow; light standards make you clear. Clarity speeds you up.

"If we measure, we must rank."
No. Measure to learn. Rank only where choices must be made.

What Counts as Memory (and What Doesn't)

A shared drive isn't a memory. A wiki isn't a memory. Even a perfect report isn't memory unless someone can *find it, trust it, and use it* at the moment of decision.

Memory is a capability, not a cupboard. It's the quiet discipline of capturing why a choice was made, what was tried, how we knew it worked (or didn't), and where it led next.

Artefacts that travel well between the two worlds:

- **Uncertainty log** in plain language—what we didn't know and how we planned to find out.
- **Experiment registry** linking tests to their purpose, variables, raw data, and who ran them.
- **Decision rationale** for irreversible choices: options, triggers, trade-offs, and the strongest doubt in the room.
- **Performance envelope** for prototypes: where it sings, where it breaks, and why that's acceptable.
- **Failure narrative**—not a eulogy, a lesson; clear enough that a stranger can avoid that corner next time.

None of this is novel. The difficulty is making it a habit within the rhythm of work, not an afterthought once sprints are over and attention has moved on.

After thirty years in innovation management, I have come to believe that the real test of an organization's memory is not what it does with its successes. It is what it does with the projects it kills. The working principle is blunt: innovation is not about creating a new product. It is about identifying, as quickly as possible, which products will never be adopted—and stopping them before they consume resources that belong to the next idea. Speed of termination is a capability, not a failure. But termination without capture is waste twice over: once when the investment is lost, and again when the next team repeats the same dead end from ignorance.

This is why a killed project should never simply disappear. It enters what we call the Purgatory—a structured transition between active portfolio and permanent memory. In Purgatory, a project is no longer funded, but it is not yet forgotten. Its assumptions are documented. Its failure modes are named. Its partial findings are tagged and indexed. Only once the extraction is complete does the project enter the organization's permanent record, where it remains available to any future team that asks a similar question. The project is dead. Its knowledge is not. A documented failure is an asset. An undocumented one is just a loss.

Pfizer learned this the expensive way, and then the lucrative one. In the early 1990s, the company was testing a compound—UK-92,480—as a treatment for angina. The trials disappointed: the effect on the heart was slight, and a pure portfolio decision would have killed the molecule and cleared the shelf. What saved it was not the drug. It was the discipline of reading the failure closely. Buried in the patients' reports of side effects was a consistent, unexpected signal about blood flow. Pfizer did not throw away the data when it abandoned the indication; it mined the post-mortem, pivoted, and in 1998, the compound that had failed at its first job was approved under a different name: Viagra. A killed project's learning, captured rather than filed and forgotten, became a product measured in tens of billions of dollars. That is what Purgatory is for.

When Memory Isn't Optional

There are places where memory is enforced, not encouraged. R&D tax credits are like that.

France (CIR/CII)	Canada (SR&ED)
The Crédit d'Impôt Recherche (CIR) returns a significant portion of eligible R&D costs; the Crédit d'Impôt Innovation (CII) extends support to certain downstream activities for SMEs. Both expect Frascati-aligned boundaries and a coherent narrative of uncertainty, experiments, and competence. Firms with strong OM produce dossiers by exporting what they already track; firms without it perform archaeology under deadline.	The Scientific Research & Experimental Development program supports a wide range of sectors with rates that vary by company size and status. The emphasis is the same: technological uncertainty; systematic investigation by qualified personnel; evidence produced in the normal course of work. Teams that treat SR&ED as a filing exercise struggle; teams that treat it as a design constraint build better memory.

For over 15 years, my professional journey has been dedicated to assisting organizations in both France and Canada in navigating the intricate landscape of government innovation incentives. I was preparing these entities to claim the substantial financial support offered by the government to organizations that demonstrate a willingness to embrace the risks inherent in innovation.

My experience with R&D tax credits has given me an understanding of the various innovation-related programs, eligibility criteria, and application processes for securing these generous government payments, ultimately fostering a culture of innovation and growth within the private sector.

Government auditors for those incentive mechanisms don't ask for glossy brochures or heroics. They ask for evidence that **uncertainty** existed, that **experiments** were undertaken to resolve it, and that **competent people** did the work. If the uncertainty was routine, if experiments were undocumented, if competence was assumed rather than shown, the answer is simple: *no.*

Countries that have established it consider the R&D tax credit as part of the innovation mix: predictable enough for CFOs, flexible enough for labs, and legible enough for auditors. Policymakers saw that firms responded not just by spending more, but by improving documentation quality. The unintended gift to companies? A forcing function for OM. Teams that learned to assemble clear evidence packs under time pressure had already built the bones of a living memory system—if they chose to keep the habit between filing seasons.

I supported organizations in countries with and without an R&D Tax Credit. I observed greater adoption of Organizational Memory mechanisms where incentives exist. However, even with a financial incentive—real money returned to the firm—many organizations struggle to produce a coherent record.

The annual scramble is familiar: reconstruct old test plans, call the engineer who "might remember," piece together commit histories, rebuild a timeline from inboxes and slides. It's archaeology under a deadline.

There's a quiet lesson here. If we struggle to remember when remembering *pays*, why would we remember better when the only reward is better decisions?

Bias and the Stories We Prefer

People are generous storytellers. We tidy a sequence to make it understandable. We keep the ending in mind and pull earlier steps into its orbit. We highlight the parts where we did well because trust is earned through competence and calm. These are virtues in life. In innovation work, they can become traps.

For instance, recency bias shapes how users judge experiences—the last ten percent can colour the whole. Teams carry the same bias inside the building. Without a record, we remember the ending and forget the map.

Human bias affecting OM
• Recency swells: the last ten percent colours the first ninety; early failures fade. • Success edits: alternative paths vanish, as if the road had always been straight. • Credit drifts: obstacles shrink and agency expands. No malice; it just adds up.

Better tools won't erase human biases. Design will. Ask for the uncertainty log as a matter of course. Make room for failure narratives. Reward the quality of the record as part of the job.

When Memory Slips

Pharma – The Missing Protocol Page

A mid-stage trial should have been confirmatory. It became a puzzle. Months earlier, the team altered an assay to meet a recruitment window. Throughput improved; sensitivity changed. The debate took place in a meeting that no one recorded. Two years later, a secondary endpoint failed. Everyone remembered the *decision*; no one remembered the *reasons*. Reconstructing context took nine months and cost a partnership window. The science was sound; the memory was not.

Automotive – The Vanishing Calibration

An OEM invested early in hybrid drivetrains. The learning ran deep—stored in personal notebooks, a deprecated server, and a retiring specialist's head. When electrification surged, new teams reran experiments because calibrations and track logs might as well have been written on water. Competitors with a living record moved faster.

Banking – The Pilot We Piloted Twice

A lab-tested biometric onboarding. Edge-case fraud and call-centre friction sank the scale-up. Three years later, a new cohort proposed the same idea with the same vendors. The old deck existed without the evidence trail—no incident tags, no post-pilot math. They reached the same conclusion. Confidence wore thin.

Public Sector – Sandboxes and Sifting

A ministry ran a privacy-preserving analytics sandbox. Pragmatic interpretations emerged—documented in minutes and inboxes. When a sister program launched, the debates restarted from zero. The law hadn't changed; the memory had.

Medical Devices – The DHF That Didn't Explain Why

A device maker's Design History File met the checklist but missed the story. A late change corrected a field failure mode, yet the rationale and conditions weren't captured. When a similar complaint surfaced two years later, the CAPA team spent weeks proving they weren't repeating an old mistake. The fix existed; the *why* didn't travel.

Energy – The Pilot That Stalled the Grid

A utility trialled advanced metering with dynamic pricing. Peaks flattened during the pilot—then spiked in rollout. The context notes (seasonality, rebate timing, a local heatwave) lived in a planner's notebook. Operations inherited the design without the caveats. Customer calls rose; trust fell; the team back-fit explanations; the memory should have carried forward.

Consumer Tech – The A/B Test That Lied in Summer

A growth team proved that a checkout nudge worked through June. In October, the results reversed. No one had logged the instrumentation change or the seasonal campaign that shifted the traffic mix. The test registry later showed a pattern: what worked for new users on mobile in the summer didn't work for returning users on desktop in the fall. The lesson stuck only after it was written down and easy to find.

These aren't failures of intelligence or effort. They're failures of drift—stories never fully written down or written down where they couldn't be found.

The Temptation of Shortcuts

Big organizations often turn to hackathons. The energy is real—people who rarely meet share whiteboards. Old code wakes up. New angles appear. For a week, the company remembers how to be porous and curious. Hackathons are useful—but they're not a memory. They're a lens that narrows for a moment. They break problems into topics and reward improvisation. They don't, by themselves, connect distant branches of the knowledge tree. Without a living system to absorb what they surface, their output is a bright flare in a dark archive.

Used well, hackathons can be harvesters. Seed teams with prior pilots and failure reports. Ask for one pattern others can reuse and one artifact that plugs into a shared ontology. Follow with a short harvest sprint to integrate what was learned. Make the flare part of a constellation.

The Craft of Evidence

Well-built memory is invisible in the moment. It rewards small acts done on time. Change a parameter? Log *why* in one sentence. Fork code? State the purpose in a single line. Stop a run early? Three words: *stopped for X*. In one lab, this produced a recognizable voice. Newcomers could read a day's work in minutes and grasp what mattered.

Elsewhere, a product group treated decisions as first-class citizens. Each irreversible choice had a one-page rationale: options, triggers, trade-offs, and the person most worried about the downside. It wasn't bureaucracy. It was a map for the next crew that would wonder why someone carried a canoe across a mountain.

A Tuesday in Retrieval

A product manager is asked whether a spec can be widened for a partner. The answer hangs on a threshold set two years ago. She types a question into a single search bar: *Who changed the sensor threshold and why?* Back comes a thread, not a dump: the week's uncertainty log; experiment entries that tipped the decision; a rationale with two options and a trade-off; an annotation in the performance envelope where the threshold is marked in red.

She doesn't need to "trust the system." She trusts the voices: an engineer who wrote "we tried the obvious thing and it failed," a statistician who noted the test's limits, a support lead who remembered returns. Her reply to the partner is simple: *We can widen it this far. Beyond that, we repeat a known failure. Here's the story.*

Good retrieval doesn't feel like a search. It feels like picking up a conversation that was waiting for you.

A Shape, Not a Recipe

Organizations ask for recipes; they tire of principles. Here's a shape that adapts without turning into a program no one owns:

- **Roles with names.** A memory steward per portfolio—vocabulary, quality, cross-project patterns. An evidence owner per project—uncertainty log, experiment registry, decision trail.
- **A light ontology.** Not an encyclopedia. A shared set of words—problem, uncertainty, experiment, failure mode, performance envelope—so artifacts connect across functions.
- **Work-in-flow capture.** Templates inside the tools people already use. Metadata captured automatically. Replace "write the report later" with "write one line now."
- **Retrieval for questions.** Organize around decisions, not departments: prior pilots by theme; known failure modes; regulatory interpretations we relied on.
- **Incentives that dignify learning.** Visible credit for the best failure write-up. Recognition for an artifact that others reuse. Dashboards that whisper rather than shout.

The point isn't to make memory heavy. It's to make it inevitable.

What to Measure (Carefully)

Some metrics warm the heart and kill the practice—page views, document counts, uploads per month. Motion isn't learning. Measure what changes decisions:

- **Reuse rate:** how often new work uses a prior artifact.
- **Time-to-insight:** median time to find a relevant precedent.
- **Avoided duplication:** experiments cancelled or redesigned because evidence said so.
- **Traceability health:** share of projects with complete uncertainty logs and registries.
- **Learning velocity:** patterns updated or retired this quarter.

Treat these as dials, not scoreboards.

The mechanics of running a Season—the budget, the boundary, the quarter-by-quarter rhythm—belong to Part III, where we build the system. Here it is enough to know that amnesia has a cure, and that the cure has to be governed, not merely wished for.

Foresight and Memory, Speaking to Each Other

Foresight scans the horizon for signals and tests the future for fit. It needs a memory to matter. A signal without a record ends up as a slide—admired and forgotten. Memory without foresight becomes a museum. In mature systems, signals are logged like experiments; scenario assumptions are tied to pilots that tried to implement them; surprising failures become weak signals, not just disappointments; patterns that recur across projects become candidates for scenarios, not myths. When the two speak, strategy stops drifting into storytelling, and execution stops repeating old debates.

This pairing clarifies a distinction that portfolio managers routinely confuse. Progression measures what the team is doing: how far an initiative has advanced through the phases. Confidence measures what the world is doing: whether the external conditions for adoption are becoming more or less favourable. They are different signals. A project can progress steadily while the market conditions for it deteriorate.

Another can stall internally while the environment outside turns sharply in its favour. Reading only one is like navigating with half a compass. The decision to accelerate, pause, or retire an initiative requires both readings simultaneously—not one mistaken for the other.

Risks, Spoken Softly

Good intentions have wrecked as many memory systems as negligence has. Over-documentation turns work into paperwork—keep the checklist short, link to raw data, ban orphan PDFs. Tool sprawl fragments context—hold the line at one search bar and a few well-integrated systems. When no one owns memory, it decays—give the job a name and a calendar slot. Fear of exposure chills learning—create access tiers, redact what must be safe, protect the earnest failure. Initiative fatigue kills trust—ship value in a quarter, retire what doesn't help, praise reuse out loud. Risks don't vanish because we name them. They become smaller because we pay attention.

A Quiet 90-Day Start

No banners required. In ninety days a small team can prove the point.

- Days 1–15: pick a portfolio, map tools, sample artifacts, and find gaps.
- Days 16–30: agree on a handful of words, publish a one-page artifact checklist, name stewards and evidence owners.
- Days 31–60: slip templates into existing tools, automate metadata, seed search with five high-value histories.
- Days 61–75: build decision-oriented views, run one portfolio learning review, write ten pattern cards.
- Days 76–90: turn on three dials, recognize the best failure write-up, decide what to scale and what to stop.

Cultures adopt new habits that prove useful fast and don't make anyone feel foolish for the old ones.

A Smaller Story

A plant's line stops after a tolerance drift. A younger engineer recalls a rumour about a similar drift from years ago. He types into the search bar and finds, to his surprise, a thread: an old uncertainty log, a failure narrative written with kindness, a rationale signed by a name on a hallway photo. The thread shows where the line held, and why. He calls the floor, makes a change, and the line hums again—no memo to the board. A little less money lost, a little less stress felt, and the next person who asks a question finds a story that's still warm. That's what memory feels like on a good day.

Why Now, and What Comes Next

Organizations are busier than ever, and attention is scarce. The temptation is to move faster and trust that learning will catch up. It won't—not without help.

The price of neglect is duplication, delay, and a quiet cynicism that creeps in when good work is forgotten and repeated. We have manuals for counting inputs and classifying outcomes.

Conventional strategy has its instruments too, refined over decades. None of them was built for the thing that actually decides whether a new initiative succeeds. Innovation is, by definition, a first-time experience. The work has not been done before—yet the organization is rarely as inexperienced as it feels. It holds overlapping experiences, good and bad, that bear directly on the new problem, if only it can find them.

What it cannot find, it repeats from scratch. The missing instrument is not another strategy method; it is a working memory of how the organization has actually solved comparable problems before—the kind of knowledge that lives in people and notebooks, not in the quarterly deck, and that never appears on a balance sheet.

Even a strong practice strains under scale. Millions of documents, dozens of systems, and the gentle drift of language across functions are more than any human steward can hold. Connecting distant branches of the organization's knowledge tree is tedious work.

It is too much for any team of human stewards—no matter how disciplined, no matter how well-resourced. That problem now has a copilot.

The Compound That Was Never Forgotten

The laboratory director would later say that the strangest thing was how long they had been looking for it.

The compound—let us call it K-7, as the actual name is proprietary—had been synthesized fourteen years earlier by a chemist who had since retired to Brittany. At the time, K-7 had shown modest activity in one assay and unremarkable results in several others. The team had moved on. The notebooks recording the synthesis were filed correctly and diligently in the archive system maintained by every pharmaceutical company to satisfy regulatory requirements. The system worked exactly as designed.

Fourteen years later, a different team, working on a different indication, encountered a signalling pathway that sparked renewed interest in a class of compounds that K-7 happened to inhabit. They searched the external literature. They searched public patent databases. They did not, because they did not know how to search their own archive. Three months into the new project, at considerable expense, a contract research organization synthesized what turned out to be—after a junior scientist had the idea of cross-referencing the new assay data against the old archive—essentially the same compound.

The compound had never been forgotten. It was exactly where it had been filed. The organization had lost the ability to ask questions of its own history.

The Mars Orbiter and the Units Problem

On September 23, 1999, the Mars Climate Orbiter fired its main engine to enter Martian orbit after a ten-month journey. Something went wrong during the burn. The spacecraft, designed to insert into a high orbit, instead entered the Martian atmosphere at an angle that subjected it to forces it was not built to survive. The mission was lost at a cost of $327 million.

The investigation revealed the cause almost immediately: one engineering team had provided navigation data in metric units while another had been calculating in imperial—newtons versus pound-force. The error was not in the spacecraft's design, not in the navigation software, not in the orbital mechanics. The error was in the interface between two groups of people who shared a project but did not share a common system of meaning.

The Mars Orbiter is routinely cited as an example of engineering failure, and that is accurate. But I want to use it differently here, as an example of memory failure at the institutional level. Both teams knew what they were doing. Both teams were competent. What neither team knew—what the project's memory system had failed to record and propagate—was the essential contextual fact that they were using different measurement conventions. The knowledge existed. The interface between knowledge domains had failed.

Organizational memory failures almost always look like this. The information is there; the connection is not. The compound is in the archive; the pathway to it is absent. The engineering data is correct; the common language is missing. And in the absence of the connection—in the absence of what I will call, throughout this book, the memory infrastructure—the organization's accumulated knowledge is technically present but functionally inaccessible.

What Amnesia Actually Looks Like

When clinicians describe anterograde amnesia—the inability to form new long-term memories, as opposed to the loss of existing ones—they often note that sufferers appear entirely normal in the present moment. They can hold a conversation, respond to questions, and make jokes. It is only when you try to test them an hour later that the deficit becomes visible: the conversation has vanished. The meeting never happened. The introduction must begin again.

Corporate organizational amnesia operates on a slower clock but with a structurally similar pattern. The organization appears to function normally. Projects complete, reports are filed, lessons-learned documents are produced. It is only when you try to access that institutional history—when you ask "what did we try in this space three years ago?"—that the deficit becomes visible. The project was completed, but the knowledge of it did not persist in a retrievable form.

The pilot ran, but nobody who remembers running it is still in the organization. The report exists in an archive folder that nobody thinks to search.

The pharmaceutical company that rediscovered K-7 is not an outlier. Studies of innovation failure rates across industries consistently find that a substantial fraction of failed innovation projects fail not because the underlying idea was wrong, but because the organization had already tried something similar, learned something important, and then forgotten what it had learned. The memory was there. The infrastructure for connecting new questions to prior knowledge was absent.

This chapter is about building that infrastructure. Not as an IT system—though IT is part of it—but as an organizational capability: the deliberate design of memory that persists across personnel changes, across reporting periods, across the quarterly rhythm that tends to overwrite institutional history with the urgency of the present.

The Four Kinds of Memory

An organization does not remember in one place. It remembers in four, and each of the four forgets in its own way.

Individual memory is the most powerful and the most fragile. A seasoned practitioner carries decades of context—why a thing was done this way and not that, what was tried and quietly abandoned, the informal political history behind a technology choice. When that person leaves, what goes is not a list of skills; it is the connective tissue between the documents and the judgment to use them. Organizations that lose a few key people often display what looks like competency amnesia—a sudden inability to do something they demonstrably knew how to do last year.

Structural memory—the policies, procedures, and processes—is more durable and far more rigid. It preserves the output of a past lesson without the reasoning behind it. A control built to prevent one specific failure becomes, over the years, simply a rule; the failure it was meant to prevent has dropped out of institutional consciousness. The process survives. The memory that justified it does not.

Cultural memory is the most powerful of all and the least visible—the shared sense of how we do things here, which ideas get taken seriously, which experiments are permitted. It encodes an enormous amount of hard-won learning, and it resists every attempt to write it down. You cannot archive a culture. You can only live in it or lose it.

External memory—the archives, the reports, the lessons-learned reviews—is the most abundant and the most wasted. Organizations generate documentation by the tonne, and most of it is unreachable, because it was filed for compliance rather than for retrieval. The information is there. The only question that matters is whether the organization can still ask it a useful question.

Building memory means designing for all four at once: capturing individual knowledge before it walks out the door, keeping structural memory legible so its reasons survive, holding cultural continuity across a change of leadership, and—above all—building the retrieval layer that lets an archive answer back.

Knowledge That Is Hidden, Not Lost

There is a darker form of forgetting that most innovation writing steps politely around. Sometimes knowledge does not leak away. It is withheld, on purpose.

It is a Tuesday afternoon, and an engineer named Sofia is hunting through a shared drive for calibration data from a project cancelled two years ago. She knows the data exists—she sat in the meeting where it was presented. The folder is empty. She emails the project's former lead, Marc, who replies three days later: "I'm not sure I still have those. Let me check." He does not check. The files are on his personal drive. He knows that surfacing them would reveal that his team's old approach was flawed—and that the same fact, raised now, would weaken the proposal he has in front of the steering committee. So he waits. Sofia rebuilds the model from scratch over six weeks and forty thousand dollars. The organization has just paid the knowledge-hiding tax, and no one will ever send it an invoice.

Organizational psychologists have a name for Marc's behaviour: knowledge hiding—the deliberate withholding of knowledge that someone else has asked for. It is not forgetting and it is not ignorance, and it is far more common than most executives believe; in survey after survey, a clear majority of employees admit to some version of it. It takes three recognizable forms. There is evasive hiding, where you protect your position by sharing less—because in an organization where sharing what you know makes you replaceable, sharing less is simply rational. There is rationalized hiding, the most corrosive of the three, where you appear to cooperate while handing over answers that are incomplete or quietly misleading; it degrades the knowledge base under cover of collaboration. And there is playing dumb—the files are "somewhere on the old server," the method was "never really documented," the contact at the partner firm "left years ago."

The effect on innovation is worse than ordinary forgetting. When knowledge is hidden, an organization does not merely fail to remember. It is deceived into believing it never knew. A team walking into a new market may have no idea that the same move was tried and abandoned three years earlier, not because the record was lost, but because the person who led it has every reason to keep that history dark.

Why Hiding Is Rational

The reason knowledge hiding survives decades of investment in knowledge management is that leaders treat it as the opposite of sharing, as if pouring more incentive into sharing would drain the hiding away. It does not. Sharing and hiding are not two ends of one dial. They are driven by different forces, and they coexist quite happily. An organization can run excellent collaboration platforms and a thriving culture of concealment at the same time.

Cross those two forces—how much people want to share, and how much they want to hide—and four states fall out, each one a Head of Innovation should be able to recognize. When the urge to share is high and the urge to hide is low, you have open collaboration: the ideal, where memory accumulates almost by itself. When both are low, you have passive silos: nobody hides anything, but nobody shares either, and knowledge sits in private drawers out of sheer indifference—this is the state most knowledge-management projects are built to fix, and it is only one of the four. When both are high, you have strategic ambiguity, the most common and most deceptive state of all: people share in the rewarded, visible places—the presentation, the formal handoff—and hide in the unmonitored ones—the corridor conversation that never gets written down, the name quietly left off an email. The surface looks collaborative. The blind spots are enormous. And when the urge to share is low while the urge to hide is high, you have active concealment, which produces the darkest outcomes and is more common than most leaders will admit.

What makes hiding so dangerous is that it feeds on itself. Person A asks B for something; B withholds it. A notices—people are remarkably good at sensing when they are being stonewalled, even when the other side believes the concealment was perfect—and begins withholding from B in turn. B senses that and escalates. Now C, who was never wronged by anyone, watches the two of them and pre-emptively closes up, because C has learned that around here the norm is to hold back. Within two or three quarters, a grudge between two people can reset the sharing behaviour of an entire team. For the practitioner, the early warning is concrete: a knowledge-reuse rate that falls quarter on quarter, even as new knowledge keeps being created, is the signature of a distrust spiral already turning.

The Judgment You Cannot Capture

There is one more way memory degrades, and it is the one organizations inflict on themselves with the best of intentions. Call it depersonalization: the habit of treating knowledge as a substance you can extract from a person and store without them—capture the what, discard the who.

It does not work because the "Who" is most important knowledge. Think of a researcher who has spent three years inside one narrow problem. What she knows is not the data she has logged. It is her instinct for which approaches are dead ends, her feel for the quirks of her own equipment, her network of contacts who will give her an off-the-record read, her judgment about when a strange result is a real anomaly and when it is just noise. Ask her to pour all of that into a standard knowledge template and you will capture perhaps fifteen percent of it.

Artificial intelligence is making this worse, not better, wherever it is used carelessly. Feed a pile of documents into a model and throw away the relationship with the people who wrote them, and you have built a system that retrieves facts but not judgment. It can tell you what the researcher wrote. It cannot tell you what she chose not to write, what she was unsure of, or what she would do differently if she started again tomorrow. That is precisely why Relational Capital is one of the four capitals and not a footnote. It is not a soft aspiration; it is a structural requirement for memory that holds. Strip the human context out of what you capture, and you end up scoring high on documented knowledge and low on knowledge that actually works when someone reaches for it.

It All Comes Down to Trust

Hiding, hoarding, and depersonalization are not really the disease. They are symptoms, and underneath almost every one of them is the same root cause: a deficit of trust. Hiding and hoarding are worth separating, by the way. Hiding is active—the deliberate concealment we have been describing. Hoarding is passive—the developer who keeps a private library of fixes and never migrates it, not out of malice but because writing it up for everyone earns him nothing. One is a decision to deny; the other is the absence of any reason to share. Both leave the organization poorer.

Trust runs at four levels, and they line up almost exactly with the four capitals. Interpersonal trust, whether colleagues feel safe enough to admit uncertainty and reveal failure, is what lets people share what they know, and it feeds Knowledge Capital. Institutional trust, whether people believe the organization will credit them fairly and not use what they share against them, is built through governance, and it feeds Process Capital. Inter-team trust, whether one team believes another will reciprocate, is what lets knowledge cross internal borders, and it feeds Memory Capital. Ecosystem trust, whether partners will co-invest and share real risk, is what makes external collaboration produce genuine value, and it feeds Relational Capital.

This is also why the cost of all this stays invisible. The project that fails because no one knew a predecessor had already hit the same wall is filed as a project failure, not a knowledge failure. The launch delayed because the original rationale for a design choice could not be found is recorded as a delay. The pattern repeats across every industry and every size of company; what varies is not whether the cost exists but whether anyone bothers to look for it. The framework rolls these conditions—hiding, distrust, lost context—into a single signal it calls Memory Fracture Risk: the odds that critical knowledge will be unreachable at the moment it is needed most. It sits on the dashboard beside ROI^2, one reading for the value your innovation is creating, one for the share of it quietly at risk. Making that cost visible is the whole point of measuring the four capitals rather than the outputs alone.

Trust is the atmospheric pressure of innovation: invisible, foundational, and decisive. A measurement system that tracks outputs while ignoring the trust beneath them is a forecast that reads the temperature and never checks the pressure. The numbers may be right today. They tell you nothing about tomorrow.

Fourteen Hundred Miles to the Right

In July 2014, I climbed aboard a sixty-five-foot racing sailboat at the port of Quebec City, Canada and did not set foot on land again before reaching Saint-Malo's port in France.

The crossing took fourteen days. The crew was fourteen people—fourteen CEOs, to be exact, assembled from a network of entrepreneurs who had dared each other into progressively more impractical challenges. The skipper was Georges Leblanc, a man who had crossed oceans before and who treated the Atlantic with the specific, unhurried respect of someone who understood what it could do.

I had been preparing for this crossing for fourteen months. That preparation was physical—training runs, sea passages in smaller boats, and emergency procedures drilled until they were automatic. But the most important preparation was not physical. It was the preparation of understanding that you were about to enter an environment that had no interest in your confidence, your professional credentials, or your prior track record. The Atlantic does not read CVs. It has its own measurement system.

On the third night out, the wind shifted unexpectedly—not dramatically, not dangerously, but enough that the sail trim we had set was now wrong. I was on watch with a very successful Canadian entrepreneur. He understood systems, risk, and decision-making under pressure. He did not understand sails. Neither of us did, fully. What saved the watch was not individual expertise; it was the accumulated learning of the crew's combined hours at sea, the informal knowledge base we had been building since departure, the ability to call on the experience of someone who had been through this before. We adjusted the sails. The boat found her rhythm again. The lesson was invisible unless you were looking for it.

What the crossing taught me—and I suspect this is what ocean passages teach most people who pay attention—is that performance in a complex system is not primarily about individual competence. It is about the memory of experience. Not human memory alone, but the distributed, institutional memory of a crew: who knows what, what was tried last time, what failed and why, what the boat will tell you if you listen to her carefully. Navigation is memory with instruments.

When I returned to land and began trying to articulate what I had learned, I found myself thinking about a framework I had been developing for several years in my consulting work—a way of categorizing the kinds of value that innovation generates, none of which appear cleanly in conventional accounting.

In Part II, I will introduce you in a more practical way to the instrument I built during this long reflection: a compass built on four capitals, calibrated by four readings, and powered by the one asset that most organizations have systematically neglected—their own memory, made readable at last by generative AI. Hold that chain; it is the spine of everything ahead: generative AI made organizational memory possible at scale, and organizational memory makes ROI^2 possible at all. You guessed right! This instrument is S4IL.

The Skipper's Log

Position — Organizations do not forget by accident; they forget by design. Incentives make hiding rational, and memory optional.

Sighted — Amnesia has two faces — knowledge lost and knowledge hidden. A shared drive is storage; memory is what answers when asked. Trust is the substrate of both.

Charted — The four kinds of organizational memory, and the craft of evidence that keeps each of them honest.

Course — Run the Tuesday test: ask a colleague to retrieve what the organization learned about a live topic three years ago. Time the search. That number is your amnesia, measured.

PART II — THE MISSING SPECIES

Picture an ecologist who has just spent two years surveying butterflies in a tropical forest. He worked methodically—walking the same transects week after week, netting specimens, recording species—and built what he took to be a comprehensive catalogue of the forest's butterflies. He identified 185 species.

He suspected he had missed some. Forests are complex. Some species are rare, some are seasonal, some hide well. But how many had he missed? He had no way of knowing what he had not seen. You cannot count an absence.

This is the problem Anne Chao, a biostatistician at National Tsing Hua University in Taiwan, took up in the early 1980s—not for butterflies in particular, but as a general question in ecological statistics: how do you estimate the total number of species in an ecosystem when your sampling is necessarily incomplete?

Her insight was elegant and unexpected. She noticed that the pattern of rare species in a sample contained information about what was missing from it. Specifically, the species seen exactly once—singletons—and the species seen exactly twice—doubletons—were not just the rarest creatures in the forest. They were signals of how many creatures remained undiscovered beyond the survey's edge. The rarer a species, the more it resembled the species that had not been seen at all.

She published her formula in 1984. Known today as Chao1, it estimates the total species richness of an ecosystem from the observed species

Applied to our ecologist's data, a formula like this estimates that the forest holds not 185 species but somewhere between 230 and 260. He had catalogued roughly three-quarters of what was there. The rest had been in the forest around him the whole time—he had simply not seen it.

The formula has since been validated across ecosystems worldwide, from the bacteria in a gram of soil to the fish in an ocean trench. It works because the rarest observed instances of a thing are the most reliable evidence of what remains invisible.

Every organization I have worked with over the past thirty years has the same problem as that forest. They believe they know what they know. They have surveys, databases, post-mortems, lessons learned, and repositories. They have catalogued 185 lessons learned.

How many did they miss?

Chapter 4: The Four Capitals of Innovation

Before leaving the house, I do the quadruple check. Every time. Wallet, phone, keys, sunglasses. In French—the language I revert to when I am talking to myself, which is more often than I would admit—it becomes a *4P framework*: Portefeuille, Portable, Porte-clés, Protection (sunglasses in summer and lip balm in winter).

I had been thinking about my own ritual one Tuesday morning in 2016, standing in the hallway of my Montreal apartment, patting my pockets in the familiar sequence, when a thought struck me sideways.

Back then, I was focusing on the "How to Get Adopted" strategies for what would become S4IL, and I was examining the foundational principles of the Marketing Discipline to understand how to better encourage an audience to adopt a novelty.

Marketing has its own 4P framework—Product, Price, Place, and Promotion—and it had been running global commerce since Jerome McCarthy codified it in 1960. Philip Kotler had built an empire on the idea that those four categories, taken together, describe the complete marketing decision space. Miss one, and the strategy has a hole.

Price. That was the word that caught me. Price is finance. Price is the number. Price is the thing every ROI calculation can see—the thing that spreadsheets were built to optimize. And yet, even in marketing, Price is only one of four. No one would accept a marketing strategy that measured only Price and ignored Product, Place, and Promotion. No one would argue that a pricing analysis, however sophisticated, constitutes a complete marketing audit. The other three dimensions carry value that pricing alone cannot capture. Everyone in marketing knows this. It is so obvious that it is not even debated.

And yet, in innovation management, this is precisely what we do.

We measure Financial Return—the Price of innovation—and call it a complete analysis. We file the other three dimensions under "intangibles" and wave them away. An innovation program that generates a billion dollars in revenue but leaves the organization no smarter, no better connected, and no more capable of innovating again has been measured as a triumph. An innovation program that generates no revenue but builds deep technical capability, opens strategic partnerships, and creates organizational memory that prevents the next cycle from repeating the same mistakes has been measured as a failure.

The quadruple check is not a metaphor. It is a diagnostic. Just as there are four things I cannot leave the house without, there are four types of capital that an organization cannot innovate without. Financial capital is one. The other three have been ignored for decades—not because they do not exist, but because no one built the instruments to measure them. The rest of this chapter builds those instruments.

Four Capitals, One ROI^2

Innovation is universally recognized as the key driver of growth, competitiveness, and resilience. Yet organizations have long struggled to answer a fundamental question: *What is the real return on innovation?* Traditional accounting systems measure tangible, predictable assets—factories, inventories, and equipment—but fail to capture knowledge, creativity, collaboration, and learning—the invisible assets that fuel progress.

The **Return on Innovation Investment (ROI²)** bridges this gap. Built upon the OECD's **Oslo Manual** (for innovation measurement) and the **Frascati Manual** (for R&D measurement), ROI² connects **knowledge creation** to **value realization**. It introduces practical methods to quantify innovation's economic, strategic, and societal contributions.

This chapter introduces the four capitals that ROI² is built from, and the two needles—Growth and Readiness—that read them.

This is not a new argument. We have been building toward it since the opening chapters, where we began to see that innovation creates four types of value—financial, strategic, intangible, and learning—and that traditional measurement captures only one of them. We have shown why ROI fails, why governance matters, why Open Innovation alone is not enough, why Organizational Memory is the missing variable, and why AI makes that memory finally tractable at scale. Chapter 7 is where those threads converge into a single, working instrument.

Conceptual Foundations: From Linear ROI to Systemic ROI²

Traditional ROI is built for predictable environments and short-term financial efficiency, making it inadequate for assessing innovation, which thrives in uncertainty and continual feedback.

The linear ROI formula is:

ROI = (Gain – Cost)/Cost

It reflects a closed, one-time cycle between investment and return. In contrast, innovation is an **open, adaptive system** where outcomes evolve through learning, iteration, and ecosystem collaboration.

ROI² extends this logic by embedding multi-period feedback loops and accounting for both tangible and intangible value creation.

Aspect	ROI	ROI²
Time Horizon	Short-term	Iterative, multi-period
Focus	Financial efficiency	Systemic value creation
Scope	Single project	Portfolio or ecosystem
Assets	Tangible only	Tangible and intangible
Risk View	Static	Adaptive and probabilistic
Feedback	Absent	Continuous through learning

Aligned with **Neo-Schumpeterian economics**, ROI² measures not only *returns on capital* but *returns on novelty*—the cumulative capability of an organization to generate and apply new knowledge. This idea is rooted in Joseph Schumpeter's theory of **creative destruction**, which describes how waves of innovation disrupt existing markets, replace outdated technologies, and create new economic structures. ROI² thus captures both the constructive and disruptive forces of innovation—

quantifying how renewal and obsolescence interact to shape long-term value creation.

The Knowledge-to-Decision Gap

Organizations carry far more knowledge than they use. The lessons from the failed 2019 pilot exist—documented, filed, and technically accessible. The team working on the same problem six years later will not find them. They will not know how to look. And even if they look, the way the old lesson was documented will not map to the language they use to frame the new problem. So, they will reinvent the failure.

This gap has a name in the research literature: the difference between potential **absorptive capacity**—what the organization knows—and realized absorptive capacity—what the organization actually uses. The gap between the two is one of the most persistent and costly inefficiencies in innovation management.

The practical test is simple. Ask: how many steps does it take for a lesson documented in one project to reach a decision-maker in a different project team working on a related problem? If the answer is more than three (find it, read it, apply it), you have a realized capacity problem.

Two organizations can possess comparable knowledge assets and exhibit radically different innovation performance trajectories. The difference is not what they know. It is how easily what they know reaches the decisions that matter.

A Compass with Two Needles

Before going further, fix the architecture in your mind. Three structures are about to do three different jobs, and only one of them is a needle. The compass has exactly two needles—Growth and Readiness, the pair you met in Chapter 2—and those are what you steer by. Beneath them sit two quartets that are not needles at all: the four reserves you accumulate, and the four readings you take. Most of the confusion in this field comes from calling all of these the same thing. We will not.

The first quartet is the **Four Capitals of Innovation**—Knowledge Capital, Relational Capital, Process Capital, and Memory Capital. These are the reserves, the accumulated assets that an organization builds over time. They represent what you have.

The second quartet is **Four Innovation Compass Readings**—Input, Throughput, Output, and Outcome. These are the flows, the dynamic measurements of how innovation moves through the organization. They represent what you do with what you have. The Capitals are the fuel. The Compass Readings are the gauges on the dashboard.

Knowledge Capital feeds every compass reading. Relational Capital lubricates the throughput. Process Capital structures the journey from input to output. And Memory Capital—the most neglected of the four—ensures that lessons from one cycle inform the next. Without Memory Capital, every innovation initiative starts from zero. With it, each cycle builds on the last.

The two needles are built from the four reserves. Growth is the return you can already bank—financial gain, drawn from Process Capital, and strategic gain, drawn from Relational Capital. Readiness is the return that has not yet surfaced—the intangible gain held in Knowledge

Capital, and the learning gain held in Memory Capital. Add what a season produces on each side, divide by what it cost, and ROI² falls out as an ordered pair: Readiness first, Growth second. The four readings are simply where, along the cycle, you take those measurements.

→The 4 Capitals are what you accumulate.

→The 4 Readings are what you measure.

→The 2 Needles are what you steer by.

Stack those three sentences and the whole instrument appears in a single picture. At the base sits everything the organization has accumulated—the four capitals, the memory of what it has tried, learned, and half-forgotten. Resting on that base are the gauges that read it: the four readings, which turn raw memory into numbers. The gauges drive one dial with two needles—Growth and Readiness, together ROI². And in the chapters ahead we will set one more storey on top: a ladder that tells you how far up this instrument your organization has actually climbed. Four storeys, each resting on the one beneath it. It is worth holding on to this shape, because the parts are about to multiply—capitals, readings, cycles, agents, postures. None of them is a rival idea competing for the same ground. Each is simply the furniture of one of these four storeys.

The Four Phases

In addition to the Four Capitals and the Four Readings, there is a third axis worth holding in mind: the stage of the innovation lifecycle a given initiative has actually reached. It is not a restatement of the other two. It is its own question.

Innovation investment does not happen in a single gesture. Each initiative moves through **Four Phases**—Where to Play, How to Win, How to Deliver, How to Get Adopted—and mistaking them for the Four Readings is the single most common category error this framework invites. A reading tells you where, in the measurement cascade, the needle is pointing right now. A phase tells you where the initiative itself has got to. They do not move in lockstep: a How-to-Deliver initiative can still be read at Input, if Input is what you happen to be tracking this cycle.

These phases align with the ISO 56002 Innovation Management System framework and echo the stages venture capital firms weigh when they invest, forming a full arc from spotting an opportunity to seeing it through. The first two are borrowed, deliberately, from A.G. Lafley and Roger Martin's *Playing to Win*—the sharpest articulation I know of what it means to choose where you compete before deciding how. The last two are mine, carrying the same logic through to delivery and adoption, where their strategic frame stops and an innovation manager's job continues.

The first phase is **Where to Play**. This is foresight work: feeding every idea this initiative will ever produce the data it needs before it exists—signals of change, emerging inventions, startups worth watching, academic and scientific literature, the trade and general press. Data without people who can interpret it is just noise, so this is also where the human network gets built: the subject-matter experts, the influencers who reach the audience you are chasing (including what Christensen would call the small worlds—the underserved sub-segments with a specific need nobody else is addressing), the pressure groups, and the regulators whose decisions will eventually bear on whether any of this ships. Where to Play does not choose a project. It chooses a territory.

The second phase is **How to Win**. The territory chosen in Where to Play now generates scenarios: ideas are produced, then clustered—not by who proposed them, but by the theme or the family of problem they collectively address. This is also where the initiative starts naming names: the people, inside the organization and outside it, without whom none of this gets built, from open-innovation partners to coopetitors willing to share a piece of the field. Proof of concept and prototyping happen here, and so does the opening move of Design Thinking, the empathy stage—focus groups, customer feedback, the unglamorous work of finding out whether anyone actually wants what you are about to spend a year building.

The third phase—and still the one most often skipped over in the innovation management literature—is **How to Deliver**. This is where an idea stops being an idea and becomes a project, with a scope someone is finally willing to commit to. Technical and human resources are mobilized to build a minimum viable product, and viable means something precise here: capable of generating value against every indicator chosen for this initiative, not only the one easiest to demonstrate at the next steering committee. It covers development, intellectual property creation, and productization. Most innovation programs that stall do not stall at the idea. They stall here, where a proven concept has to become a deliverable artifact, and nobody budgeted for how unglamorous that step would be.

The fourth phase is **How to Get Adopted**. A market-penetration strategy is defined and then executed—growth hacking, gamification, incentivization—in search of whatever mechanism will actually move a sceptical early-majority audience to adopt something a handful of early enthusiasts already love. Market entry, scaling, and impact measurement take centre stage. A product that exists but is not adopted has not completed the innovation journey. It has just finished a very expensive prototype.

→4 Capitals. 4 Phases. 4 Readings

Capital: which kind of value this initiative is building—Process, Knowledge, Memory, or Relational. **Phase**: where this initiative has actually got to on the ground—Where to Play, How to Win, How to Deliver, How to Get Adopted. **Reading**: where, in the measurement cascade, you are taking the pulse—Input, Throughput, Output, Outcome. Three different questions.

Miss any one of them, and the compass gives a false reading.

What Each Capital Actually Tracks

The four capitals—Knowledge, Relational, Process, and Memory—are not abstract categories. Each has a specific set of measurable indicators that together produce a comprehensive picture of innovation health. Understanding what each capital actually tracks, at the operational level, is essential for implementing the framework effectively.

Knowledge Capital. Knowledge Capital measures the organization's ability to generate and hold useful knowledge. Its indicators include: the number of new knowledge assets created per quarter (research papers, technical reports, market analyses, competitive intelligence documents); the diversity of knowledge domains represented in the portfolio (an organization with deep knowledge in one domain but no knowledge in adjacent domains is strategically fragile); the currency of the knowledge base (what percentage of knowledge assets have been reviewed or updated in the last twelve months); and the accessibility of knowledge (what percentage of employees can find and access the knowledge they need within fifteen minutes).

Relational Capital. Relational Capital measures the organization's network of trust and collaboration that enables knowledge to flow. Its indicators include: the density of cross-team collaboration (measured by joint projects, shared deliverables, and cross-functional team assignments); the strength of external partnerships (measured by joint publications, co-development agreements, and ecosystem participation rates); psychological safety scores (measured by validated survey instruments that assess whether employees feel safe sharing failures, uncertainties, and dissenting opinions); and the employee turnover rate among key knowledge holders (high turnover among experts is a leading indicator of Relational Capital erosion).

Process Capital. Process Capital measures the maturity and effectiveness of the organization's innovation processes. Its indicators include: decision latency (the time from insight to decision, and from decision to action); governance maturity (whether innovation decisions are made through structured, evidence-based processes or through ad hoc judgment); resource allocation efficiency (whether resources flow to the highest-value opportunities or are locked into legacy commitments); and the ratio of exploration to exploitation activities (the ambidexterity balance described in Chapter 7).

Memory Capital. Memory Capital measures the organization's ability to learn from its own experience over time. Its indicators include: the Reuse Rate (described in Chapter 5); the Memory Fracture Risk score (introduced in Chapter 3); the knowledge contribution rate (what percentage of employees actively contribute to the organizational memory system per quarter); and the Factorless Income Residual (described in Chapter 8)—the ultimate measure of whether accumulated organizational memory is producing compounding returns.

Together, the four capitals and their indicators produce what we call the Innovation Compass Score. This single composite metric tells the board of directors whether the organization's innovation capability is strengthening, stable, or eroding.

> **→The compass does not replace detailed analysis—you still need to read the individual indicators to understand why the score is moving.**

But it provides the high-level signal that busy executives need: Are we heading in the right direction?

The North Star Metric: Choosing Your Primary Signal

While the Innovation Compass Score provides an overall health signal, every organization should also define a **North Star Metric.** This single number best captures the organization's most important innovation objective for the current strategic period.

The North Star Metric is not the most comprehensive. It is the most clarifying metric—the one number that, if it improves, signals that the organization's innovation strategy is working. Different organizations in different strategic positions will choose different North Stars:

- An organization that is investing heavily in R&D but struggling to translate research into commercial products might choose the Reuse Rate as its North Star, signalling that the priority is knowledge application rather than knowledge creation.
- An organization that is acquiring smaller companies for their innovation capability might choose the knowledge absorption score as its North Star, signalling that the priority is absorbing and integrating external knowledge.

- An organization that is launching a major innovation program might choose the Factorless Income Residual as its North Star, signalling that the priority is to demonstrate that innovation investment is producing compounding returns beyond what individual projects deliver.
- An organization battling talent attrition in key innovation roles might choose the Relational Capital retention rate as its North Star, signalling that the priority is stabilizing the human network through which knowledge flows.

The North Star Metric should be reviewed annually and updated as the organization's strategic priorities evolve. It should be visible to everyone in the organization who is related to Innovation—not buried in a dashboard but displayed prominently as the primary measure of collective progress.

Enabling Organizational Memory with Generative AI

The promise of Organizational Memory has always been limited by a practical constraint: capturing, organizing, and retrieving institutional knowledge at scale requires effort that most organizations cannot sustain. Post-mortems go unread. Lessons-learned databases become digital graveyards. The knowledge exists, but the cost of making it accessible exceeds the perceived benefit—until now.

Generative AI changes this equation fundamentally. A large language model, fine-tuned or prompted with an organization's innovation history, can serve as a persistent copilot that remembers what humans forget. It can surface relevant prior art during ideation sessions. It can flag when a new project resembles a failed initiative from three years ago—and explain why it failed. It can synthesize lessons across hundreds of project reports in seconds.

But the copilot is only as good as what it is fed. The real breakthrough is not the AI itself—it is the disciplined practice of capturing both declarative knowledge (what we know explicitly: reports, patents, data) and tacit knowledge (what we learn implicitly: patterns across failures, tacit expertise, contextual judgment). An AI copilot that learns from both types becomes an organizational asset that appreciates with every project cycle.

The copilot does not replace human judgment. It amplifies institutional memory. The copilot co-drives innovation initiatives by providing continuity that no single person can offer. When a key engineer leaves, the copilot retains their documented reasoning. When a market pivot requires revisiting abandoned concepts, the copilot retrieves them instantly. Organizational Memory, enabled by Generative AI, transforms from an aspiration into infrastructure.

The Knowledge Withholding Problem

There is a darker obstacle to Organizational Memory than any technology can solve, and Chapter 3 examined it in full: knowledge withholding, the deliberate hoarding of what one knows because, in a resource-competitive culture, knowledge is power. It is worth naming again here only for where it lands on the ledger. Withholding does not drain some abstract resource—it attacks two of the four capitals at once, starving the Relational Capital that depends on exchange and corroding the Memory Capital that depends on lessons being written down at all. The structural and technological countermeasures belong to later chapters; the copilot of Chapter 6 will show how to make sharing so frictionless that withholding loses its advantage. For now, hold the cost in view.

> **→ The most dangerous knowledge loss is not accidental. It is the knowledge that people choose not to share.**

The Four Compass Readings

The Four Compass Readings—Input, Throughput, Output, and Outcome—are the operational heart of the measurement system. While the four capitals describe what is measured, the compass readings describe how measurement is structured across the innovation lifecycle. Each reading captures a different stage of the value creation process.

Input: What We Invest. The Input reading measures what goes into the innovation process: the resources, knowledge, relationships, and infrastructure that the organization invests. Input indicators include R&D spending, headcount allocated to innovation, the number of active partnerships, available knowledge assets, and the quality of the organizational memory system. Input indicators are necessary but not sufficient—high inputs without corresponding outputs indicate a process problem, not an investment problem.

Throughput: How We Process. The Throughput reading measures the health and efficiency of the innovation process itself: how effectively does the organization convert inputs into activities? Throughput indicators include decision latency (how quickly does the organization move from insight to action?), pipeline velocity (how quickly do ideas move through the innovation funnel?), collaboration density (how many cross-functional interactions occur per initiative?), and knowledge synthesis rate (how quickly is raw experience converted into reusable knowledge?). Throughput indicators reveal process bottlenecks before they affect outputs.

Output: What We Produce. The Output reading measures the tangible deliverables produced by the innovation: prototypes built, patents filed, products launched, processes improved, and knowledge assets created. Output indicators are the most visible and the most tempting to over-emphasize. But outputs without outcomes are activity without impact. A patent filed is an output; a patent that generates licensing revenue or blocks a competitor is an outcome.

Outcome: What Value We Create. The Outcome reading measures the ultimate value that innovation creates: revenue from new products, cost savings from process innovations, strengthened strategic positions, developed capabilities, and—above all—accumulated organizational learning. Outcome indicators are the hardest to measure because they lag behind outputs (sometimes by years) and because they are influenced by factors beyond the innovation team's control. But they are the only indicators that ultimately matter to the board of directors.

The discipline of the Four Compass Readings does not mean measuring everything, but measuring at least one indicator in each reading for every innovation initiative. An initiative that tracks only outputs ('we built a prototype') without tracking throughput ('how efficiently did we build it?') or outcomes ('did the prototype generate customer value?') is navigating with one instrument instead of four. The compass requires all four readings to produce a reliable navigational signal.

Before the next chapter puts this framework to work, one orientation will save you from a confusion I have watched derail many first attempts. The compass is read in two different modes, and mixing them is the fastest way to get lost.

The first mode is reading a situation. You have an opportunity in front of you, and you want to know its health: which capitals it is building, where it sits in its lifecycle, and at which point you are measuring it. Here, the four lenses are flat—four independent questions you ask about one thing, in any order. The second mode is establishing a season. Now you are not diagnosing a single initiative but designing a whole portfolio—deciding how much to invest, over how many cycles, and whether to weight it toward Growth or Readiness. Here, the lenses are not flat; they cascade, each decision constraining the next, from company strategy down to the indicators on a single initiative. That cascade is the subject of Chapter 9. For now, hold only this: the same four lenses answer a diagnostic question when you read a situation, and drive a design sequence when you establish a season.

The four lenses, and when each was set

Lens	What it shows	The question it answers	Introduced
Needles	The two ROI² readings you report	Are we winning, and are we getting readier?	Chapters 7–8
Capitals	The four assets an initiative builds	What did this initiative actually produce?	Chapter 4
Phases	The four stages of the innovation lifecycle	Where in its life is this initiative?	Chapter 4
Readings	The four measurement points	At which moment are we measuring?	Chapter 4

Keep this table beside you through Part III. When a chapter feels abstract, find which lens it is turning—and whether it is asking you to read a situation or to establish a season. Almost every difficulty with the framework, in my experience, dissolves the moment that distinction is clear.

The four capitals are defined. The four readings are calibrated. The framework exists. But a framework on paper is just a diagram. The question that separates organizations that measure innovation from organizations that merely talk about it is this: What does it actually look like when memory works? Not in theory. Not in a model. In a real organization, on a real Tuesday morning, when someone needs to find something the organization learned three years ago.

Four capitals, phases and readings, all set—now what?

The framework is complete—in theory. But theory without practice is just another slide deck in a shared drive. The next chapter takes you inside an organization that actually built this system and shows what innovation memory looks like when it works.

The Skipper's Log

Position — The compass exists: four capitals, four phases, four readings — and two needles, Readiness and Growth, read together, never collapsed into one.

Sighted — Each capital pays its return in a different way. Measuring only what markets price leaves half the instrument dark.

Charted — Knowledge, Relational, Process, Memory — and the Input, Throughput, Output, Outcome readings that track them through a season.

Course — Sort your current initiatives by the capital each one actually builds. The empty columns are not gaps in the model. They are gaps in the portfolio.

Chapter 5: What Memory Looks Like on a Good Day

Every sailor knows about barnacles. They attach themselves to the hull in clusters so small you barely notice them. Individually, each barnacle is trivial. Collectively, they add drag that can reduce a vessel's speed by thirty per cent. The cure is not to sail harder. The cure is to haul out the boat and scrape the hull clean. Organizational memory works the same way. Forgotten lessons, duplicated efforts, and lost contacts accumulate invisibly, one small failure at a time, until the entire innovation system is dragging through the water, wondering why nothing moves fast enough.

The call had been scheduled for nine o'clock. The engineer had been working on the new production process for seven months. She knew the system better than anyone currently in the building.

The problem was the phrase 'currently in the building.' The person who knew why the pressure settings were configured as they were had retired in 2019. The documentation said what the settings were; it did not say why. The engineer had spent the last three days trying to reverse-engineer the reasoning from first principles, using thermodynamic models that worked in theory and kept producing numbers that didn't match the observed process behaviour.

At 9:47, she found it. Not in the official documentation, not in the engineering system, but in a collection of digitized lab notebooks that had been uploaded to the company's intranet as part of a knowledge preservation initiative four years ago and never indexed. The relevant entry was from March 2017: a brief note, three sentences, in the handwriting of the retired engineer. It explained, in the casual shorthand of someone noting something obvious, exactly why the pressure settings were what they were. The reasoning had been obvious—to him, then. It was not obvious now.

The three sentences had been there for four years. They had been accessible for four years. They had not been found because no one had made the connection between the question asked in 2024 and the answer recorded in 2017. The memory was intact. The retrieval infrastructure did not exist.

The archive was immaculate. Three hundred and twenty-seven project files, each tagged with a project number, a date, and a status. The search function worked. The metadata was clean. The Head of Innovation showed it to me with the quiet pride of someone who had spent eighteen months building a system that no predecessor had attempted.

I asked a question: "Can you show me a case where a current project team found and used a lesson from a past project—where the archive actually changed a decision?"

There was a pause. Not an embarrassed pause—a genuinely puzzled one. The system had been designed to store. No one had designed it to be used.

This is the difference between a storage system and a memory system, and it is the most expensive confusion in knowledge management.

The Difference Between Storage and Memory

There is a distinction that cognitive scientists make between storage and retrieval that is essential for understanding organizational memory. A memory system that stores perfectly but cannot retrieve is not functional. It is an archive. An archive is useful for compliance and legal purposes; it is not useful for organizational learning.

Human memory is not primarily a storage system—it is primarily a retrieval system. What makes human memory functional is not the capacity to retain information but the capacity to surface relevant information in response to the demands of a specific situation. This is why experts are experts: not because they remember more than novices, but because their memory systems have been structured by experience to surface the right associations when the right problems arise. The senior engineer does not consciously remember every process decision she has made; she has internalized the patterns of those decisions in a form that her brain can access efficiently.

Organizational memory that mimics this architecture—organized not for storage but for contextual retrieval—is qualitatively different from the archive-based knowledge management systems that organizations currently maintain. The distinction matters enormously for how you design the system.

Archive-based systems ask: "Where should we put this so we can find it again?" They organize knowledge by its origin: project name, date, author, and document type. This works well if you know what you are looking for. It fails when you are asking a question whose answer might exist in material you would not have thought to search.

Memory-based systems ask: "What questions might someone ask about this in the future, and how should we structure this knowledge so those questions get answered?" They organize knowledge by the context in which it is likely to be useful. The difference in design philosophy produces entirely different capabilities.

What Organizational Memory Actually Looks Like

In the organizations I have worked with that have built effective innovation memory systems, the common elements are surprisingly consistent. They are not primarily technological—though technology enables them—but rather organizational design choices.

The first element is captured at the point of decision. The most valuable organizational memory is not the summary report written three months after the project was completed; it is the note written the day the team decided to change course, explaining why. The reasoning, the alternatives considered, the evidence that tipped the decision: this is the knowledge that allows future teams to avoid relearning what was already known. Organizations that routinely capture this knowledge—as a normal part of project management rather than a retrospective exercise—build compounding memory.

The second element is structured reflection. Beyond individual decisions, the pattern of decisions over time contains knowledge that individual decisions alone do not reveal. Why have we tried this approach three times and abandoned it each time? What distinguishes the innovation projects that reached adoption from the ones that stalled? What is the signature of a successful sponsor? Answering these questions requires connecting multiple data points over time, which in turn requires that the data points have been captured consistently, tagged with comparable metadata, and structured in a way that allows for pattern analysis.

The third element—and this is the element that AI is beginning to make genuinely feasible at scale—is intelligent retrieval. The lab notebooks that the engineer found at 9:47 on Tuesday were retrievable only because she already knew what she was looking for. An intelligent retrieval system would have surfaced them in response to her original query, recognizing the connection between her current problem and the 2017 entry without requiring her to know it existed in advance. This is the promise of AI-augmented organizational memory: not that the machine remembers, but that the machine can find the connection between what you are asking now and what was learned before.

Memory is not storage. Memory is the living relationship between what an organization has learned and what it is trying to do. Building that relationship, maintaining it, and making it queryable is the most important and most neglected capability in innovation management.

The Reuse Rate

If memory is not storage but retrieval, then the most important metric for organizational memory is not how much knowledge is captured but how often captured knowledge is actually used again. This is the Reuse Rate.

> **→ The ratio of knowledge assets that are accessed and applied in subsequent projects to the total knowledge assets available.**

The Reuse Rate is deceptively simple, yet one of the most powerful diagnostic indicators in the framework. A high Reuse Rate means that the organization's memory is functional—knowledge created in one context is successfully transferred to another. A low Reuse Rate means that the organization is spending money to create knowledge that nobody ever uses again.

In practice, most organizations have never measured their Reuse Rate. They know how many documents are in their knowledge repository. They know how many people have access to the knowledge platform. They may even know how many downloads or views each document receives. But they do not know whether any of that accessed knowledge was actually applied—whether it changed a decision, prevented a mistake, or accelerated a development cycle.

The framework measures the Reuse Rate through four complementary indicators:

- **Citation frequency.** The number of explicit citations of prior knowledge in project proposals, business cases, and design documents. If teams are building on prior work, they should be referencing it.
- **Time-to-reuse latency.** The average time from knowledge creation to first reuse by a team other than the creating team. Short latency indicates functional retrieval. Long latency (more than two quarters) suggests that knowledge exists but is not findable.
- **Cross-team reach.** The number of different teams that have accessed and applied a given knowledge asset. Knowledge shared across multiple teams has greater organizational value than knowledge confined to its original team.
- **Portfolio linkage rate.** The proportion of projects in the current quarter that reference knowledge from prior quarters. A

healthy innovation portfolio should show that at least 40% of current projects build on documented prior knowledge.

Together, these four indicators produce a Reuse Rate that ranges from near zero (the organization creates knowledge that is never used again) to a target in which each knowledge asset is accessed and applied multiple times over its lifetime, rather than once by the team that created it and never again. In organizations that have built mature memory systems, this multiplier effect is among the most visible returns on the investment in organizational memory.

→ **The gap between the current Reuse Rate and the Target Rate is one of the most actionable numbers on the dashboard.**

Evidence from Healthcare Innovation Hubs

The principles of functional organizational memory are not confined to private-sector innovation. Some of the most compelling evidence for the value of structured knowledge reuse comes from healthcare, where the consequences of institutional amnesia are measured in patient outcomes rather than market share.

When England's Health Foundation set out to help the NHS become a better adopter of innovation, it funded four dedicated innovation hubs—in Bradford & Craven, Cambridgeshire & Peterborough, Dorset, and Greater Manchester—to build exactly this kind of dedicated infrastructure for innovation memory. Each hub was established to serve as a bridge between clinical practice and innovation, with three core functions: identifying unmet clinical needs, connecting clinicians with innovators, and—most of all—capturing and disseminating the knowledge generated by those connections.

Research on knowledge brokering in collaborative networks, together with the design of hubs like these, points to a set of conditions that separate effective innovation infrastructure from ineffective. Four of them map directly to the framework's four capitals:

- **Knowledge Capital:** The hubs' ability to capture and codify clinical needs, innovation opportunities, and lessons from failed attempts—what the framework calls the Input compass reading for Memory Capital.
- **Relational Capital:** The trust relationships between clinicians, innovators, and hub staff that enable honest sharing of both successes and failures—what the framework measures through Relational Capital indicators, including psychological safety scores and cross-boundary collaboration rates.
- **Process Capital:** The structured processes for needs assessment, innovator matching, and follow-up—what the framework tracks through Process Capital indicators, including decision latency and governance maturity.
- **Memory Capital:** The documented outcomes and learning loops that allow each hub to build on prior experience—the accumulated organizational memory that distinguishes mature hubs from newly established ones.

The most consistent theme in this research is what scholars call 'boundary spanning'—the ability to transfer knowledge across organizational boundaries. The most effective collaborations do not merely store knowledge; they actively broker it, connecting a surgeon's frustration with a specific instrument design to an engineering team that has solved a similar problem in a different context. This brokering function—which is precisely what an AI-enabled organizational memory system automates—is repeatedly identified as one of the strongest levers on innovation outcomes.

The implication for the framework is direct: memory infrastructure must be designed not just for storage and retrieval but for connection. The most valuable function of organizational memory is not answering the question 'What do we already know about this?' but answering the question 'Who else in the organization has faced a similar problem, and what did they learn?'

Three Roles That Memory Cannot Do Without

Every memory system, regardless of how sophisticated its technology, depends on three human roles that no algorithm can replace. Organizations that skip these roles deploy expensive architecture on a foundation that is not there.

The memory holder. Long-tenured employees who know why processes were adopted, which approaches were tried and discarded, and where the real pitfalls lie. They are the living index of what the organization has actually attempted—as opposed to what it officially recorded. The memory holder is not a historian. They are a navigator who can say, in real time, "We went down that road in 2019, and here is what we found." Identify them before they retire. Give them a formal role in onboarding new initiatives—not as teachers of the past but as navigators of precedent. When they leave without a knowledge transfer protocol, an irreplaceable layer of contextual memory leaves with them.

The storytelling ritual. Humans remember stories far better than reports. Post-mortems, brown-bag lunches, failure fairs—these are not soft culture activities. They are the mechanism through which tacit knowledge moves from one person's experience into the organization's shared vocabulary. The ritual must be blameless by design: if people fear the story, they will not tell it. And if they do not tell it, it dies with the project. One well-documented, findable failure narrative is worth more to future teams than ten polished success case studies.

The knowledge broker. Someone whose explicit job is to connect people with knowledge across organizational silos. Not a librarian—a navigator. Someone who knows that the team in one division solved a version of what a different team is struggling with right now, and who picks up the phone. The brokering function is repeatedly identified in the research on collaborative networks as one of the strongest levers on innovation outcomes—and it is the function that AI-enabled memory systems are beginning to automate. But until the automation is mature, the human broker is the connective tissue that prevents the organization's knowledge from remaining a collection of isolated islands.

These three roles are the human infrastructure on which any technology investment must rest. An AI-enabled memory system amplifies human judgment. It does not replace the social fabric that makes knowledge worth sharing in the first place.

Why Your Best People Don't Share

Every Head of Innovation has experienced the same frustration at some point. The team knows something. The knowledge exists. Someone in the building could save the new project six months of wrong turns if they shared what they learned the last time. But they don't. And the new team reinvents the failure.

The temptation is to attribute this to culture ("people here don't share") or structure ("we need a better knowledge platform"). Both are partially true, and both miss the point. Knowledge hiding—the deliberate withholding of knowledge from colleagues, examined in Chapter 3—is driven by incentives that are largely rational from the individual's perspective.

The researcher who documented why the compound failed does not share that documentation because, in most organizations, a documented failure is a career liability. The senior engineer who knows how a process actually works—not the approved procedure but the real one—does not write it down because their expertise is their job security. The business unit director with deep customer intelligence does not share it with the R&D team because, in a resource-competitive organization, information is power.

The consequence: deploying an AI memory system atop an organization where knowledge hiding is the norm yields an expensive, well-organized database of what people are comfortable sharing. Which is not where the real learning lives.

Psychological Safety Is Infrastructure, Not Culture

The practical implication is one that most technology-led implementations miss. Before you build the memory system, you have to build the conditions under which people will actually put their real knowledge into it. This is not a soft topic. It is a system design question. The three interventions that work:

Blameless post-mortems are structurally enforced. Not a gentler conversation about failure—a formal protocol in which the question is never "who made this decision" but always "what information was missing or misread when this decision was made." That distinction must be explicit, enforced by facilitation, and visibly backed by leadership.

- Separation of project evaluation from person evaluation. In most organizations, project and performance reviews are intertwined. What people document about project failures should not be the same as what their manager cites in their annual review. Separate the channels.
- Anonymous contribution pathways for early-stage and sensitive knowledge. Not all knowledge can be attributed without political cost. A mechanism for contributing anonymously—especially for observations about what's not working or internal capability gaps—captures knowledge that would otherwise stay locked inside individual heads.

None of these requires a budget. They require policy. And they require a Head of Innovation who is willing to have the conversation with HR, Legal, and the executive team about why the standard performance framework creates the wrong incentives for organizational learning.

Designing Efficient Retrospective Meetings

The following questions are designed to move a post-mortem from single-loop to double-loop. They should be asked only after the standard "what happened" review is complete, as a separate phase:

- What assumption—not action—led to this outcome? Every failure has a decision behind it, and every decision has an assumption behind it. The assumption is where the real learning is won.
- If we had correctly understood the situation from the start, what would we have done differently? Not "what would we have done better" but "what would we have done differently?"

- What does this failure reveal about a recurring pattern in how we make decisions? If this has happened before in a different form, the pattern matters more than the specific incident.
- What would have to change in our governance or incentive structure to make the right decision easier to make next time? Not "make the wrong decision harder"—"make the right decision easier."

The outputs of this phase should be stored differently from standard post-mortem documentation. Standard post-mortems inform future projects of the same type. Double-loop outputs inform governance design. They should reach the people who own the process, not just the teams who run the projects.

The Four Stages of Institutional Learning

The post-mortem process described above is one mechanism for organizational learning. But for an organization to build genuine memory—not just records, but the capacity to learn from experience—it needs a more comprehensive learning architecture. This architecture has four stages, each corresponding to one of the Four Compass Readings.

- **Stage 1: Capture (Input).** Learning begins with experience. Every innovation project generates data—customer feedback, technical results, market responses, and team dynamics. The input stage captures this raw experience in a structured form, making it available for analysis. The key metric is the capture rate: what percentage of project experience is documented within 30 days of the experience? Most organizations capture less than twenty percent.

- **Stage 2: Synthesize (Throughput).** Raw experience must be interpreted before it becomes useful knowledge. The synthesis stage involves structured reflection—connecting individual experiences to broader patterns, identifying root causes rather than surface symptoms, and translating project-specific lessons into generalizable principles. The key metric is the synthesis rate: what percentage of captured experience is analyzed and interpreted within one quarter?
- **Stage 3: Codify (Output).** Synthesized knowledge must be made accessible in a format that enables action. The codify stage creates reusable knowledge assets—decision frameworks, design patterns, failure catalogues, best-practice guides—that can be applied to future projects. The key metric is the codification rate: the percentage of synthesized insights that are translated into reusable knowledge assets.
- **Stage 4: Apply (Outcome).** The ultimate test of institutional learning is whether codified knowledge actually changes behaviour. The apply stage measures the Reuse Rate introduced earlier in this chapter: are future teams building on the knowledge generated by past teams? The key metric is the application rate: the percentage of codified knowledge referenced in subsequent project decisions.

The four stages form a cycle, not a sequence. Applied knowledge generates new experience, which feeds back into the capture stage. Each cycle through the loop strengthens the organization's memory. The framework measures the health of this learning cycle by tracking the conversion rate between each stage. A healthy organization shows positive conversion at each stage: captured experience becomes synthesized insight, synthesized insight becomes codified knowledge, and codified knowledge becomes applied learning. The specific rates will vary by organization and sector—but the direction of travel is diagnostic. When conversion collapses at any one stage, the bottleneck reveals exactly where the intervention is needed.

When conversion rates are low at any stage, the bottleneck reveals the necessary intervention. Low capture rates require better documentation tools and incentives. Low synthesis rates require dedicated analysis time and structured reflection practices. Low codification rates require better knowledge management platforms and editorial support. Low application rates require better retrieval systems, which is precisely what the AI-OM Orchestrator and Contextual Recall Sidecar described in Chapter 6 are designed to provide.

Memory infrastructure works. The evidence is clear. But it asks something most organizations cannot supply by human effort alone: the discipline to surface the right knowledge at the right moment, across thousands of projects, millions of documents, and decades of accumulated experience. A memory that can be stored but never retrieved is not a memory at all—it is an archive with good intentions. This is the condition the whole chapter reduces to: until what an organization has learned can be found at the moment it is needed, nothing built on top of it has anything to read.

THE SKIPPER'S LOG

Position — Memory is not what an organization stores. It is what an organization can retrieve at the moment of decision.

Sighted — The Reuse Rate as the honest metric of memory — and the quiet, rational reasons your best people do not share what they know.

Charted — The three roles no memory system survives without, and the four stages of institutional learning.

Course — Compute one rough Reuse Rate: of the lessons documented last year, how many were referenced by a later project? Expect a single digit. That is the baseline, not the verdict.

Chapter 6: The Copilot in the Engine Room

For thirty years, I saw organizations confusing storing knowledge with having it. The distinction sounds academic. It is not. It is the difference between an archive and a memory—and it is the reason that the engineer in Chapter 5 spent three days searching for a pressure setting that had been sitting in a digitized notebook—accessible, indexed, and completely invisible until she knew where to look.

The architectural assumption behind every knowledge management system of the last three decades was the same: build a repository, train people to fill it, and hope they search it before reinventing what already exists. The result was always the same. The repository was filled with what people were comfortable documenting. The search returned results only if you already knew roughly what you were looking for. And the knowledge that mattered most—the reasoning behind a decision, the context around a failure, the informal workaround that a technician built on a Thursday afternoon and never wrote down—stayed exactly where it had always been: in someone's head, until that someone left.

The engineer who spent three days reverse-engineering that pressure setting did not fail because the knowledge was gone. She failed because the knowledge was stored as an answer to a question no one was asking anymore. The notebook said what the setting was. It did not say why, because in 2017, the why was obvious to everyone in the room. By 2024, those people had moved on—the why had become invisible.

This is the specific failure that every knowledge management system over the last three decades has been unable to solve. Not the storage problem—organizations have always been able to store. The retrieval problem: surfacing the right knowledge at the right moment for a question that was never anticipated when the knowledge was captured. The bottleneck was always human bandwidth. Someone had to tag correctly, index deliberately, and search with the right vocabulary. If the question was different from the answer, the system returned nothing.

→ Generative AI changes Organizational Memory at the root.

Not because it is more intelligent than previous systems. It cannot assess whether a past experiment remains relevant in a changed market, cannot read the political dynamics in a governance meeting, and cannot decide that a reported success is being overclaimed. What it can do—and this is the specific shift—is understand meaning rather than match keywords. The engineer asking *why this pressure setting is at this value* can now receive, in response, the 2017 notebook entry that never uses those words but explains exactly the relevant reasoning. The connection is made not by a human who knew to look there, but by a system that understood what both texts were about.

This is what organizational memory has always needed and could never have: a layer that makes the implicit explicit, connects what was captured to what is being asked, and does so across the entire accumulated history of the organization—simultaneously, continuously, without requiring anyone to have anticipated the future question when recording the past answer.

The chapters that follow show what this looks like in practice—its capabilities, its limits, and the governance decisions that determine whether it becomes an asset or an expensive illusion.

The Smoke Before the Fire

An AI system called ALERTCalifornia—operated by the University of California San Diego across a network of more than a thousand cameras on the state's wildfire-prone hills—now routinely catches the first wisp of smoke from a new ignition before any human reports it; more than half of its detections arrive before the first 911 call. The system had learned, over years of monitoring, what early ignition looks like: not a plume, not a visible flame, but a specific signature of light scatter and atmospheric disturbance that precedes the visible fire by enough minutes to make the difference between a controlled burn and an uncontrolled one.

This is not a story about artificial intelligence replacing human judgment. The ALERTCalifornia system does not call the fire department. It does not assess wind conditions, fuel moisture, or access routes. What it does is transform an unstructured, high-volume perceptual environment—more than a thousand cameras watching California's wildfire-prone backcountry—into a specific, actionable signal. It converts noise into knowledge. The human judgment about what to do with that knowledge remains irreducibly human. But the human is now working with information they could not have had before the machine was watching.

This is the Centaur Principle, named for the Greek mythological figure that combined human reason with equine power: not human versus machine, but human plus machine, each contributing what it does better. The machine sees more than the human can see. Humans understand more than machines can understand. The combination produces capabilities that neither possesses alone.

What Generative AI Can Actually Do for Organizational Memory

The application of Generative AI to organizational memory is, in 2025, at roughly the same stage of development as GPS was in the early 1990s: technically feasible, increasingly reliable, and still poorly integrated into most organizations' workflows. The gap is not primarily technical. It is organizational. The systems exist; the decisions about how to use them—and, above all, how to structure the organizational knowledge that feeds them—have not yet been made by most enterprises.

There are four specific capabilities that Generative AI brings to organizational memory that deserve careful attention.

The first is **contextual retrieval**. Traditional document management systems surface documents when you search for specific terms that appear in the document. AI-based retrieval systems surface documents based on semantic similarity—what the document is about, in a functional sense—allowing queries that would fail in a keyword search. The engineer asking "why is the pressure setting at this value" can now receive, in response, a decades-old lab notebook entry that never uses the phrase 'pressure setting' but explains exactly the relevant reasoning. The connection is made not by keyword matching but by an understanding of meaning.

The second is **pattern recognition** across time. Individual innovation projects generate data that, taken in isolation, is only locally useful. But the pattern across dozens of projects—the signature of what makes a pilot succeed, the common feature of failed technology bets, the correlation between team composition and adoption outcomes—is invisible without a system that can process all the projects simultaneously. AI-based pattern recognition can surface these structural insights from organizational history, converting a collection of project reports into a learning system.

The third is **automated capture**. Much of the most valuable organizational knowledge is currently not captured at all because it requires deliberate effort from people with many other demands on their time. AI systems that can extract insights from meeting notes, email threads, and collaboration tool activity—with appropriate privacy considerations—can dramatically reduce the friction of knowledge capture, allowing organizations to build memory from the normal flow of work rather than requiring separate documentation effort.

The fourth is **anomaly detection** in innovation performance. A well-instrumented innovation measurement system generates continuous data on project progress, resource allocation, and outcome metrics. AI-based monitoring of this data can surface early warning signals—a project that is consuming time without generating learning, a technology bet that contradicts the pattern of past successes, a capability gap that appears repeatedly across multiple unrelated projects—that human reviewers reading periodic reports would miss. The system does not make the decision; it changes the quality of the information available when the decision is made.

The Limits of the Copilot

The centaur principle requires an honest account of both sides of the pairing. The machine sees more; the human understands more. Understanding this asymmetry clearly is essential for avoiding the failure modes that accompany premature AI automation of organizational judgment.

The most public attempt to hand that job to a machine came from Klarna. In 2024, the Swedish fintech moved much of its internal knowledge and workflow onto AI agents built with OpenAI, retired tools from vendors like Salesforce and Workday, and froze hiring—its people now served the context they needed at the moment of decision rather than hunting for it across silos. For the internal work of organizational memory, this is the very shift this book argues for. But Klarna pushed the logic too far, replacing front-line customer-service staff with the same automation—and by 2025 it was quietly hiring humans back, its chief executive conceding that the company had "overestimated AI's capabilities and underappreciated the human aspects" of the work. The lesson is not that the copilot fails. It is that it is a copilot. It carries the volume and the recall; the judgment stays human.

AI systems learn from the data they are given. If an organization's memory contains primarily its successes—the projects that worked, the decisions that proved correct, the innovations that reached market—then the AI trained on that memory will systematically underweight the lessons of failure. Organizational memory that captures failure honestly is not simply more complete; it is qualitatively more useful for learning. Building the capture process in a way that makes recording honest failure the path of least resistance rather than the politically risky alternative is an organizational design challenge that no AI system can solve for you.

AI systems also cannot provide the contextual judgment that experience-based human knowledge provides. The lab notebooks that recorded why the pressure settings were set as they were proved valuable precisely because they contained the reasoning of someone who understood, at a deep level, why that reasoning was relevant. An AI system can surface the connection between the current question and the old reasoning; it cannot assess whether that reasoning remains valid in a changed technological environment. The centaur needs a capable rider.

Finally, AI systems for organizational memory are only as good as the data governance decisions behind them. What gets captured? Who decides what is private and what is shared? How is knowledge tagged so that the retrieval system can find it? These decisions are not technical—they are organizational decisions about what an organization believes its knowledge is worth. Organizations that have not explicitly made these decisions will find that their AI systems produce sophisticated retrieval from an impoverished memory. The machine is powerful. The machine needs feeding.

The AI-OM Orchestrator: Four Agents for Organizational Memory

The centaur principle established earlier in this chapter describes the collaboration between human judgment and machine capability. But what does this collaboration look like in practice when applied specifically to organizational memory? The answer is an orchestration architecture that deploys four specialized AI agents—each aligned with one of the framework's four capitals—and coordinates them through a central orchestration layer.

This is not science fiction. The individual components exist today in varying stages of maturity. What the framework provides is the governance architecture that determines how these agents work together and—critically—how their outputs are validated by human judgment before they influence decisions.

The four agents correspond to four distinct functions:

- **The Retrieval Agent.** Responsible for finding and surfacing relevant knowledge from the organizational memory in response to queries. This is not a simple keyword search—it is semantic retrieval that understands context. When a product team asks, 'What do we know about customer resistance to subscription models?', the Retrieval Agent does not just find documents containing those keywords. It identifies relevant experience from across the organization: a failed subscription pilot in another division, customer research from two years ago that identified price-sensitivity thresholds, and a competitive analysis documenting how a rival handled the same transition. The Retrieval Agent maps to Knowledge Capital in the framework.
- **The Policy Alignment Agent.** Responsible for ensuring that retrieved and generated knowledge aligns with organizational policies, regulatory requirements, and strategic direction. Before a piece of prior knowledge is surfaced to a decision-maker, the Policy Alignment Agent checks whether the context has changed—whether the regulatory environment has shifted, whether the strategy has pivoted, and whether the data is still current. This agent maps to Process Capital, ensuring that the memory system operates within the governance architecture.
- **The Market Intelligence Agent.** Responsible for incorporating external signals—market trends, competitor moves, emerging technologies, patent filings, regulatory changes—into the organizational memory. Innovation does not happen in a vacuum, and an organizational memory system that looks only inward is incomplete. The Market Intelligence Agent continuously scans external sources and connects external signals to internal knowledge. This agent enriches Relational Capital by extending the organization's knowledge network beyond its boundaries.

- **The Risk, Failure, and Synthesis Agent.** Responsible for two critical functions: identifying patterns of failure in the innovation portfolio and generating novel combinations of existing knowledge. The first function is diagnostic—detecting that three different teams have independently encountered the same technical obstacle, or that a pattern of late-stage project cancellations correlates with a specific type of early-stage assumption. The second function is generative—proposing connections between knowledge assets that no human has explicitly linked. This agent maps to Memory Capital, turning accumulated knowledge into forward-looking insight.

The orchestration layer coordinates these four agents, resolving conflicts (when the Market Intelligence Agent surfaces an opportunity that the Policy Alignment Agent flags as outside strategic scope), managing priorities (ensuring that urgent queries receive faster processing), and maintaining an audit trail that allows human reviewers to understand how a particular recommendation was generated.

The four-agent architecture is not arbitrary—it mirrors the four capitals because the capitals represent the four dimensions of innovation value that the organization needs to manage. An AI system that retrieves knowledge but does not check policy alignment is dangerous. An AI system that checks policy but does not incorporate market intelligence is myopic.

→ The four-agent architecture ensures that the AI copilot operates across all four dimensions simultaneously.

The Contextual Recall Sidecar

One of the most powerful applications of the AI-OM Orchestrator is the Contextual Recall Sidecar—a lightweight AI companion that operates alongside the innovation team's existing workflow, rather than requiring them to switch to a separate knowledge management system.

The concept is simple: as a team works on a project—drafting a business case, conducting a design review, planning a market entry—the Sidecar monitors the content being created and proactively surfaces relevant prior knowledge. The team does not need to stop and search. The relevant context appears alongside their work.

Consider a product development team drafting a business case for a new software module. As they write the market analysis section, Sidecar surfaces a customer research study from eighteen months ago that identified the same market need—along with a note that the previous team abandoned the initiative due to integration complexity, not market demand. As they draft the technical approach, the Sidecar surfaces a patent filing from the R&D team that addresses exactly the integration challenge that killed the earlier project. As they estimate the budget, the Sidecar surfaces the actual costs from three comparable projects, adjusted for inflation and complexity.

The Sidecar does not make decisions. It provides context. The human team retains full authority to accept, reject, or modify the surfaced knowledge. But by making relevant prior knowledge available at the moment of decision—rather than requiring a separate research effort that most teams skip due to time pressure—the Sidecar dramatically increases the probability that organizational memory will actually influence innovation decisions.

In the framework's terms, the Sidecar is the mechanism that converts Memory Capital from a passive asset ('we have this knowledge somewhere') into an active input ('this knowledge is influencing today's decisions'). The Reuse Rate—the metric introduced in Chapter 5—is the primary indicator of Sidecar effectiveness. When the Sidecar is functioning well, the Reuse Rate climbs because knowledge is being applied rather than just stored.

The mapping between agents and capitals is architectural, not decorative. The Retrieval Agent serves Knowledge Capital—it surfaces what the organization knows. The Policy Alignment Agent serves Process Capital—it keeps what is surfaced inside the governance, regulation, and strategy currently in force. The Risk, Failure, and Synthesis Agent serves Memory Capital—it turns the accumulated record of what was tried, and what failed, into forward-looking insight. The Market Intelligence Agent serves Relational Capital—it extends the network of knowledge beyond the walls of the firm, binding external signal to internal memory. Each agent feeds the capital it serves. Remove one, and the corresponding capital goes dark on the dashboard.

A Head of Innovation should think of the four agents as the four crew members on a small racing yacht: the navigator (Retrieval), the quartermaster (Policy Alignment), the lookout (Market Intelligence), and the skipper who turns failure and pattern into a course correction (Risk, Failure, and Synthesis). No single crew member sails the boat. The boat sails because they work in concert—each contributing what the others cannot see.

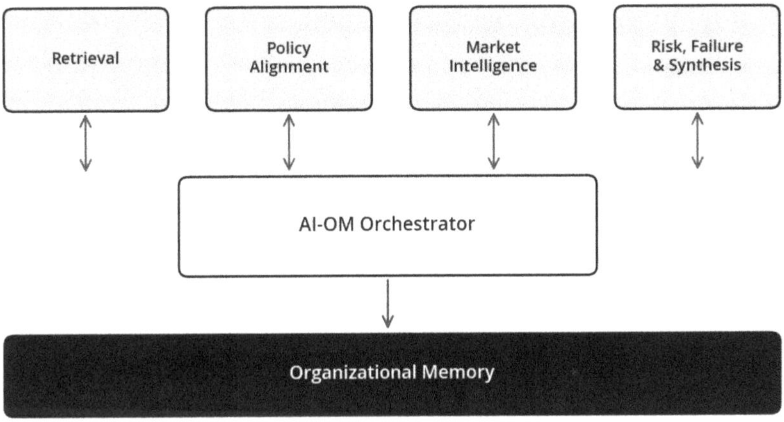

Figure: The AI-OM Orchestrator—four agents reading from a single organizational memory.

Data-Driven Innovation: From Intuition to Evidence

The AI-OM Orchestrator operates on the organization's internal knowledge. But innovation increasingly depends on a second dimension of intelligence: data-driven insight drawn from the intersection of customer behaviour, market signals, and operational patterns.

Organizations attempting to integrate data analytics into their innovation process run into four recurring challenges. Understanding these challenges is essential for building an AI copilot that actually works.

- **The Relevance Challenge.** Most organizations have data in abundance, but struggle to identify which data is relevant to innovation decisions. The innovation team drowns in dashboards and reports without gaining insight. The framework addresses this by defining the Four Compass Readings—Input, Throughput, Output, Outcome—as the organizing structure for innovation data. Data that does not map to one of these four readings is, by definition, not innovation data.

- **The Integration Challenge.** Even when relevant data exists, it often resides in systems that do not communicate with each other. Customer feedback is in one system, project data in another, and financial data in a third. The AI-OM Orchestrator addresses this by serving as the integration layer—not by replacing existing systems but by connecting them through a shared knowledge graph.
- **The Interpretation Challenge.** Innovation teams often lack the analytical skills to extract insight from raw data. They can read a chart but cannot design a meaningful experiment. The Contextual Recall Sidecar addresses this by providing interpreted insights rather than raw data—telling the team not just that customer satisfaction declined by twelve points but that a similar decline in a previous product launch was caused by onboarding friction, which was resolved by a specific intervention.
- **The Action Challenge.** Once an insight is generated, organizations struggle to translate it into action. The insight exists in a report; the action requires changes to process, budget, or strategy. The governance architecture addresses this by connecting measurement to decision rights—ensuring that the people who see the data have the authority to act on it.

The four challenges map precisely to the four capitals. Relevance is a Knowledge Capital problem. Integration is a Process Capital problem. Interpretation is a Memory Capital problem—it requires prior knowledge to contextualize new data. And Action is a Relational

Capital problem—it requires the trust, authority, and collaborative relationships that enable decisions to be made and implemented.

The AI copilot, then, is not a single tool. It is a system that operates across all four capitals simultaneously—retrieving knowledge, aligning with policy, incorporating external intelligence, and synthesizing patterns—while the human crew retains the judgment, the strategic vision, and the accountability that no machine can provide. The compass does not steer the ship. The captain steers the ship. But a captain without a compass is navigating by hope.

The Copilot in Practice

The organizations I have observed that have begun to implement AI-augmented memory systems share a common starting point: they began not with the technology but with the question. What questions do we wish we could ask about our organizational history? What knowledge do we repeatedly need but cannot reliably find? Where does the gap between what we know and what we can access cost us the most?

Starting with the question rather than the technology produces a fundamentally different implementation path. It focuses on the quality and structure of the underlying knowledge base before the retrieval layer is built. It forces the organizational design decisions—what to capture, how to tag it, who maintains it—before the AI is deployed. And it establishes a clear success criterion: can the system answer the questions we most need answered?

The ALERTCalifornia system works because decades of wildfire observation were captured, structured, and made available to the learning algorithm. The machine learned what early ignition looks like because thousands of examples of early ignition—and thousands of examples of non-ignition events that resembled it—were in the training data. The AI is the copilot. The data is the flight manual. The organization that built the data is the only reason the copilot can fly.

The wildfire model learned because someone had first captured the fire—thousands of ignitions, observed, recorded, and structured until a machine could recognize the pattern. The same principle scales all the way down to a single desk, and there it wears an unlikely face. In 2025, that face belonged to Obsidian—at first glance a humble note-taking application: a place to write things down in plain text. What makes it different is that every note can link to every other note, and the software draws the result as a graph—a living map of what its owner knows and, more revealing, of how the pieces connect. Feed it for a year and the graph stops resembling a filing cabinet and starts resembling a mind. Ideas jotted months apart, in unrelated contexts, turn out to sit two clicks from each other. The tool did not invent that connection. It made visible one that already existed and would otherwise have stayed buried in a single head—unretrievable, and therefore, for every practical purpose, lost.

This is what it means to domesticate knowledge. Most of what an organization knows is wild: tacit, scattered, lodged in the heads of people who will eventually walk out the door, written in documents no one can locate, encoded in decisions whose reasoning was never recorded. Wild knowledge is not worthless—but it is unharvestable. It cannot be counted, it cannot be reused, and it cannot be built upon, because there is no way to reach it on demand. To domesticate it is to do the reverse: to capture it, connect it, and make it answer when called. A personal graph does this for one person. The organizational version is the same task multiplied by every employee, every project, every season—and until very recently, at that scale, it was simply not tractable.

What changed is that the graph can now be read by a machine that understands language. A knowledge base a human would need weeks to traverse can be searched, cross-referenced, and synthesized in seconds by a generative model given access to it—the architecture the field calls retrieval-augmented generation: memory on one side, reasoning on the other. By 2026, tools had begun to occupy precisely that gap. A skill such as Hermes—named, fittingly, for the messenger of the gods—gives an assistant like Claude structured access to an organization's accumulated memory, so that a question no longer merely searches a database but activates the whole archive: it retrieves what is relevant, joins what was written separately, and surfaces what the organization knew but had forgotten it knew. The distinction is not cosmetic. A stored document is a fossil. An activated memory answers back.

The pattern from one year to the next is already legible: Obsidian in 2025, Hermes in 2026, and no reason to expect the queue to stop forming. The division of labour is legible too. Public generative models will keep getting better at what humanity knows collectively—the published, the indexed, the open. The systems that matter inside an organization will turn the other way, toward the internal information and proprietary data no public model will ever see. The largest players did not wait for the queue: in 2024, Saudi Aramco unveiled Metabrain, a model trained on seven trillion data points drawn from ninety years of the company's own records—nine decades of proprietary memory turned into an instrument. By the time you read these pages, the tool names will have changed. The direction will not.

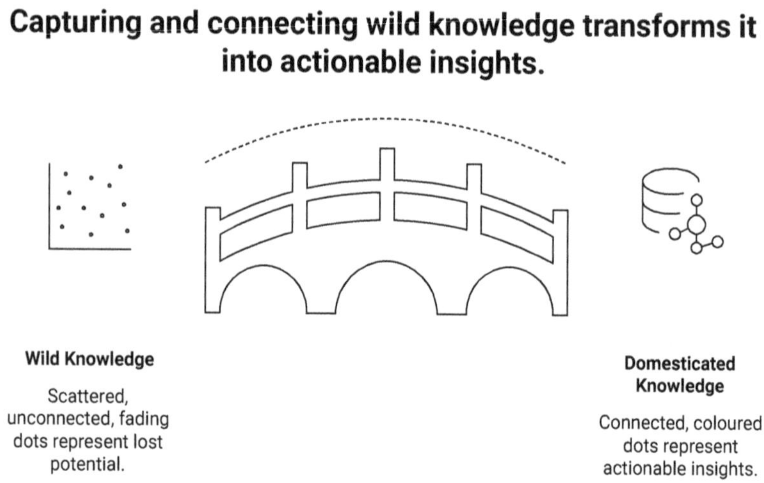

And here is the part most treatments of knowledge management walk straight past. Domesticated, activated memory does two jobs at once, and the second is the one that pays. The first is measurement. Once an organization's knowledge is reachable, the four taxes stop being rhetoric. The Duplication Tax becomes visible, because the system can see that the problem in front of the Singapore team was solved in Munich two years ago. The Amnesia Tax becomes computable, because you can finally measure what fraction of hard-won lessons is ever reused. Reuse Rate, the Factorless Income Residual, the entire memory side of ROI²—none of it can be calculated until the knowledge has been domesticated. But measurement is the smaller prize. The larger one is stimulation. The same activation that lets you count duplication is what prevents it—surfacing the prior work at the moment the new idea is forming, not in a post-mortem two years too late. The same layer that measures the Coordination Tax is what dissolves it, connecting two teams who never knew they were neighbours. Memory that can be read at the speed of a question does not merely audit innovation. It feeds it.

This is the asymmetry that separates the organizations that understand memory from those that keep it as an archive. An archive depreciates—heavier, slower to search, less trusted with every passing year. Domesticated memory does the opposite: it compounds. Each season's lessons sharpen the next season's ideation; the graph grows denser, the connections multiply, the taxes shrink as the generative surface widens. An organization that leaves its knowledge wild pays the four taxes indefinitely and files them under the cost of doing business. An organization that domesticates it turns the same liability into an engine—and every season, the distance between the two widens.

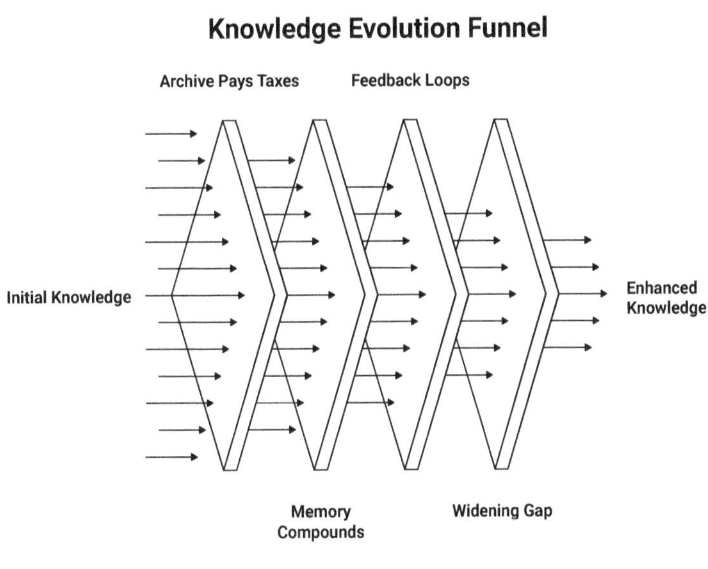

And innovation will not keep this advantage to itself. A memory that can answer questions about failed prototypes can answer questions about failed negotiations, churned customers, and successful hires;

every managerial function that depends on what the organization already knows—which is to say, all of them—will eventually lean on the same activated layer, and every function that joins adds capture where there was none, shrinking the innovation tax from angles the innovation team never controlled. Two consequences matter for this book. The first is that the old wall between R&D and innovation management—one producing knowledge, the other struggling to find it and put it to work—becomes a doorway, because both draw on the same living archive. The second is that ROI² becomes calculable on both of its dimensions at last. Growth was never the hard half: revenue, market share, and strategic position leave tracks the P&L already reads. Readiness was the dark half—the knowledge built, the lessons banked, the capability accumulated for seasons that have not yet arrived. Activated memory is what makes that half countable. An organization that domesticates its knowledge does not simply measure its innovation better; it can finally prove the value of the initiatives whose only output, this season, was becoming more ready.

The compass has been calibrated. The four capitals are defined, the four readings are understood, and the AI copilot stands ready to surface what the organization knows but has forgotten it knows. But the machine is only ever as good as the memory beneath it and the judgment beside it. It amplifies a well-kept memory and exposes a neglected one; it sharpens a capable reader and misleads a careless one. The copilot is not the navigator—it is the instrument that lets a navigator see further, and an organization with neither memory nor judgment will only arrive at the wrong place faster.

The Skipper's Log

Position — Generative AI finally makes organizational memory operable at scale. But the copilot is an instrument, not a navigator.

Sighted — The machine amplifies the memory beneath it and the judgment beside it. Given neither, it arrives at the wrong place faster.

Charted — The AI-OM Orchestrator's four agents, and the Contextual Recall Sidecar that brings what the organization knows to the moment it is needed.

Course — Choose one recurring decision and wire retrieval into it, so the relevant history surfaces at the point of use. One decision made with memory teaches more than any archive.

PART III — THE PILOT'S KNOWLEDGE

Ignoranti quem portum petat, nullus suus ventus est.

"For one who does not know which port he is sailing to, no wind is favourable."

— Seneca, Letters to Lucilius, Letter 71, c. 65 AD

On a spring morning in 2019, a Panamax bulk carrier loaded with grain departed the port of Montreal heading downriver for the Gulf. The ship was 225 metres long. It carried more than thirty thousand tonnes. Its bridge was equipped with GPS, AIS transponders, radar, an electronic chart display, real-time current data, and weather-routing software updated every six hours.

The ship's master had navigated the Saint Lawrence for eleven years.

At Les Escoumins, 320 kilometres downstream, the ship slowed. A small pilot boat came alongside. A man in an orange survival suit climbed a rope ladder up the hull. He reached the bridge, shook hands with the master, glanced at the instruments, and took the wheel.

For the next eighteen hours, the Pilot—not the ship's master, not the GPS, not the routing software—was responsible for the vessel. The master, who owned legal command of his ship, became an observer on his own bridge.

This is not a courtesy. It is the law. Under the Pilotage Act, every foreign vessel over 35 metres on the Saint Lawrence between Les Escoumins and Montreal must carry a licensed Pilot. The St. Lawrence Pilots Corporation has been active in some form since the mid-seventeenth century. Today, its members serve one of the most technically demanding navigation corridors in the world: a river whose tides exceed six metres, whose currents run in multiple directions simultaneously, whose fog can appear in minutes, and whose channel shifts subtly with every season's scouring of the riverbed.

The question a shipowner sometimes asks is reasonable: if my captain has GPS, electronic charts, and eleven years of experience, why does he need a Pilot?

The answer is not that the Pilot has better instruments. He boards with the same instruments that are already on the bridge. The answer is that the Pilot has memory that no instrument carries. He knows that at a particular bend near Île d'Orléans, the current runs two knots faster than the charts indicate in late April because of snowmelt. He knows which buoys drift off-station in freezing weather and which the coast guard corrects within forty-eight hours. He knows the signature of the fog patterns near Rimouski—which ones burn off by mid-morning and which ones deepen. He knows because his predecessors knew, and because the Corporation is, among other things, a living repository of everything the Saint Lawrence has done to ships for three and a half centuries.

French-Canadian explorer, René-Robert Cavelier de La Salle, left Lachine in July 1669 with nine canoes and twenty-four men, convinced that a great river to the south would lead him to China. He was brave, driven, and wrong. His maps were inaccurate. His astrolabe gave faulty latitude readings. On his final expedition, fifteen years later, he arrived at Matagorda Bay in Texas—800 kilometres from the mouth of the

Mississippi, where he had sought, because his instruments told him he was in the right place. He trusted the instrument. He had no Pilot who knew the difference. His own men murdered him in the spring of 1687.

The lesson is not that courage fails. La Salle had courage. The lesson is that in the most complex and consequential navigation, instruments are necessary but not sufficient.

What makes the difference is the knowledge that cannot be encoded in a chart—the pattern recognition built from thousands of crossings, the anomaly memory that says *this is not right, something the instrument cannot see is wrong here.*

Watch the Pilot work and you notice something the shipowner's question misses entirely. He does not steer the river with one instrument. In the wide reach below Québec he leans on radar and the chart; at the bend off Île d'Orléans he ignores both and reads the current against the hull; in the narrows he calls for the lead line the bridge had stopped using a generation ago. No single instrument is right for the whole river. Each answers one question, at one moment, and is useless at the next. The craft is not in any one of them—it is in knowing which to trust where, and binding them together with the memory of what the river did the last thousand times.

Innovation is navigated the same way, and for the same reason: because it is an economic discipline, not a mood. You invest in it with a purpose, and you are owed a way to measure whether the investment is working. But no method answers that for the whole voyage. Scanning the horizon tells you where to play; it says nothing about how to win. A prototype settles how to win; it cannot make a market adopt what you built. Gamification turns an addressable market into an addressed one; it has nothing to say about whether you explored the right territory in the first place. Every method in this field is an instrument—precise at its moment, blind everywhere else. The practitioners who get results are not the ones with the best single method. They are the ones who orchestrate: combining methods, sometimes fragmenting them, applying each to the phase of the lifecycle that needs it.

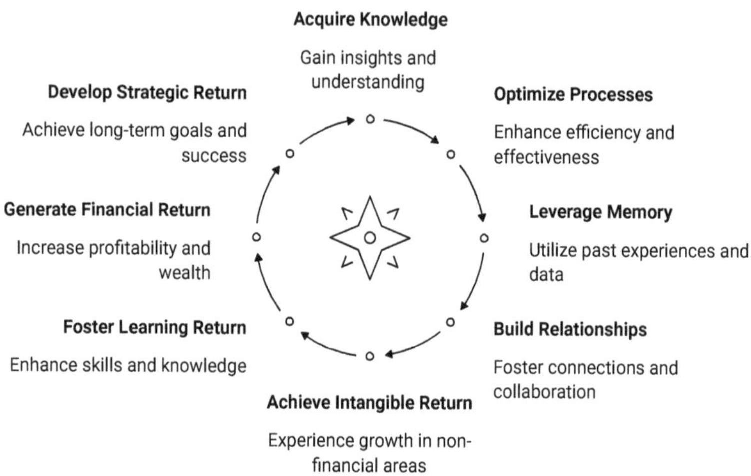

That orchestration is what the framework organizes, and it is best held as a chart rather than a list. The innovation lifecycle has four phases—Where to Play, How to Win, How to Deliver, How to Get Adopted—and you may enter at any of them and loop back freely; the river does not run in a straight line either. Beneath all four sits the one thing that lets the phases teach one another instead of repeating each other's mistakes: organizational memory, held as the Four Capitals. And across the whole chart you read two needles—Growth and Readiness—which together are ROI². That single picture is the instrument panel for the entire voyage. Everything that follows is a tour of it: which method to reach for at each phase, how to measure what it produces, and how to keep the memory beneath it compounding instead of evaporating.

The Four Readings will give you your ROI²—your customized innovation navigation instrument; we will build it in Chapter 7. But an instrument without a Pilot who carries the river's memory is a GPS on a ship that has never been here before.

Part III is about building the Pilot's knowledge—the memory beneath the chart—and then learning to orchestrate the instruments above it: the right method, at the right phase, measured honestly, and made to compound across generations of crews.

Chapter 7: The ROI^2 Scorecard

Day One of the rollout at a mid-sized aerospace firm looked nothing like the brochure. The CFO sat in the back row with his arms folded, radiating skepticism the way a radiator emits heat—silently, but unmistakably. "Another framework," he muttered to the VP of Engineering beside him. "How long before this one joins the graveyard?"

The VP shrugged. She had survived three transformation programs in four years. She had learned to nod at kickoffs and wait for the inevitable fade. What neither of them expected was that six months later, the CFO would be the system's most vocal advocate—not because a compelling slide had converted him, but because the governance structure had quietly answered every objection he had ever raised about innovation spending.

The CFO had earned his arms-folded posture, and it is worth pausing on why, because his skepticism is the most rational position in the room. Consider what an honest ROI^2 actually asks an organization to keep track of. Four capitals, measured across every initiative in the portfolio. Four readings per initiative per cycle—what went in, what is moving, what came out, what it changed. A curated indicator set per initiative, drawn from a catalogue of nearly two hundred, weighted by horizon and by season. Every significant decision logged with its reasoning. Every abandonment recorded with its lesson. Every reuse traced back to its source, because the Reuse Rate is a fraction and fractions need numerators. External signals bound to the bets they bear on. And beneath all of it, the comparison that quantifies the Duplication Tax: every new project checked against everything the organization has ever tried—a task that grows not with the size of the portfolio but with the length of the organization's entire history.

Read that list again, slowly, and imagine assigning it to a team. Not designing it—running it, every cycle, for years. No analyst does this. No department of analysts does this. I have spent three decades inside organizations that innovate, and I have never once seen the full ledger kept by hand—not because the people were lazy, but because the task is insurmountable in the only currency that matters, which is sustained human attention. Somewhere around the third quarter, under deadline pressure, the logging quietly stops. The channels close. The ledger goes dark.

Do not take my word for it. NASA—an organization with a mandated, purpose-built Lessons Learned Information System—was audited twice by the Government Accountability Office and once by its own Inspector General. The findings read like a diagnosis of the species: lessons not routinely captured, managers unaware of what other centres had learned, the cited barrier being the one that matters—no time—and, a decade after the first warning, eight of ten centres still not compliant. If the people who land robots on Mars cannot keep the ledger by hand, your organization will not either.

And this—precisely this—is where Innovation Theatre comes from. The theatre of Chapter 1 is not a moral failure; it is what rational people stage when the honest number is unreachable. If you cannot compute what innovation built, you count what innovation did: the ideas submitted, the workshops held, the prototypes paraded. Vanity metrics are not chosen because anyone believes them. They are chosen because they are countable by hand. The dishonesty of innovation measurement has always been, at bottom, a problem of arithmetic capacity.

What changed is not that the arithmetic got easier. It is that the bookkeeper changed species. A generative model connected to the organization's memory does not find the ledger insurmountable, because reading everything, remembering everything, and comparing everything is the one thing it does without fatigue. The Decision Log writes itself into the record at the moment of decision; the comparison against all prior work runs while the new idea is still being framed; the four capitals are tallied continuously instead of reconstructed quarterly under protest. Chapter 6 showed what this looks like in the engine room. Here is what it means for measurement: every method stacked in the chapters ahead—the scorecard, the cascade, the formula, the season—is executable, for the first time, because none of it any longer depends on human clerks doing inhuman clerical work. And none of this retracts the minimum viable set of Chapter 1—four data points per initiative per month is the on-ramp a crew keeps by hand; the full ledger is what the new bookkeeper keeps once the voyage is long.

This is the spine of the book, and it deserves one line of its own: generative AI made organizational memory possible at scale, and organizational memory makes ROI^2 possible at all. Without the memory, the best you will ever compute is an approximation of Growth—the half that leaves tracks in the P&L anyway—while Readiness stays dark and the theatre reopens for another season. With the memory, the full number is within reach of any organization willing to keep its channels open. The CFO in the back row did not become the system's most vocal advocate because the slides improved. He became its advocate the day the number in front of him stopped being staged.

Implementation is the stretch most readers will want to skip. It sounds procedural, bureaucratic, the opposite of the creative spark that draws people to innovation. But implementation is what separates a system from a stunt. Without it, every other chapter in this book is a theoretical exercise.

The three chapters ahead are your playbook. They walk you through the methodology step by step, from building the foundation to calculating a portfolio-level ROI² score. Together they provide the complete technical toolkit for a successful implementation: the indicator library, measurement formulas, dashboard blueprints, and implementation worksheets that translate the conceptual framework from Part II into operational practice. Each step in this journey builds on the previous one.

Before the playbook begins, hold the destination in view, because it is easy to lose in what follows. Everything in the three of them converges on a single number you can set in front of a board—ROI², the two needles of Growth and Readiness—and the formula that produces it arrives at Step 5. The steps before it are the build: Steps 0 through 2 stand up the memory foundation and decide what is worth measuring; Steps 3 and 4 are the measurement machinery, where the long indicator library is a reference to draw from, not a passage to read end to end. Step 5 is where that machinery resolves into the formula. Steps 6 and 7 lift the result from a single initiative to a portfolio and a dashboard; Chapter 9 turns it into a planned investment season. Build, then read, then pilot.

On a first pass, read for the spine and skim the catalogues. The indicator set and the dashboard blueprints are built to be consulted later, with a spreadsheet open—not memorized now. What has to land by the end is simple: how a column of raw figures becomes one defensible pair of needles, and why that pair, not a slide of disconnected metrics, is what finally earns innovation a hearing in the room where the money is decided.

Organizational Memory + ROI² = S4IL

The CEO wanted growth weighted at seventy percent. This was not unreasonable—the organization was at a stage where growth was the primary strategic priority, the board was asking growth questions, and the management team had been hired with growth mandates. Seventy percent on growth, fifteen percent on efficiency, fifteen percent on resilience: the weights seemed to reflect the strategy.

The problem was that the weights, once set, would affect every subsequent measurement. A portfolio optimized for a 0.7 growth weight would systematically deprioritize projects in the efficiency and resilience categories, even when those projects were generating superior epistemic returns and building knowledge capital that the growth projects would eventually need. It would also systematically overvalue early-stage growth projects relative to late-stage efficiency projects, because growth potential is visible from the start, while efficiency gains only appear at deployment.

The question the CEO was really asking—though she did not frame it this way—was: what do we want our innovation portfolio to optimize for over the next three years? And the answer to that question, properly understood, is not simply a matter of strategic priorities. It is a matter of what the organization's memory infrastructure can actually support.

An organization that has strong knowledge capital in growth-oriented innovation but weak knowledge capital in efficiency and resilience innovation will not benefit from weighting growth at 70%—it will simply invest in growth without the organizational memory to execute well. Conversely, an organization with deep institutional knowledge in a specific efficiency domain might rationally place greater weight on that domain than strategic priorities suggest, because it can generate superior returns in a domain where its memory is strong.

The governance of an innovation measurement system is ultimately about aligning what the organization says it is doing, what it measures, and what it actually knows how to do. When these three things are aligned, measurement systems reinforce capability development. When they are misaligned, measurement systems create the appearance of strategy while eroding its reality.

The Three Governance Postures

The Compass framework identifies three distinct governance postures for innovation management, each corresponding to a different organizational situation and requiring a different measurement configuration.

The first posture is **Exploration Governance**, appropriate for organizations in the early stages of building innovation capability or entering new domains. In this posture, the measurement emphasis is on learning quality—the richness of insights generated, the speed of hypothesis testing, the quality of knowledge capture—rather than on commercial outcomes, which are premature to measure at this stage. The risk in Exploration Governance is over-measurement of inputs and under-investment in the knowledge capture infrastructure that will allow exploration results to compound. Organizations in this posture should resist pressure to demonstrate ROI from early-stage investments; instead, they should demonstrate the quality of their learning.

What follows is evidence from organizations that have made this transition: from episodic innovation performance to a systematic learning capability. The patterns are consistent enough to have generated a practical implementation framework—one that the plant engineer at the centre of this chapter could use to make her eleven years of accumulated knowledge an organizational asset rather than a personal one.

The second posture is **Translation Governance**, appropriate for organizations that have established exploratory capability and are working to convert research and pilot results into commercial deployment. In this posture, the measurement emphasis shifts to adoption drivers: what is slowing the transition from pilot to deployment, where knowledge transfer between R&D and implementation teams is breaking down, and which organizational capabilities are limiting the translation of innovation investment into commercial return? The signature failure mode of Translation Governance is over-optimism about the difficulty of adoption; organizations in this posture benefit from systematic measurement of the gap between what works in the lab and what works at scale.

The third posture is **Optimization Governance**, appropriate for organizations managing a mature innovation portfolio with established deployment processes. In this posture, the measurement emphasis is on portfolio efficiency—the return per unit of investment, the distribution of risk across horizons and domains, and the sustainability of the knowledge infrastructure over time. The signature failure mode of Optimization Governance is the gradual elimination of genuine Exploration investment in favour of incremental improvement, driven by the pressure to demonstrate returns within measurement cycles that are too short for exploratory work. Maintaining a deliberate allocation to Exploration—even when the returns are not visible in the current period—requires explicit governance protection.

Building the Governance Architecture

A governance architecture for the Compass comprises three levels, corresponding to the three time horizons of the measurement system.

At the operational level—quarterly—the governance focus is on portfolio tracking: are projects progressing according to plan, are learning artifacts being produced and captured, are resources allocated in proportion to the current weight configuration? At this level, the governance tool is the portfolio dashboard, which should provide a real-time view of the current state of innovation investment across all horizons and domains.

At the management level—annually—the governance focus is on trajectory analysis: is the portfolio generating better returns this year than last, is the knowledge infrastructure improving, and is the organization building the capabilities its strategy requires? At this level, the governance tool is the trend report, which requires the longitudinal data consistency discussed in the previous chapter.

At the strategic level—every three to five years—the governance focus is on architecture review: do the current weight configurations still reflect the organization's strategic reality, has the portfolio's balance across horizons and domains shifted in ways that require correction, has the external environment changed in ways that make the existing measurement framework inadequate? At this level, the governance tool is the strategic review, which should include external benchmarking, stakeholder input, and a reassessment of the fundamental assumptions underlying the measurement system.

The CEO who wanted growth weighted at seventy percent was right to think about weights. She also needed a governance process to review those weights as her organization's situation evolved—because the most dangerous measurement system is one optimized for a strategic situation that no longer exists.

Step 0: Build the Foundation—Organizational Memory, Amplified by AI

Before any ROI² calculation can begin, the organization must have one thing in place—and it is a discipline before it is a system: the habit of capturing, organizing, and retrieving innovation knowledge, kept alive through the channels of Appendix I. That discipline is the non-negotiable prerequisite of the entire methodology. The AI layer is not the prerequisite. It is the amplifier—the mechanism that carries the discipline past the third quarter, where hand-kept ledgers historically go dark, and that lights the Readiness needle to its full depth.

What does this system look like in practice? It can take several forms. It may be an Innovation Management System (IMS) with built-in AI capabilities. It may be a set of AI tools—large language models, knowledge graphs, recommendation engines—that collectively feed a central database. Or it may be a distributed architecture in which multiple databases are connected via APIs, and a machine learning layer synthesizes insights across them. The specific technology matters less than the principle: there must be a persistent, AI-powered layer that collects the cloud of information generated by every innovation initiative.

This machine learning layer does three things. First, it captures both declarative knowledge (explicit documents, reports, patents) and tacit knowledge (patterns inferred from project histories, failure modes, contextual judgment). Second, it makes this knowledge retrievable—not just searchable, but contextually relevant at the moment of decision. Third, it learns: with every project cycle, the system becomes more valuable, not less.

→ Without organizational memory, ROI² is a formula with only unknown variables.

You can begin without the amplifier. A first season at the second rung of the measurement maturity ladder (Chapter 8) runs on a spreadsheet, finance extracts, and the knowledge audit—soundings by lead line, honest and coarse. What you cannot begin without is the discipline, because a memory that was never kept cannot later be retrieved, by any intelligence. Lay the keel by hand if you must. Motorize before the ocean.

Step 1: Understand the Problem—Why the Boardroom Needs a Compass

There was a pause. The CIO had last year's portfolio. It existed as a separate document, from a separate review cycle, organized under a slightly different taxonomy, using different stage definitions, and produced by a different team. It was accurate and thorough. It was simply not comparable to this year's version in any rigorous way.

"We can work on that," the CIO said.

The CFO, to her credit, was not asking to obstruct. She was asking because she understood, from years of financial analysis, that the only meaningful measurement of a portfolio is longitudinal. A snapshot tells you the current state. A sequence of snapshots tells you whether you are improving. A management system that cannot produce comparable sequential data is not a measurement system; it is a reporting system. Reporting systems describe the present. Measurement systems track change.

What the CFO was asking for—and what most organizations lack—is an innovation measurement system that is sufficiently stable to be analytically meaningful. Not stable in the sense of unchanging (the taxonomy should evolve as the organization's innovation strategy evolves), but stable in the sense of maintaining consistent definitions, comparable units, and a continuous thread of data that allows genuine trend analysis.

Building the ROI² Scorecard

The ROI² framework introduced in Chapter Two organizes innovation measurement across two layers: financial return and epistemic return. At the portfolio level, translating this framework into a practical scorecard requires addressing three specific design problems.

Step 2: Know What to Measure—The Curated Indicator Set

For practical organizational use, the Oslo Manual's comprehensive indicator set needs to be curated: reduced to a working set that is measurable within normal organizational data collection, comparable across organizational functions, and stable enough to allow trend analysis over multiple reporting cycles. The following core indicators have been selected based on these criteria.

Input indicators measure what the organization is investing in innovation: total innovation expenditure as a percentage of revenue; headcount allocated to innovation activities (full-time equivalents); external knowledge acquisition (licensing, partnerships, university collaborations). These are the easiest indicators to measure and the least informative on their own—they tell you what you are spending, not what you are getting.

Throughput indicators measure the quality of the innovation process: time from idea to pilot (speed); percentage of ideas that advance to pilot (selectivity); abandonment rate with documented learning versus abandonment without documented learning (memory quality). The last indicator—which most organizations do not currently track—is arguably the most important, because it measures whether the organization is building knowledge capital from its abandonment decisions.

Output indicators measure what the organization produces: revenue from products and services introduced in the last three years; the number of patents filed and maintained; and process efficiency improvements attributable to innovation investments. These are the indicators that appear in most existing innovation dashboards, and they are valuable as far as they go, which is only to the end of the commercial deployment horizon.

Outcome indicators measure the lasting consequences of innovation: market share movement in innovation-intensive categories; customer retention in product lines that have been significantly improved; talent acquisition and retention in innovation roles (a proxy for the organization's reputation as an innovative employer). These indicators typically require a two- to four-year lag before the data are meaningful.

Memory indicators—the dimension that distinguishes the Compass from conventional dashboards—measure the quality of the organization's learning infrastructure: percentage of projects that produce documented learning artifacts beyond the final report; retrievability score (percentage of questions about past projects that can be answered from existing documentation); knowledge transfer rate (percentage of key insights from completed projects that have been actively communicated to new projects in the same domain). These indicators are the least conventional and the hardest to benchmark externally, but they are the most diagnostic of long-term innovation capability.

Governing the Compass

The first problem you will hit at this stage is normalization. Innovation investments vary enormously in scale, time horizon, and domain. A five-million-dollar manufacturing process improvement and a fifty-thousand-dollar exploratory research project are both innovation investments; comparing their returns directly produces meaningless numbers. The scorecard must be normalized across scales before aggregating. The standard approach—which I will develop in detail in Appendix A—uses an intensity measure (innovation investment as a percentage of revenue or of the R&D budget) rather than an absolute number, and tracks return in basis points of margin improvement rather than in absolute revenue.

The second problem is horizon alignment. The same dimensions should not be used to measure early-stage innovation projects as those in deployment. A three-year-old exploratory research project should be measured primarily on learning outcomes: what do we know now that we did not know before? What hypotheses have been validated or invalidated? What capabilities has the organization built? A late-stage deployment project should be measured primarily on adoption and financial return. A measurement system that applies the same metrics to both produces distorted signals.

The Compass framework addresses this through a horizon structure inspired by McKinsey's three-horizon model but adapted for measurement rather than strategy.

- Horizon 1 investments—projects within eighteen months of commercial deployment—are measured primarily on adoption and financial return.
- Horizon 2 investments—projects two to five years from deployment—are measured on capability development and validated learning.
- Horizon 3 investments—exploratory research beyond a five-year horizon—are measured on knowledge capital creation and option value.

Each horizon has different indicators; each contributes to the overall portfolio score in different proportions.

Why Your H1 Machine Is Slowly Killing Your H3 Capability

The three-horizon structure described above is a portfolio framework. But it masks a dynamic that every Head of Innovation needs to understand explicitly: the organizational systems that make H1 execution efficient are, by design, hostile to H3 exploration. This is not a failure of will or imagination. It is a structural consequence of how organizations work.

H1 investments succeed through discipline, predictability, and efficient execution. The governance systems that support H1—stage-gate reviews, return hurdle rates, quarterly reporting cycles, risk minimization protocols—are calibrated for a world where the question is "how efficiently can we do what we already know how to do?" Apply those same systems to an H3 project, and you will systematically kill it—not because it lacks merit, but because it will fail every review designed for a different kind of work.

The research term for managing both simultaneously is organizational ambidexterity. The practical implication for a Head of Innovation is blunt: if your innovation portfolio aspires to include H3 investments but uses the same governance, incentive, and measurement framework across all three horizons, your H3 pipeline will drift toward H1 over time. Not because leadership changed its mind. Because the system was selected for it.

When the Compass dashboard flags "H1 Starvation Risk"—meaning the portfolio is overweight on core investments—it is rarely because the organization decided to under-invest in the future. It is usually because the governance systems applied uniformly across the portfolio quietly eliminated everything uncertain enough to be transformational.

The Ambidexterity Diagnostic

Before attributing portfolio imbalance to strategic intent, check the systems. Ask these questions for each horizon tier in your portfolio:

- **Review gate criteria:** Are the same stage-gate criteria applied to H1 efficiency projects and H3 exploratory bets? If yes, your H3 projects will die at the first gate.
- **Success metrics:** Are H3 teams measured on adoption timelines, revenue targets, or ROI within 12–24 months? Those are H1 metrics applied to H3 work.
- **Personal career risk:** What happens to the career of an H3 project lead whose three-year exploratory project does not convert? If the answer involves significant negative consequences, your best people will not volunteer for H3 work.
- **Time allocation:** Is the time allowed for reflection, experimentation, and iteration genuinely protected in H3

projects? Or does operational urgency continuously redirect that time toward H1 deliverables?

The goal is not to eliminate the process. It is to have different processes for different kinds of work: tight governance, where predictability is the value, loose governance, where learning is the value. The Compass framework supports this through its horizon-differentiated measurement approach, but only if the governance structure outside the measurement system is also differentiated.

The third problem is memory integration. The most valuable dimension of innovation measurement—and the one most consistently absent from existing systems—is the longitudinal record that connects current investments to the organizational learning they build on. What prior knowledge enabled this project? What did the last attempt at this problem teach us? What would we do differently if we attempted this again? These questions are not answerable from a portfolio review alone; they require access to the organization's innovation memory.

This is where the Compass connects its measurement function to its memory function. A portfolio review conducted without reference to organizational memory is a snapshot. A portfolio review conducted with reference to organizational memory is a trajectory analysis, and only trajectory analysis can tell you whether your innovation capability is improving.

Aligning S4IL with ISO 56002

The framework does not exist in a vacuum. For organizations operating in regulated industries or multinational environments, alignment with international standards is not optional—it is a prerequisite for credibility. ISO 56002, the international standard for

Innovation Management Systems, provides the most closely aligned institutional framework with the measurement approach described in this book.

Where this sits on the compass. ISO 56002 is not a method at any one phase; it is the ring around the whole compass. Where Chao1, prioritization, and the diffusion mechanics each act at a single point in the cycle, the standard governs all of them at once—giving the orchestration external credibility and a vocabulary auditors and regulators already trust. OKRs, in the section that follows, do the complementary job: they translate the same compass into the targets a team is actually held to. Neither one measures innovation; both make the measurement legible to the organization around it.

ISO 56002 defines an innovation management system as a set of interrelated elements that establish innovation policies and objectives, along with the processes to achieve them. The standard follows the familiar Plan-Do-Check-Act cycle and addresses eight elements: the organization's context, leadership, planning, support, operations, performance evaluation, improvement, and innovation management system techniques.

For the practitioner, the alignment is natural. ISO 56002's 'performance evaluation' element requires the organization to define what needs to be monitored and measured; the methods for monitoring, measurement, analysis, and evaluation; when monitoring and measuring shall be performed; and when results shall be analyzed and evaluated. The framework provides specific answers to each of these requirements through the Four Compass Readings, the curated indicator set, and the ROI² calculation methodology.

The evidence from organizations that have implemented structured innovation management systems is consistent: standardization does not constrain creativity—a common fear among innovation teams—but rather provides the structural foundation that allows creative work to be sustained, measured, and scaled. Organizations with mature innovation management systems outperform their peers on both radical and incremental innovation, not because structure generates ideas, but because structure ensures that ideas are captured, evaluated, and built upon rather than lost.

→More structure produces more creativity, not less.

The mechanism is straightforward: standardization reduces the cognitive overhead of managing the innovation process, freeing the innovation team to focus on the creative work itself. When the measurement system is well-defined, the team does not spend time debating how to report progress. When the governance architecture is clear, the team does not spend time navigating organizational politics to secure resources.

Innovation Ambidexterity: Balancing Explore and Exploit

The earlier discussion of Horizon balance targets introduced the concept of balancing exploration and exploitation. ISO 56002 elevates this balance to a systemic requirement, and the research evidence provides empirical support for what many innovation leaders have suspected: the ability to pursue both explorative and exploitative innovation simultaneously—innovation ambidexterity—is one of the most robust predictors of sustained innovation performance.

The four-capital structure of the framework provides a natural architecture for ambidexterity. Each capital has both an explorative and an exploitative dimension:

- **Knowledge Capital.** Explorative dimension: discovering new knowledge domains, building capabilities in emerging technologies, and understanding unfamiliar markets. Exploitative dimension: deepening existing expertise, codifying best practices, optimizing known processes.
- **Relational Capital.** Explorative dimension: building new external partnerships, engaging with non-traditional collaborators (startups, academic institutions, cross-industry partners). Exploitative dimension: strengthening existing supplier and customer relationships, deepening internal collaboration networks.
- **Process Capital.** Explorative dimension: designing agile, experimental processes for Horizon 3 initiatives. Exploitative dimension: standardizing and optimizing processes for Horizon 1 operations. The governance architecture described in Step 0 should explicitly assign different process models to different horizons.
- **Memory Capital.** Explorative dimension: capturing knowledge from failed experiments, abandoned approaches, and emerging signals. Exploitative dimension: maintaining and updating the knowledge base for current products, markets, and processes.

The ambidexterity diagnostic introduced earlier in this chapter should be conducted quarterly, with the results plotted on a four-quadrant map that shows the balance between exploration and exploitation for each capital. An organization that is heavily exploitative across all four capitals is optimizing for the present at the expense of the future. An organization that is heavily explorative across all four capitals is investing in the future but starving current operations. The ideal state—innovation ambidexterity—strikes a balance across all four, with specific ratios calibrated to the organization's strategic position and competitive environment.

The Explore-Exploit Measurement Architecture

Lewrick's Problem-to-Growth-and-Scale Framework provides a useful complement to the framework for understanding how measurement requirements change as an innovation initiative matures. In the early stages—problem definition, solution building, MVP testing—the appropriate metrics are exploration metrics: are we learning? Are we reducing uncertainty? Are we getting closer to problem-solution fit? In the later stages—launch, execution, growth—the appropriate metrics shift to exploitation metrics: are we scaling efficiently? Are we achieving product-market fit? Are we generating sustainable revenue?

The framework accommodates this progression across four maturity stages—a complementary lens to the Four Phases of Chapter 4. Each stage shifts the indicator set accordingly:

- **Stage 1 (Discovery)—m**inimum viable exploration metrics. Focus on learning velocity, hypothesis testing rate, and pivot frequency. The goal is not financial return but uncertainty reduction.
- **Stage 2 (Validation)—b**alanced exploration and exploitation metrics. Focus on customer validation, technical feasibility, and initial business model testing. The goal is evidence of desirability, feasibility, and viability.
- **Stage 3 (Scaling)—p**rimarily exploitation metrics with continued exploration. Focus on adoption rates, unit economics, and operational efficiency. The goal is to demonstrate scalability.
- **Stage 4 (Optimization)—f**ull exploitation metrics with strategic exploration. Focus on market share, profitability, and ecosystem contribution. The goal is sustainable value creation.

The discipline of matching metrics to maturity stage is one of the most common failures in innovation measurement. Organizations that apply Stage 4 metrics to Stage 1 initiatives kill innovation by demanding financial proof before the initiative has had time to learn. Organizations that apply Stage 1 metrics to Stage 4 initiatives waste resources by continuing to 'explore' when the time for exploration has passed.

The Curated Indicator Set

The OECD Oslo Manual provides the most widely used international framework for innovation measurement, covering the full innovation cycle from R&D inputs to market outcomes. It is thorough, rigorous, and designed for national statistical collection. It is not designed for organizational management.

Step 3: Select Indicators for Each R&D&I Initiative

Here is the critical principle that makes the framework practical: not every initiative uses the same indicators. Each R&D&I initiative—whether a core product improvement, an adjacent market experiment, or a transformational moonshot—selects its own set of indicators from the catalogue. The selection depends on the initiative's type, horizon, and strategic intent.

For example, a Horizon 1 product extension might track Revenue from New Products, Process Efficiency Index, and Time-to-Market. A Horizon 3 exploratory bet might instead track Experiment Success Rate, Knowledge Recombination Score, and Capability Uplift. The indicators are different because the initiatives are fundamentally different in nature.

The catalogue of indicators in Appendix A provides the menu. Each initiative team, guided by the innovation governance framework, selects the indicators most relevant to its work. The only constraint is that every indicator must pass four criteria: Alignment with one of the four ROI^2 components, Measurability, Causality (a clear link to innovation performance), and Actionability (it must inform decisions).

> **→Different initiatives, different indicators. Same methodology, same compass.**

The power emerges at aggregation—Step 6.

One selection criterion deserves its own diagnostic, because it polices the memory the whole system rests on. Before locking any initiative's indicator set, put four questions to its team about the search that preceded their proposal:

- Did the team search for prior work before starting? What did they search for, and where?
- Did they find anything useful? If not, why not—wrong search terms, wrong system, didn't know where to look?
- Would an expert in the organization have known where to point them? Why didn't that connection happen?
- Were there relevant lessons documented somewhere that the team never reached? How far away were they?

The answers will reveal whether your problem is a knowledge capture problem (the lessons were never written down), a knowledge findability problem (they exist but no one can surface them), or a knowledge translation problem (they exist and are findable, but the vocabulary used to store them does not match the vocabulary used to search).

Each requires a different solution. Most organizations assume the first and ignore the second and third entirely.

Read the four layers that follow as the Four Compass Readings in economic dress—Input, Throughput, Output, Outcome—not as a rival taxonomy. Each layer names what the corresponding reading is worth in currency, and Chapter 8 supplies the pricing:

1. **Investment Layer (Inputs):** Quantifies all resources dedicated to innovation—financial, human, technological, and collaborative capital. This layer evaluates both tangible and opportunity costs, including **Total Addressable Market (TAM)** assessments and **Cost of Opportunity Pursued (COP)**. For example, an IP licence's TAM can estimate potential future revenue streams if the innovation is commercialized, while COP quantifies the foregone benefits of choosing one innovation path over another. By mapping investments to their alternative value scenarios, organizations can better understand innovation trade-offs and prioritize high-impact opportunities.

2. **Transformation Layer (Throughputs):** Measures the efficiency of converting inputs into prototypes, patents, and validated concepts. This layer is where **most visible** change occurs: new ideas challenge and replace older processes or technologies, leading to renewal and obsolescence. Schumpeter introduced the creative destruction dynamic, which captures how experimentation and prototyping dismantle outdated practices and enable innovative replacements that fuel progress.

3. **Output Layer (Deliverables):** This layer captures tangible innovation results such as new products, services, or intellectual property assets. For instance, **IP licensing revenues**, **process**

cost reductions, and **new market product launches** are measurable outputs that directly enhance organizational value.

4. **Outcome Layer (Impact):** Evaluates broader, long-term effects of innovation, including market expansion, social or environmental benefits, and brand equity improvement. Examples include **societal impact from sustainability initiatives**, **public value creation through digital inclusion**, and **economic growth through ecosystem partnerships**.

The framework is flexible enough to incorporate **IP valuation** metrics, including patent evaluation, licensing potential, and protection strength. Even unsold patents or unused discoveries—documented through lab notebooks or prototypes—hold value as **intangible evidence of risk and learning**. These can be estimated through reuse potential, cost contribution, or similarity to market benchmarks.

Example indicators include *knowledge reuse rate*, *prototype repurposing ratio*, *failed experiment insight index*, and *IP licensing efficiency*. Tracking these enables firms to identify value hidden within non-commercialized results.

Examples of indicators that an organization can include in the ROI² framework

Before using the following table, readers should consider how to adapt or prioritize indicators based on their organization's innovation strategy. Those focusing on market expansion may emphasize output and outcome indicators, while research-driven organizations may weigh inputs and throughputs more heavily. The goal is to select metrics that best align with strategic objectives, available data, and the maturity level of innovation practices.

The table below presents a curated selection of indicators—chosen from the comprehensive ROI² Indicator Catalogue in Appendix A—that represent the most broadly applicable metrics across the Four Capitals.

These are a starting point, not a ceiling. The full catalogue in Appendix A contains every indicator I have been able to identify and validate over thirty years of innovation management practice. It is almost certainly not exhaustive, and I actively encourage innovation practitioners to contact me with additional indicators they have found effective in their own organizations.

Notice that the table includes a Horizon column rather than a fixed measurement frequency. This is deliberate. Every indicator is measured according to the investment cycle of the initiative it serves—not on a rigid calendar schedule. The Horizon column indicates which types of initiatives each indicator is most relevant to, listed in order of priority. An indicator marked "H3, H2" is most naturally suited to transformational and adjacent initiatives but may also apply to core innovation in certain contexts. An indicator marked "H1, H2, H3" is broadly applicable across all horizons.

Category	Indicator	Description	Formula	Horizon	Focus	Orientation
Input	R&D Intensity	% of revenue allocated to R&D	R&D Spend / Total Revenue	H1, H2, H3	R&D	Growth
Input	TAM Utilization	Proportion of total addressable market targeted	Target Market / TAM	H1, H2	R&D	Growth
Input	Cost of Opportunity Pursued (COP)	Opportunity trade-off value	Value of Chosen Path – Best Alternative	H2, H3	R&D	Readiness
Throughput	Idea Conversion Rate	% of ideas reaching prototype stage	Prototypes / Ideas	H1, H2, H3	Innovation	Growth
Throughput	Collaboration Index	Efficiency of cross-department collaboration	Collaborative Projects / Total Projects	H1, H2, H3	R&D	Growth
Throughput	Experiment Success Ratio	% of successful experiments	Successful Tests / Total Tests	H2, H3	R&D	Readiness
Throughput	Process Efficiency Index (PEI)	Measures innovation throughput efficiency	Weighted Output / Weighted Input	H1, H2	Innovation	Growth
Output	Product Innovation Rate	New products as % of total portfolio	New Products / Total Products	H1, H2	Innovation	Growth

Category	Indicator	Description	Formula	Horizon	Focus	Orientation
Output	IP Licensing Revenue	Licensing revenue contribution	Licence Income / Total Revenue	H2, H3	R&D	Growth
Output	Patent Utilization Ratio	Active vs. dormant patents	Active Patents / Total Patents	H2, H3	R&D	Readiness
Output	Cost Reduction Index	% operational savings from innovation	(Baseline – New Cost) / Baseline	H1	Innovation	Growth
Output	Process Automation Impact	Productivity gain from automation	Output After / Output Before	H1, H2	Innovation	Growth
Output	Knowledge Reuse Rate	Reused knowledge from prior projects	Reused Insights / Total Insights	H1, H2, H3	R&D	Readiness
Outcome	Market Share Growth	Market share gained through innovation	(New – Old) / Old	H1, H2	Innovation	Growth
Outcome	Customer Adoption Rate	Adoption rate of new product/service	New Users / Total Users	H1, H2	Innovation	Growth
Outcome	Ecosystem Leverage	Partner-driven innovation outcomes	Co-Developed Projects /	H2, H3	Innovation	Growth

Category	Indicator	Description	Formula	Horizon	Focus	Orientation
			Partnerships			
Outcome	Environmental Efficiency Gain	Environmental performance improvement	Reduced Emissions / Baseline	H2, H3	Innovation	Growth
Outcome	Failed Experiment Insight Index	Value extracted from failures	Lessons Captured / Failures	H3, H2	R&D	Readiness
Intangible	IP Portfolio Strength	Weighted patent quality	(Patent Quality × Remaining Life)	H2, H3	R&D	Readiness
Intangible	Knowledge Capital Growth	New knowledge creation rate	Knowledge Created / Period	H3, H2	R&D	Growth
Intangible	Learning Return	Skills applied post-training	Applied / Trained Employees	H1, H2, H3	Innovation	Readiness
Intangible	Organizational Agility Index	Ability to adapt through innovation	Rapid Pivots / Total Projects	H2, H3	Innovation	Readiness
Strategic	Competitive Resilience Index	Recovery speed post-disruption	Time to Recover Benchmark	H2, H3	Innovation	Readiness
Strategic	Ecosystem Position Strength	Innovation influence in networks	Centrality Score / Total Partners	H2, H3	Innovation	Growth

Category	Indicator	Description	Formula	Horizon	Focus	Orientation
Strategic	Strategic Alignment Index	Project alignment to strategic goals	Strategic Projects / Total Projects	H1, H2, H3	Innovation	Readiness
Strategic	Transformation Impact Score	Extent of business model renewal	New Business Models / Total	H3, H2	Innovation	Growth
Learning	Experiment Learning Ratio	Insights reused from failed tests	Lessons from Failures / Total Failures	H3, H2	R&D	Readiness
Learning	Knowledge Diffusion Index	Learning spread across teams	Teams Applying Learnings / Total Teams	H2, H3	Innovation	Growth
Learning	Innovation Capability Maturity	Readiness of innovation systems	Weighted Maturity Assessment	H1, H2, H3	Innovation	Readiness
Learning	Learning Transfer Efficiency	Lessons integrated into future projects	Projects Applying Learnings / Projects with Learnings	H2, H3	Innovation	Growth

These indicators serve as an example of a flexible library for innovation management practitioners to design an **ROI²** aligned with their organization's innovation strategy, including priorities, objectives, and competitive environments.

To determine whether an indicator is relevant to ROI^2, it should reflect the dual objectives of R&D and innovation: **R&D** aims to transform investment into knowledge, while **innovation** converts that knowledge into new value. Together, these processes enable organizations to **grow** and **adapt to change**. Therefore, indicator criteria must reflect both growth potential and adaptability. An indicator is relevant to ROI^2 when it meets the key criteria of *alignment, measurability, causality,* and *actionability*:

- **Alignment:** The indicator must directly support one of the four ROI^2 components (Financial, Intangible, Strategic, or Learning) and reflect the organization's innovation objectives.

- **Measurability:** It should be quantifiable or convertible into measurable proxies supported by reliable data sources.

- **Causality:** There must be a clear cause-and-effect link between the indicator and innovation performance or outcomes, avoiding vanity or correlation-only metrics.

- **Actionability:** Finally, it must inform decisions—showing where to invest, improve, or scale innovation activities.

Indicators that fail to meet these criteria—such as those that are too subjective, loosely connected to innovation outcomes, or lacking measurable data—should be excluded. This ensures that each metric included in an ROI^2 framework truly contributes to understanding and improving the value of innovation.

Quantifying Inputs: Establishing the Innovation Baseline

A critical aspect of defining innovation inputs is understanding how **Total Addressable Market (TAM)** and **Cost of Opportunity Pursued (COP)** guide investment prioritization. TAM helps quantify the potential market value of an idea, product, or intellectual property licence—thereby informing whether an opportunity is worth scaling. COP, on the other hand, measures the organization's sacrifice in choosing one innovation path over another.

Together, these two indicators encourage decision-makers to weigh strategic ambition against opportunity risk, ensuring that resources are allocated to initiatives with the highest expected value and the greatest alignment with long-term goals.

Step 4: Measure Each Initiative—The Four Compass Readings

With indicators selected, measurement begins. Each initiative is measured across the four compass readings: Input (what you invest), Throughput (how you transform), Output (what you deliver), and Outcome (the impact you create).

The tables below provide the measurement framework for each reading.

Inputs are the fuel of innovation—financial, human, and knowledge resources.

Category	Example Metrics	Data Source	Example Calculation
Financial Inputs	R&D budget, innovation operating budget, venture participation	Finance	Total R&D cost / Total revenue
Human Inputs	% of workforce in innovation, training hours, and intrapreneurship rate	HR	Employees in innovation / Total employees × 100
Knowledge Inputs	Research collaborations, patents-in-progress, reusable datasets	R&D	Σ of monetized knowledge inputs — each converted by its catalogued method (Chapter 8), then summed in currency

$I^{(total)} = I^f + I^h + I^k$

Measuring Throughputs: Capturing the Innovation Process

Throughputs are the **engine** of innovation—transforming ideas into validated outcomes.

Indicators: Idea conversion rate, experimentation rate, collaboration index, and prototyping velocity.

$PEI = (\Sigma\ (w(i) \times n(i))/\Sigma\ w(i))$

The **Process Efficiency Index (PEI)**, adapted from productivity analysis, gauges how effectively resources and experiments translate into tangible outcomes.

A high PEI reflects strong innovation processes that strengthen ROI[2] through higher throughput performance.

Measuring Outputs: Tangible Deliverables

Outputs are the immediate, measurable deliverables of innovation.

Type	Indicator	Formula	Notes
Product Innovation	Revenue from new products	New product revenue / Total revenue	Must meet Oslo definition
Process Innovation	Operational cost savings	(Baseline – New Cost) / Baseline	Post-implementation validation
Organizational Innovation	Productivity increase	Output after / Output before	Based on HR metrics
Marketing Innovation	Customer acquisition growth	New customers / Total customers	Attribution required

$$DIV = \Sigma\ (O^i \times W^i)$$

Direct Innovation Value (DIV) aggregates output performance into a single measurable value, where each weight W is assigned at season design and the weights sum to one—the same governance that sets the capital weights, one level down.

Measuring Outcomes: Strategic and Intangible Impact

Outputs represent *creation*, while outcomes measure *impact.* Outcomes include market, brand, and ecosystem effects.

Category	Example Metric	Formula	Source
Brand Equity Gain	Brand awareness × Sales uplift	Survey × Revenue	Marketing
Capability Uplift	Employees applying new skills	Trained / Total	HR
Ecosystem Leverage	Co-developed projects	Partnerships / Year	PMO
Learning Return	Knowledge reused	Reused learnings / Total learnings	OMS

$$OS = (0.3 \times BEG) + (0.3 \times CU) + (0.2 \times EL) + (0.2 \times LR)$$

The weights on OS are set at season design, exactly like the capital weights of Chapter 8—the 0.3/0.3/0.2/0.2 above is an illustration wearing default clothes, not a recommendation.

Connecting S4IL to OKRs

John Doerr's Objectives and Key Results framework, popularized through his work at Intel and later at Google, provides a natural bridge between the measurement system and organizational execution. The connection is not accidental: both frameworks share the conviction that what gets measured with precision gets managed with purpose.

The integration works at two levels. At the strategic level, each of the Four Capitals becomes an Objective. At the operational level, the ROI^2 indicators become Key Results. This translation is powerful because it converts the Compass from a reporting tool into a management system—one that connects the boardroom's strategic intent to the innovation team's daily work.

Memory Capital OKRs

Objective: Build an organizational memory infrastructure that prevents knowledge loss and accelerates future innovation cycles.

- **KR1:** Increase Memory Retention Score from 45% to 70% by the end of Q2 (measured by the percentage of completed innovation projects with fully archived decision rationale, test results, and failure analysis).
- **KR2:** Reduce Knowledge Rediscovery Time from 3 weeks average to 3 days by deploying AI-assisted retrieval across the top 20 innovation project archives.
- **KR3:** Achieve 80% coverage of Lessons Learned documentation across all active portfolio initiatives, with quarterly audit by the Innovation Memory Steward.

Process Capital OKRs

Objective: Establish repeatable innovation processes that compound organizational capability with each cycle.

- **KR1:** Reduce average time-to-first-prototype from 90 days to 45 days by standardizing the Stage 0 knowledge audit across all new initiatives.
- **KR2:** Implement portfolio-level learning reviews in 100% of quarterly governance cycles, with documented pattern cards feeding back into the Knowledge Base.
- **KR3:** Achieve a Process Maturity Score of 3.5/5 on the self-assessment by the end of the fiscal year, up from the current baseline of 2.1.

The discipline of OKR integration forces a critical conversation that many innovation teams avoid: what does progress actually look like? When the Objective is "Build organizational memory," and the Key Result is "80% Lessons Learned coverage," the team can no longer claim success by pointing to workshops attended or ideas generated.

→The compass needle moves only when the organization's memory actually improves.

→

THE SKIPPER'S LOG

Position — The scorecard is the page leadership actually reads. Organizational memory plus ROI² is the system behind it.

Sighted — Vanity indicators crowding out value — and the discipline of a curated set aligned with ISO 56002 rather than invented beside it.

Charted — The ROI² Scorecard's structure, its governance rhythm, and its coupling to OKRs, so that the needle moves only when reality does.

Course — Draft the one-page version now: a short, curated indicator set per capital, each with a target and an owner. If it does not fit on one page, it is not yet a scorecard.

Chapter 8: Computing ROI²

The Measurement Cascade

A persistent challenge in innovation measurement is ensuring that the metrics visible to the board of directors meaningfully connect to those visible to individual innovation teams. Too often, boardroom metrics and team metrics exist in separate worlds: the board sees portfolio-level aggregates that feel remote from daily work, while teams, in contrast, see project-level indicators that feel disconnected from strategic direction.

The framework addresses this through a Measurement Cascade—a deliberate architecture that links metrics at four organizational levels:

- **Board Level.** ROI² aggregate, Innovation Compass Score, North Star Metric, Factorless Income Residual, Horizon balance, Memory Fracture Risk aggregate. These metrics answer the question: Is our innovation capability producing strategic value?
- **Portfolio Level.** Portfolio ROI², capital-level scores (Knowledge, Relational, Process, Memory), ambidexterity balance, Reuse Rate, and knowledge absorption score. These metrics answer the question: Is our innovation portfolio healthy and balanced?
- **Initiative Level.** Initiative-level Four Compass Readings (Input, Throughput, Output, Outcome), curated indicator set performance, OKR progress, and Adoption Compass metrics. These metrics answer the question: Is this specific initiative progressing as expected?

- **Team Level.** Weekly activity metrics, knowledge contributions, collaboration actions, and "InnoPoints" balance. These metrics answer the question: Am I contributing to the innovation mission?

The cascade is not just a reporting structure—it is a governance mechanism. When a team-level indicator changes, the cascade shows how that change propagates through the initiative, portfolio, and board levels. When a board-level metric declines, the cascade enables rapid drill-down to identify which initiatives and which specific indicators within those initiatives are driving the decline.

The Governance Rhythm: When to Measure What

The Measurement Cascade defines what is measured at each level. The Governance Rhythm defines when each level is reviewed. The framework recommends a four-cycle governance rhythm that ensures regular measurement without creating bureaucratic overhead:

- **Weekly: Team Health Check.** Teams review their own activity metrics, knowledge contributions, and InnoPoints. Duration: fifteen minutes. Format: self-service dashboard review, no formal meeting required.
- **Monthly: Initiative Review.** Initiative leaders review Four Compass Readings, OKR progress, and Adoption Compass metrics for their initiatives. Duration: one hour. Format: structured review meeting with a standardized agenda.
- **Quarterly: Portfolio Assessment.** Portfolio managers review capital-level scores, Horizon balance, Reuse Rate, and the ambidexterity diagnostic. This is the meeting where portfolio rebalancing decisions are made. Duration: half day. Format: working session with the decision authority.

- **Annual: Strategic Innovation Review.** Board receives ROI² aggregate, Innovation Compass Score, Factorless Income Residual, and strategic recommendations. Duration: one hour as part of a regular board meeting—format: executive presentation with drill-down available on request.

The governance rhythm ensures that measurement is embedded in the organization's operational cadence rather than bolted on as a separate reporting exercise. Each review cycle feeds into the next: weekly data informs monthly reviews, monthly reviews inform quarterly assessments, and quarterly assessments inform the annual strategic review.

The four-cycle rhythm is designed to be lightweight at the team level (fifteen minutes per week) and substantive at the strategic level (half-day quarterly).

This inversion is deliberate: innovation teams should spend their time innovating, not reporting. The measurement system should serve them, not the other way around.

The Indicator Selection Meeting

Maria Torres—the plant engineer we follow through Part III—sat through her first indicator selection meeting the way a musician sits through a lecture on acoustics: understanding every concept, impatient with every slide. She had spent eleven years accumulating exactly the kind of knowledge the framework was designed to capture. She knew which experiments had been tried. She knew why three of them had failed. She knew the workaround that a technician had built in 2019 that no one had documented and that was now the only thing preventing a recurring defect.

What she did not know, until the meeting, was that none of this appeared in any measurement system. The Knowledge Contribution Rate was zero—not because she had contributed nothing, but because the system had never been configured to see her type of contribution. The Memory Retention Score for her division was in the bottom quartile—not because knowledge had been lost, but because it had never been captured in the first place. It lived in her head, in her hands, in the particular way she tilted her ear toward a machine that was beginning to misbehave.

"You are telling me," she said to the facilitator, "that the system measures what I write down, not what I know?"

"That is exactly the problem this framework is designed to fix," the facilitator replied.

The indicator selection meeting was the moment Maria understood that S4IL was not being built for the innovation team. It was being built for people like her—the domain experts whose knowledge is the organization's real innovation portfolio, and whose contribution has never been visible in any dashboard.

The formulas that follow are the instruments that make that visibility possible.

Pricing the Cargo: Three Ways to Value a Return

Ask a marine surveyor to value a sailboat before a purchase, and at the end of a day spent aboard with a moisture meter and a notebook you will be handed not one number but three. What she could earn in a season of charter—the income view. What a comparable hull had sold for that spring, two pontoons over—the market view. What it would cost to build her again from the keel up—the cost view. The three numbers will not agree, and no good surveyor is embarrassed by that: when they sit close together, trust the middle; when one runs away from the others, that is where you look. The buyer pays for the survey and receives, without knowing it, the entire discipline of intangible valuation for the price of an afternoon.

Accountants hold the same three views, and have held them for a century. The income method asks what an asset produces. The market method asks what a comparable asset trades for. The cost method asks what it would take to replace the asset—or what its absence would force you to spend. Nothing in this book invents them; the valuation professions codified them long ago. What this book does is assign them: every indicator in the catalogue of Appendix A carries not only a formula but a conversion—the rule that turns its reading into currency, and the method family that rule belongs to. The gap most measurement systems die in is exactly here, between the percentage on the dashboard and the dollar in the boardroom. The conversion rules are the plank across that gap, and there are only four shapes of plank.

Investment × multiplier. When the indicator is a spend—R&D investment, capability building, infrastructure—its expected return is the amount invested, multiplied by a sector return multiplier, adjusted by a time-discount factor for the lag before monetization. The multipliers are not invented in-house: decades of published econometrics on returns to R&D put pharmaceutical multipliers far above process-industry ones, and the honest builder cites the study, not the wish. Provenance: peer-reviewed.

Rate × reference budget × capture. When the indicator is a rate or a coverage—adoption of a new practice, share of time on innovation, reuse of prior work—the rate alone is a percentage going nowhere.

Multiply it by the budget it governs to get addressable value, then by a capture rate calibrated to your market phase to get realized value: early markets capture perhaps five to fifteen percent of what they address, saturated ones sixty to eighty-five. Provenance: industry benchmark, phase-calibrated, declared.

Benchmark delta × volume. When the indicator is a gap against a reference—time-to-market against the peer median, recovery time against the industry norm—the value is the delta priced at the cost or margin it moves, multiplied by the volume it applies to. Faster by six weeks, on a launch worth so much per week, across three launches: the arithmetic is short, and the reference must be named.

Direct value. Some cargo arrives already priced. Licensing income, a validated post-implementation saving, the budget of a duplicated project that was caught and cancelled—these need no conversion, only attribution and evidence. They are the easiest numbers in the ledger and the ones a finance partner will test first, precisely because they can be tested.

Two disciplines make the conversions defensible, and both cost less than the meeting where their absence is discovered. First, every coefficient carries its source and a provenance flag—peer-reviewed, industry benchmark, or internal estimate—so that when the CFO challenges a number, the conversation starts from a citation instead of a confession. A coefficient without a source is an opinion in a costume. Second, illustrative defaults are declared as illustrative and re-derived at season design; a default that quietly survives three seasons has stopped being a default and become a fiction. With the conversions in hand, F, I, S, and L stop being letters. They become sums of priced cargo—and the formula that follows can finally be computed rather than admired.

The ROI² Formula

The ROI² composite resolves into two needles—Readiness (Intangible and Learning returns) and Growth (Financial and Strategic returns)—each weighted to reflect the season's innovation strategy:

Step 5: Calculate ROI² for a Single Initiative

Recall the two needles from Chapter 2. ROI² is not a single number; it is a pair—a Readiness reading and a Growth reading—and you compute each needle before combining them. Each needle is the sum of two capital returns, divided by the initiative's total cost.

Before you compute anything, be clear about which half of this pair your data can honestly support. The Growth needle is the forgiving one: Financial and Strategic returns leave tracks in systems you already run—revenue, contracts, market position. An organization with no organizational memory at all can still approximate Growth, and most do. The Readiness needle is different in kind. Intangible and Learning returns are made of exactly the material that evaporates when nobody captures it: what was learned, what was documented, what was reused. There is no system of record for Readiness except the organizational memory itself. Compute ROI² without one and you have not computed a smaller ROI²—you have computed a different number wearing its name: Growth, alone, dressed as the whole. That is the arithmetic definition of Innovation Theatre, and the reason this book spent two chapters on memory before letting you anywhere near the formula.

And if the distinction feels academic, consider who else has reached it. Since 2023, Saudi Aramco—the world's largest oil producer—has reported a self-defined, non-IFRS indicator it calls Technology

Realized Value: the actual cashflow benefit of deployed technologies, measured against a defined business baseline. By the end of 2025 the cumulative figure stood at $11.3 billion. Read that carefully: an organization with every accounting resource on earth had to invent its own instrument, because the standard ledger could not see what its technology was returning. That is the Growth needle, formalized at industrial scale. The Readiness needle still awaits the same discipline—and it is the harder half, because its raw material is memory.

Growth = $w_F \times (F/C) + w_S \times (S/C)$—the returns already being realized: Financial (F), from Process Capital, and Strategic (S), from Relational Capital.

Readiness = $w_I \times (I/C) + w_L \times (L/C)$—the returns not yet visible to financial analysis: Intangible (I), from Knowledge Capital, and Learning (L), from Memory Capital.

$$ROI^2 = [\ \textit{Readiness},\ \textit{Growth}\ ]$$

The single composite a board reads is simply the two needles added together: composite

***ROI²** = **Growth** + **Readiness** =* $w_F \times (F/C) + w_I \times (I/C) + w_S \times (S/C) + w_L \times (L/C)$.

Always compute and display the two needles first—their balance is the strategic signal that a single blended number hides.

Where:

- **F** = Financial gain (revenue, cost savings)—feeds Growth, from Process Capital
- **I** = Intangible gain (brand value, IP, knowledge)—feeds Readiness, from Knowledge Capital
- **S** = Strategic gain (market share, resilience)—feeds Growth, from Relational Capital
- **L** = Learning gain (organizational maturity)—feeds Readiness, from Memory Capital
- **C** = Total investment cost

The weights shown here—w_F 0.35, w_S 0.25, w_I 0.25, w_L 0.15—are one illustration, not a recommended setting. Read together, they place sixty percent of the weight on Growth ($w_F + w_S$) and forty percent on Readiness ($w_I + w_L$): a configuration tilted toward near-term realized return. The weights are where innovation strategy becomes innovation investment strategy. At the start of each investment season, the governance team must derive them from explicit, rational criteria aligned with that season's strategy—how much the organization is choosing to invest in growing now versus becoming ready for what comes next—and revise them whenever the strategy shifts. The only structural constraints are that the four weights sum to 1.0 and that none is zero: assigning zero weight to Learning Return, for instance, formally declares that the organization does not care whether its innovation capability improves over time, which the framework does not permit.

One rule keeps the ledger honest, and it belongs here, before any arithmetic: each unit of value enters the ledger once. The sub-scores for Financial, Intangible, and Strategic gain are sums of monetized indicators, and sums have an appetite. Two indicators that price the same underlying substance—an R&D-intensity reading and an innovation-budget reading, converted by the same multiplier—will book the same money twice, and the composite will grow with the length of your indicator list rather than the health of your portfolio. The discipline is selection, not subtraction: one anchor indicator per conversion shape per capital, and when two candidates monetize overlapping substance, keep the better-sourced one and demote the other to context. Memory is the exception, by design—its three readings, a few pages ahead, are averaged rather than added, because they are three estimates of one stock, not three cargoes in one hold. A CFO will find double counting in an afternoon. Find it first.

Connection to Sub-Indicators: The **Direct Innovation Value (DIV)** derived from measurable outputs flows directly into the **Financial (F)** component, while the **Outcome Score (OS)**—which aggregates strategic and intangible effects—feeds into the **Strategic (S)** dimension. This ensures that tangible results and long-term strategic outcomes are fully integrated into the ROI^2 framework for complete coherence.

Where do four such numbers come from? Trace one mid-size portfolio before running the formula on it. Its Financial gain is the direct kind: validated post-implementation savings of $1.2M and attributable first-year revenue of $0.8M—F = $2M, no conversion required, only evidence. Its Intangible gain is priced by method: the income view of a licensed patent family, $0.9M of expected licensing over its remaining life, discounted; plus a capability uplift converted by rate × reference budget × capture, $0.6M—I = $1.5M. Its Strategic gain is a co-development pipeline priced at contracted value times a phase-calibrated capture rate—S = $1M. And its Learning gain is not summed at all: the income view (a memory bonus of $0.55M—the calculation follows shortly), the cost view (avoided duplication of $0.5M, priced from the knowledge audit), and the market view (a conservative slice of latent asset value, $0.45M) are three estimates of the same stock, so L is their mean—$0.5M, with a spread of twenty percent, inside tolerance. Every figure above is illustrative. Every method is not.

Worked example. Take F = \$2M, I = \$1.5M, S = \$1M, L = \$0.5M, C = \$5M, at the illustrative weights above. Growth = $0.35 \times (2/5) + 0.25 \times (1/5) = 0.14 + 0.05 = 0.19$. Readiness = $0.25 \times (1.5/5) + 0.15 \times (0.5/5) = 0.075 + 0.015 = 0.09$.

So ROI^2 = [Readiness 0.09, Growth 0.19], a composite of 0.28—or 28%. The number to act on is not "28%"; it is the balance, 0.09 against 0.19: a growth-tilted initiative, returning realized value but building little future capability. A whole portfolio shaped like this looks healthy this season and starves the next.

This is why you compute ROI^2 for each initiative but read it across the portfolio. A single initiative's pair is a building block; the season's decision rests on the portfolio's combined Readiness and Growth, exactly as Chapter 2 set out when it cautioned against judging innovation project by project.

Project Scorecard Example:

Project	F (\$M)	I (\$M)	S (\$M)	L (\$M)	Cost (\$M)	ROI^2 (%)	Phase
A	3.2	2.5	1.0	0.4	5.0	41	Scaling
B	1.1	0.9	0.5	0.2	3.0	26	Experimentation
C	4.5	3.5	2.0	1.0	6.0	52	Commercialization

Operationalizing the Readiness Needle: The Factorless Income Residual

The Readiness needle answers a question a single composite cannot: how much value is the organization building that its financial statements do not yet show? The Factorless Income Residual is how you put a number on it. It is not a fifth dimension beyond ROI²—it is the monetary read of the Readiness half of the pair, expressed in the language a board already understands.

There is a question that haunts every CFO who has tried to reconcile an organization's market value with its book value: where does the gap come from? A company with ten billion dollars in physical assets—factories, equipment, inventory—that trades at forty billion on the stock exchange has thirty billion dollars of value that does not appear on any balance sheet. Accountants call this intangible value. Economists have a more precise name for it: factorless income.

The term comes from a line of research in macroeconomics that asked a deceptively simple question. If you add up all the labour an economy uses and all the physical capital it deploys, the total output should equal the combined contribution of those two factors. It does not. There is a residual—a portion of output that cannot be explained by the labour and capital that produced it. Economists call this the factorless income residual, and for decades they debated what it represented. The answer, established by a series of landmark studies, is intangible capital: the accumulated knowledge, organizational capability, software, data assets, brand equity, and institutional learning that generate economic value but appear on no ledger.

At the firm level, the same residual exists and the same explanation applies. When Organization X generates one hundred million dollars in revenue, and its labour costs and physical capital explain seventy-five million, the remaining twenty-five million is the return on intangible capital. It is the value generated by the organization's accumulated memory, the relationships it has built, the processes it has refined, and the knowledge it has retained. This is the factorless income residual—and it is the single most important number for any Head of Innovation who wants to prove that innovation investment compounds.

Consider a practical illustration. A mid-sized industrial company runs its dashboard for three consecutive seasons. In Season 1, the factorless income residual—estimated as revenue minus the contribution of measured labour and capital—represents eighteen percent of total revenue. In Season 2, after implementing structured knowledge capture and a retrieval system, the residual rises to twenty-two percent. In Season 3, it reaches twenty-six percent. The physical inputs have not changed. The headcount has not changed. What has changed is the organization's ability to reuse what it already knows—to avoid duplicating past work, to make faster decisions based on accumulated evidence, and to build on previous experiments rather than starting from zero.

That eight-point increase across three seasons is the compounding return on organizational memory. It is real. It is measurable. And it is invisible to any accounting system that tracks only physical capital and labour.

In the framework, the Factorless Income Residual is the lagging read of the Readiness needle. It moves slowly, it requires at least three measurement seasons to become meaningful, and it cannot be gamed by short-term action. Its value is precisely that patience: it tells the board, with the authority of a number that aggregates everything the organization does, whether the cumulative investment in innovation capability is producing compounding returns or slowly eroding.

The number does not tell you where the value comes from; the four capitals tell you that. But the Factorless Income Residual tells you something no single capital can: whether the Readiness needle—the half of ROI^2 that financial statements never show—is genuinely rising.

It is fair to ask where these two needles come from, and whether they are simply a tidy invention dressed up in a formula. They are not. The line this book draws—between the value an organization can bank today and the capability it is quietly building for tomorrow—is the same line that national economists have spent two decades learning to draw. They found that a great deal of what makes an economy grow never shows up in this year's output: it sits in skills, in relationships, in accumulated know-how, in the intangible capital that decides who pulls ahead next. ROI^2 is that distinction brought down from the scale of a nation to the scale of a single firm. The four capitals beneath it are borrowed in the same honest way—they are the standard map organizational researchers have long used for the places a company keeps what it knows: in its people, its relationships, its processes, and its records. None of it was chosen for the pleasing symmetry of the number four. It was chosen because it already rhymes with how the rest of the economy accounts for the invisible—which is exactly why a CFO is likelier to accept it than a metric invented for a single book.

A word, too, on where this instrument lies to you—because every instrument does, and the ones that pretend otherwise are the dangerous kind. ROI^2 can only read a memory that exists. An organization that has written almost nothing down—no searchable trace of what it tried, no record of why a decision was made—will find the Readiness needle stuck near the floor, and the reason will not be that its readiness is genuinely low. The reason will be that there is nothing underneath the needle to measure. There is a harder version of this, and it is worth saying plainly, because it is the one most likely to bite. The organizations that would gain the most from reading both needles are often the ones least able to compute them. The firm with the thinnest memory is usually the one quietly repeating its own mistakes—and the one for which ROI^2 is hardest to calculate honestly. The instrument does not dissolve that tension; nothing does. It only tells you where you are standing on it. So if the Readiness needle will not move, do not reach first for a conclusion about your innovation. Reach for a conclusion about your memory. That, more often than not, is the real finding.

Memory Capital, Read Three Ways

The surveyor's lesson applies with full force to the one capital nobody can invoice. Memory Capital is valued by all three methods at once—not for elegance, for defence. A number that three independent routes fail to contradict is a number a board can stand on.

The income view is the Factorless Income Residual just described, brought down to firm scale as a memory bonus: the season's innovation output, minus what labour, tangible capital, and codified knowledge alone would predict—Memory Bonus = Output − (labour share × labour cost + capital share × capital cost + documented knowledge inputs). The factor shares are calibration parameters, taken from industry benchmarks or the firm's own estimates and recorded as such. Deducting the documented inputs is the point of the exercise: it separates what the library explains from what only the crew's accumulated judgment can—and the residual is the judgment, priced. Two indicators strengthen the evidence on this side: the Failure Correction Rate, the share of documented past failures actually avoided in new projects, and the Knowledge Recombination Score, the share of new concepts that draw on three or more distinct memory domains. Both are retrieval made visible.

The cost view asks what memory saved, and it is the view a first-season crew can compute with no instrumentation at all. The four components of the Innovation Tax, read in reverse, become avoided cost: duplication caught before budget was spent, relearning that did not have to happen, decisions that did not wait, coordination that did not thrash. The knowledge audit of Chapter 11—interviews and an inventory—produces these figures in days, which is why the cost view is where honest Memory measurement begins.

The market view asks what the unexplored is worth: the Latent Asset Value of Chapter 12, where the estimated extent of your innovation surface, minus the part you have visited, is priced at the average value of an explored domain. It is ready the day your idea platform can be exported, and it sharpens as the memory's traces densify.

Then the criterion that turns three numbers into one defensible one. When two or more views are available, compute the spread: the largest minus the smallest, divided by their mean. Under thirty percent, the triangulation holds—report the mean and sleep. Above thirty percent, do not average your way past a disagreement: the outlier is a data-quality finding, and the finding is usually worth more than the number. Data-poor contexts—public agencies above all—may legitimately run cost-only for a season or two; the obligation is to declare the single view in the logbook rather than dressing one view as three. A declared limit is a measurement. A hidden one is a liability with a delay.

Memory Fracture Risk, Defined

The dashboard's second Readiness gauge has carried its name since Chapter 3; here is how to compute it without mystique. Memory Fracture Risk estimates the odds that critical knowledge will be unreachable at the moment it is needed. Three observable components, each scored between zero and one, each checkable by an auditor in an afternoon.

Channel exposure: the share of the seven input channels of Appendix I that are not currently open. A memory fed by two channels out of seven scores 0.71—most of what the organization learns has nowhere to land.

Succession exposure: the share of identified critical knowledge holders without a completed transfer—one minus the Expert Knowledge Succession Rate of Appendix A. This is the single-point-of-failure reading: the pilot who holds the passage in his head.

Reuse decay: one if the Reuse Rate has fallen for two consecutive cycles while knowledge creation kept rising—the distrust-spiral signature of Chapter 3—half for one cycle, zero otherwise.

Memory Fracture Risk is the mean of the three. Below 0.25, a sound hull. Between 0.25 and 0.5, watch—and schedule the repairs this season. Above 0.5, fracture is likely: run the exit debriefs and reopen the channels before the departure that makes the number academic. It is an estimate built from proxies and says so—a lead line, not sonar—but every component is observable, which is more than can be said for the risk it measures.

The Measurement Maturity Ladder

A question reaches me in every rollout, usually from the person holding the spreadsheet: do we need the AI layer before we can compute anything? No—and pretending otherwise is how measurement programs die in procurement. What you can compute depends on which rung you stand on, and there are five.

Rung one, ad hoc. No monetary tracking of innovation at all. ROI^2 is not computable, and the honest reading is "not yet." Writing that down is already progress; most organizations have never written it down.

Rung two, emerging. The cost method runs on Process indicators: a spreadsheet, finance extracts, and discipline. The Growth needle is approximated; the Readiness needle is dark. Most organizations reading this book start here, and a first season here is legitimate—soundings by lead line.

Rung three, structured. The market method joins: comparable transactions for intellectual property, and a first latent-asset estimate from an idea-platform export. Memory's cost view arrives through the knowledge audit. Both needles are readable; Readiness is still coarse.

Rung four, integrated. The AI-amplified memory comes aboard, and with it the income method—the memory bonus needs longitudinal output and factor data that only a kept memory supplies. Strategic outcomes aggregate from ecosystem data. Memory is triangulated in full, and the instrument stops estimating and starts measuring.

Rung five, predictive. Trajectory modelling, cross-validation between methods, and the estimators of Chapter 12 running on live traces rather than quarterly exports. Few boats need this rung in their first year. All of them should know it exists.

The ladder is also the honest restatement of Step 0. The non-negotiable prerequisite is the memory discipline—channels open, decisions logged, abandonments recorded. The AI layer is what carries that discipline past the third quarter and lights the Readiness needle to full depth. Climb a rung per season. Do not buy a bridge before you have a hull.

The Tide Tables: Adjusting for Time-to-Value

Two portfolios can post the same composite and be entirely different boats. One monetizes inside the budget year; the other's value arrives with the spring tide, three seasons out. Boards feel that difference even when the number hides it—so give the number tide tables.

The method is standard present-value discipline, applied per capital. Each capital carries a horizon profile—the share of its value expected in the current cycle, the adjacent horizon, and the transformational one—and each horizon carries a time-to-monetization. Discount each share by a present-value factor, $\exp(-r \cdot \tau)$ at your cost of capital, blend the factors, multiply each sub-score by its blend, and recompute the composite. Call the result the horizon-adjusted reading, ROI^2-HA. Sensible defaults behave the way sailors expect: Process is short-cycle, with most of its value inside the year; Knowledge is mid-cycle; Memory pays early through avoided cost and then compounds; Relational is the long-cycle cargo.

Read the gap between the raw composite and the adjusted one. Under ten points, a portfolio that pays within its own cycle. Ten to twenty-five points, the normal lock-up of a balanced multi-horizon book—nothing to fix, something to explain. Beyond twenty-five, a fleet heavy with long-cycle cargo: strategically defensible, politically exposed on the day budgets tighten, and better disclosed by you than discovered by an auditor. Report the adjusted figure whenever seasons are compared across time; keep the raw one for in-season governance. The tide does not care which number the committee prefers.

Portfolio Aggregation

Step 6: Aggregate—From Initiatives to Portfolio

This is where the architecture reveals its power. When individual initiatives are aggregated into a portfolio view, identical indicators across initiatives are consolidated. Revenue from New Products from Initiative A combines with Revenue from New Products from Initiative C. Knowledge Reuse Rate from Initiative B combines with Knowledge Reuse Rate from Initiative D. The portfolio scorecard shows the organization's composite innovation performance—not as an average of disconnected projects, but as a coherent picture where each dimension has depth.

The aggregation follows horizon categories. Core (H1) initiatives cluster together, Adjacent (H2) initiatives form their own group, and Transformational (H3) initiatives are measured on their own terms. The portfolio-level ROI^2 is a weighted composite across all three horizons.

Step 7: Build the Dashboard

Executive Level

- **Purpose:** Strategic visibility for leadership.
- **Metrics:** Portfolio ROI^2, category ROI^2, ROI^2 YoY, Innovation Efficiency Ratio.
- **Visuals:** Donut charts, trend lines, and financial overlays.
- **Insight:** Transformational projects generate 40% of ROI^2 using 25% of the total budget.

Operational Level

- **Purpose:** Manage process execution and innovation flow.
- **Metrics:** Idea-to-Prototyping Rate, Experiment Success Ratio, Cost per Learning, PEI, Time-to-Adoption, Innovation Throughput Rate.
- **Visuals:** Pipeline charts, throughput gauges, variance trackers.
- **Insight:** A 10% increase in PEI correlates with a 5% ROI² uplift.

Policy / Ecosystem Level

- **Purpose:** Measure national or ecosystem-wide innovation performance.
- **Metrics:** National ROI² Index, Adoption Rate, R&D Efficiency, Knowledge Capital Formation, Collaboration Density.
- **Visuals:** Heatmaps, geographic dashboards, benchmarking grids.
- **Insight:** Ecosystems with higher collaboration density display greater ROI² sustainability.

Intangible Asset Evaluation

Category	Proxy	Method	Value ($M)	Weight (%)
Brand	Awareness × Sales uplift	Income	0.9	25
IP	Licensing potential	Market	1.3	35
Capability	Training ROI × Score	Cost	0.7	20
Partnerships	Pipeline value	Hybrid	0.6	20
Total I			3.5	100

A destination note on this table, because the letters matter. The brand, intellectual property, and capability proxies price the Intangible gain (I); the partnership proxy prices the Strategic gain (S). Learning gain (L) never passes through a proxy table at all—it is triangulated, as shown above, precisely because no single proxy deserves its weight.

Beyond the organizational level, ROI² reinforces the dynamics of **creative destruction** at the national scale. By systematically measuring how innovation replaces outdated practices and enables new growth sectors, it helps governments and policymakers identify the pulse of renewal in their economies.

In this sense, ROI² serves as both a diagnostic and strategic tool, guiding national innovation policies, resource allocation, and competitiveness strategies. It closes the loop between micro-level innovation management and macro-level industrial evolution—exactly as Schumpeter envisioned when describing innovation as the engine of economic transformation.

The worked layouts for these dashboards—the one-page scorecard, the quarterly review, the annual report, the horizon planning sheet—live in Appendix B, drawn to be copied into whatever instrument you assemble from Appendix J rather than admired here. What belongs here is the harder skill: reading the number the dashboard produces.

Reading the Number

A first composite lands and the first question follows it into the room: is 0.28 good? It is the wrong first question, but it deserves an answer. In practice, organizations in their first measured seasons—the second and third rungs of the measurement maturity ladder—commonly read between 0.3 and 0.6. Readings above 1.0, where weighted value exceeds the season's cost, are not errors; they appear once intangible capitals begin to compound, and they are legitimate provided two things survive scrutiny: the horizon-adjusted figure beside them, and the non-overlap rule behind them. Readings below 0.3 usually indict the instrument before the innovation—unpriced indicators, an empty memory, weights at war with the actual portfolio. Treat these bands as coastline, not berth. Targets are set at season design, in Appendix E, against your own trajectory. Not against a stranger's.

Then three readings before any conclusion. The pair before the composite: a 0.09/0.19 split is a different vessel from a 0.19/0.09 split, at the same 0.28. The composition against the declared weights: a capital delivering far above or far below the weight the strategy assigned it is, more often than not, the season's real finding. And the trajectory: three seasons of 0.32, 0.38, 0.45 outrank any single 0.6 that cannot say where it came from. The composite is a position. The pair, the composition, and the trend are the course. A position without a course is a fix without a chart, and no navigator ever staked a voyage on one.

What Maria Saw on Her First Dashboard

Three months later, Maria Torres looked at her division's first dashboard. The numbers were rough—some cells were estimates, some indicators were proxies—but the shape was unmistakable.

Her division scored well on Knowledge Capital. That surprised no one who worked there. It scored poorly on Memory Capital. That surprised no one who had watched colleagues leave without transferring what they knew. The Reuse Rate was eleven percent. Eleven percent of documented knowledge had been referenced by a subsequent project. The other eighty-nine percent sat in a shared drive, technically accessible, functionally invisible.

The number that changed the conversation was the Innovation Tax. When the CFO saw the estimated cost of duplicated effort—projects that had unknowingly repeated work already done elsewhere in the division—the question shifted from "why should we invest in organizational memory?" to "why haven't we invested in it already?"

Maria did not need a formula to know this. She had watched the duplication happen in real time, project after project, year after year. What the formula did was translate what she already knew into a language the boardroom could hear.

THE SKIPPER'S LOG

Position — ROI^2 is auditable arithmetic: a sub-score per capital, weights that sum to one, and a cost line every number traces back to.

Sighted — Three ways to price a return — income, cost, market — and the Innovation Tax, which translates forgotten knowledge into a language the CFO hears.

Charted — The two needles of the formula, the Measurement Cascade from team to board, and the horizon-adjusted reading, ROI^2-HA.

Course — Run the computation once on last season's numbers, however rough. The first honest pass teaches more than a year of planning the perfect one.

Chapter 9: Planning the Investment Season

The Innovation Investment Planning Matrix

Before each investment cycle—whether annual, semi-annual, or quarterly—the innovation portfolio requires a planning instrument that connects project selection to measurement discipline.

The Innovation Investment Planning Matrix serves this purpose. It ensures that every project in the portfolio is measured across all four value capitals, mapped to the appropriate horizon, and subjected to the Vanity Metrics Cap.

The matrix operates on a simple principle: for each project type in your portfolio, you must select at least one indicator from each of the four capitals (Financial, Intangible, Strategic, Learning).

This ensures that no project is measured solely on financial returns, and no project escapes measurement entirely by hiding behind "it's too early to measure."

Table: Innovation Investment Planning Matrix by Project Type and Capital

Project Type	Horizon	Financial (F)	Intangible (I)	Strategic (S)	Learning (L)
Opportunity Exploration	H2-H3	Market size estimate; Revenue potential	New domain expertise; IP landscape mapping	Market positioning options; Ecosystem access	Customer insight depth; Problem validation quality
Challenge / Ideation Campaign	H1-H2	Cost avoidance from solved challenges	Employee engagement index; Brand innovation score	Pipeline diversity score; Cross-unit collaboration rate	Ideation capability maturity; Creative confidence index
Proof of Concept (POC)	H2-H3	Unit economics validation; Cost-to-learn ratio	Technical feasibility confidence; Partnership value	Option value created; Adjacent market signals	Technical skill acquisition; Failure pattern library growth
Minimum Viable Product (MVP)	H1-H2	Revenue from first adopters; Margin trajectory	Customer relationships created; Brand equity contribution	Competitive moat contribution; Platform leverage	Go-to-market playbook maturity; Adoption model validation

Designing the Innovation Investment Season

That shortlist does not appear from nowhere. It is the last strategic decision in a chain that starts well above the innovation department. Company strategy sets the direction; innovation strategy translates that direction into Where-to-Play themes—the industries, technologies, or customer segments the organization has decided are worth its attention. From there, the innovation investment strategy commits actual resources: how much the organization will spend, and over how many investment cycles that commitment holds. This is also where the season's Growth-Readiness balance gets set—the target split between building what pays off now and building what the organization will need later, expressed as the weights that feed the ROI^2 formula later in this chapter. Only once that balance is fixed does the portfolio get split across horizons, and only then does the question this section exists to answer arrive: which indicators, from the full catalogue in Appendix A, will this Season actually track. Skip a link in that chain and the shortlist floats free of strategy—precise, perhaps, but answering a question nobody asked.

Appendix A contains the complete ROI^2 Indicator Catalogue—a comprehensive menu of every metric the Compass framework can track across the Four Capitals. That catalogue is deliberately exhaustive. No single organization, and certainly no single investment season, should attempt to measure everything in it.

Selecting a shortlist from that catalogue is not an administrative exercise. It is, in itself, one of the most consequential strategic decisions an innovation leader makes. The indicators you choose define what "innovation success" means for this season. They translate your organization's strategic priorities into measurable ROI^2 criteria that will govern every investment decision in the portfolio. Choose indicators that emphasize Knowledge Capital, and you are signalling that this season is about building absorptive capacity. Choose indicators weighted toward Process Capital, and you are declaring that this season is about scaling and efficiency. The shortlist is your strategy made visible.

This is a two-level process. First, the Head of Innovation—working with the executive team—selects the season's strategic indicator shortlist from the full catalogue. This shortlist defines the ROI² criteria that the entire portfolio must satisfy by the end of the investment season (see Template E.1 in the Appendix). Second, each Innovation Manager—supporting an innovation champion or project manager—selects the subset of those season indicators that applies to their specific initiative (see Template E.2 in the Appendix).

The critical principle is this: no single initiative is expected to cover every indicator on the season's shortlist. Each initiative tracks only the subset relevant to its scope, horizon, and strategic intent. But at the end of the season, the compounded value of all initiatives must collectively cover every chosen indicator. It is the aggregate portfolio—not any individual project—that produces a complete ROI² reading. Think of it as a mosaic: each tile contributes a fragment of colour; only the full assembly reveals the picture.

This portfolio-level completeness check is what transforms a collection of isolated experiments into a strategically coherent innovation program. If, at mid-season review, you discover that no initiative in the portfolio is tracking a particular indicator from your shortlist, you have a strategic gap—not a project management problem. That gap tells you something important about where your portfolio is under-invested relative to your declared strategy.

The remedy is not to force an existing initiative to adopt an indicator it was never built for. It is to go looking for the initiative that was. A coverage gap is, in effect, an invitation: launch a Hackathon, an Ideathon, a Competition, an Incubator cohort, or bring in an Entrepreneur-in-Residence or an Intrapreneur program, with a brief narrow enough to target exactly the indicator the portfolio is missing. None of these formats produce value by themselves—each can just as easily generate noise without adoption, which is why Chapter 13 has more to say about which mechanisms actually convert energy into results. Aimed here, at a specific coverage gap, they stop being generic innovation theatre and become a precision instrument.

The Innovation Season: Boundaries Create Freedom

A sailing race has a start and a finish. The distance between them is known. The weather is uncertain, the route is debatable, and the outcome is unpredictable—but the race has a boundary. That boundary is what makes strategy possible. Without it, the crew is not racing. The crew is wandering.

Two units of time matter here, and conflating them is the fastest way to lose the thread. The Investment Cycle is the recurring budget period—the interval at which the organization commits a fixed amount to the innovation portfolio and reviews what it got for it. The Investment Season is the longer span over which one innovation investment strategy holds: the multi-cycle arc across which the Where-to-Play themes, the horizon split, and the season's Growth-Readiness balance stay fixed, before the organization revisits any of them. A Season is made of Cycles, not the other way around.

Both durations are a business decision, not a rule this book can hand you. A Cycle might run a quarter, six months, or a year; a Season might run two Cycles or five. To keep the arithmetic legible through the rest of this chapter, the examples that follow use one illustrative pairing—a one-year Cycle and a three-year Season, three Cycles long—but nothing in the framework requires those specific numbers. What the framework does require is that the Season behaves like a race leg: a bounded investment period during which the innovation portfolio operates under a defined budget, a defined set of indicators, and a defined accountability structure. When the Season closes, the results are measured, the portfolio is reassessed, and the next Season opens with updated assumptions.

The concept is deceptively simple, and its consequences are profound. Without Seasons, innovation becomes an unbounded commitment. Projects accumulate without ever being formally evaluated against each other. Budgets roll forward because no one has defined a moment at which the question "was this worth it?" must be answered. Knowledge generated by one cycle of projects never reaches the next cycle, because there is no structural boundary at which the organization pauses, extracts what it learned, and carries that learning forward.

Seasons create three things that unbounded innovation programs lack. The first is comparability. When every initiative in a Season is measured against the same indicator set—agreed before the Season opens, not retrofitted after the results are in—the portfolio becomes genuinely comparable. One project's Financial Return can be set beside another's Learning Return without a taxonomy dispute. The second is accountability. A Season has a governance review at its close. That review is not optional, not deferrable, and not subject to the "we just need a few more months" extension that kills measurement discipline. The third is compounding. Season-over-season, the aggregate ROI² score becomes a trajectory. A trajectory is what governance actually needs—not a snapshot of this quarter's results, but a trend that reveals whether the organization's innovation capability is strengthening or eroding.

The practical mechanics of Season design are covered in the planning process that follows and in the templates provided in Appendix E. But the conceptual point must be established here, because it is one of the four disciplines on which the framework rests: innovation investment that is not bounded by time is not investment. It is spending.

The Five-Step Planning Process

With the season's strategic shortlist established, the Innovation Investment Planning Matrix guides you through five steps to operationalize it across the portfolio.

- **Step 1: Inventory your portfolio.** List all active and planned innovation initiatives. Classify each as Opportunity Exploration, Challenge/Ideation Campaign, POC, or MVP. Initiatives that span categories should be split into measurable phases.

- **Step 2: Select initiative-level indicators from the season shortlist.** For each initiative, select 2–3 indicators per capital from the season's strategic shortlist (established in the section above). Use Template E.2 to guide this selection. The key constraint is that every initiative must have at least one indicator from each capital. Remember: no single initiative needs to cover every shortlisted indicator. But across the full portfolio, every shortlisted indicator must be tracked by at least one initiative.

- **Step 3: Map to horizons.** Map each initiative to its primary horizon (H1, H2, or H3). Then check the portfolio-level allocation against the target ranges below.

- **Step 4: Apply the Vanity Metrics Cap.** Count your total indicators. If more than 20% of them are activity-based metrics (ideas submitted, workshops held, prototypes built), you have exceeded the Vanity Metrics Cap. Replace excess vanity metrics with outcome-linked, capability-linked, or position-linked alternatives.

- **Step 5: Set capital weights per initiative.** These are the same w_F, w_I, w_S, and w_L weights the ROI^2 formula uses later in this chapter—here, tuned per initiative around the season-level Growth-Readiness balance the investment strategy already fixed, not invented fresh for each project. Assign weights to each capital based on the initiative's horizon and strategic intent. H1 projects typically weigh Financial at 40–50%; H3 projects should weigh Learning at 30–40% and Financial at no more than 15%.

Table: Horizon Balance Targets

Horizon	Target Allocation	Risk Profile	Measurement Focus
H1 (Core)	50–70% of portfolio	Low risk, predictable returns	Efficiency gains, margin improvements, cost savings
H2 (Adjacent)	20–35% of portfolio	Moderate risk, medium-term	New market revenue, capability building, partnership value
H3 (Transformational)	5–15% of portfolio	High risk, long-term options	Learning value, strategic positioning, knowledge capital

Table: The Vanity Metrics Cap

The 20% Vanity Metrics Cap is not arbitrary. It reflects a practical observation: organizations that measure innovation primarily through activity metrics—ideas submitted, workshops held, hackathons organized—create the illusion of progress without the substance. These metrics are easy to collect, satisfying to report, and almost entirely uncorrelated with actual innovation value creation.

> **→A small allocation is acceptable because Vanity metrics can serve as leading indicators during early-stage work. But when they dominate the ROI², the compass is pointing at the crew, not the destination.**

Metric Category	Example	Classification	Max Allocation
Activity counts	Number of ideas submitted, workshops held	Vanity	≤20% of total
Throughput volume	Number of prototypes built	Vanity	≤20% of total
Outcome-linked	Revenue from new products, cost savings	Value (Financial)	No cap
Capability-linked	Skills acquired, knowledge retention score	Value (Learning)	No cap
Position-linked	Market options created, ecosystem access	Value (Strategic)	No cap
Asset-linked	IP portfolio strength, brand equity	Value (Intangible)	No cap

The Investment Season Planning Cycle

The matrix is designed to be used at the beginning of each investment cycle. The recommended cadence:

- **Month 1 (Audit):** Inventory existing portfolio. Conduct a one-day review of all active initiatives using the matrix template.

Identify measurement gaps (initiatives with fewer than one indicator per capital). Score the current Vanity Metrics ratio.

- **Month 2 (Calibration):** Calibrate the scorecard for the coming period. Set horizon allocation targets. Assign capital weights per initiative. Ensure Vanity Metrics remain below 20%. Present the calibrated matrix to the governance board for approval.
- **Month 3 (Lock and Launch):** Lock the measurement framework and begin the investment period. New initiatives added mid-cycle must pass the matrix test before entering the portfolio. Quarterly reviews assess indicator performance, not just project performance.

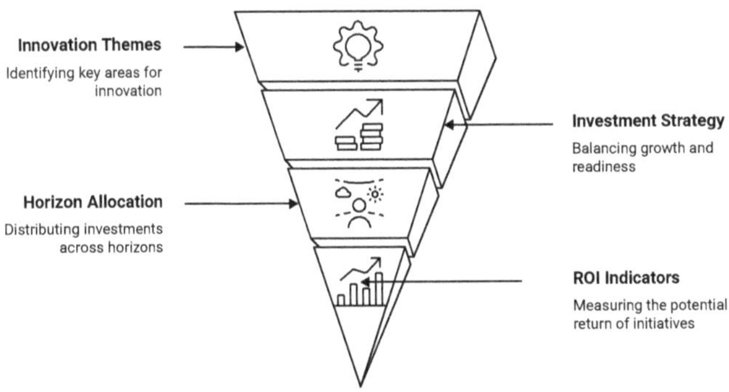

The Boardroom Problem

Step 8: Value the Intangibles

Innovation creates value the financial statements miss—brand equity, intellectual property, organizational learning, strategic resilience—and Chapter 8 built the pricing house for it: three valuation views, four conversion shapes, and the triangulation of Memory. Step 8 applies that house under season rules, and the rules are what keep the numbers defensible twelve months later. Choose the method for each indicator at selection time, not at reporting time; a method chosen after the results are known is an alibi, not a valuation. Record the choice, the coefficient, and the coefficient's source beside the indicator, with its provenance flagged—peer-reviewed, industry benchmark, or internal estimate. Hold the method constant for the season; if the world forces a change, log the deviation and the reason where an auditor will find them. And where a method's data does not yet exist—the income view of Memory before the ladder's fourth rung—value with what you have and declare the view you used. Intangibles do not forgive improvisation. They forgive honesty about limits.

Step 9: Implement the Full S4IL System

One clarification before the checklist, because it decides everything downstream: the full S4IL system is not a product you procure. It is an instrument you build—and the hull is yours to choose. A spreadsheet on a shared drive. A small program. An internal web page. A configuration of the innovation-management platform you already run. The seven stations of the instrument are identical in every hull, and Appendix J—the shipwright's yard—specifies each station precisely enough to build from, whatever material you build in. Chapter 11 tells you when, in the ninety days, the keel gets laid. What follows is the order of assembly.

Implementation Steps:

1. Develop project scorecards.
2. Aggregate at the portfolio level.
3. Visualize via BI tools.
4. Review quarterly and recalibrate weights.

Common Implementation Pitfalls and How to Avoid Them

The framework has been designed for practical implementation. But implementation experience reveals four common pitfalls that can undermine even well-intentioned deployments. Forewarned is forearmed.

- **Pitfall 1: Measurement Overload.** The temptation to measure everything is strong. Innovation teams, excited by the four-capital framework, attempt to track thirty or forty indicators simultaneously. The result is measurement fatigue—teams spend more time reporting than innovating, data quality declines, and the dashboard becomes a wall of numbers that nobody reads. The remedy: start with four indicators per initiative—one per capital, chosen so that between them the four readings are covered—and let this be the first-season on-ramp, not the destination. Grow toward the cruising configuration of the Five-Step Planning Process, two to three per capital, only when the first four are producing reliable, actionable signals.
- **Pitfall 2: Measurement Without Governance.** Organizations deploy the framework without connecting it to the processes by which budgets are allocated, projects are approved, and people are evaluated. The dashboard exists, but it does not influence decisions. The remedy: every metric must be linked to a specific decision right. If the Reuse Rate declines, who is responsible for diagnosing why? If the Horizon balance shifts, who has the authority to reallocate resources? Metrics without decision rights are decoration.
- **Pitfall 3: Top-Down Imposition.** The innovation team builds the measurement system in isolation, without engaging the

people and teams whose work will be measured. When the system launches, it faces resistance not because it is wrong but because it was imposed. The remedy: involve representative stakeholders in the indicator selection process. Let teams propose their own indicators within the four-capital framework. People support what they help create.

- **Pitfall 4: Static Implementation.** Organizations implement the measurement system once and then leave it unchanged as the organization's strategy, competitive environment, and capabilities evolve. An indicator that was relevant two years ago may be meaningless today. The remedy: conduct a formal indicator review at the annual Strategic Innovation Review. Retire indicators that no longer provide actionable signals. Introduce new indicators that reflect current priorities. The measurement system is a living instrument, not a permanent installation.

The meta-lesson across all four pitfalls is the same: the measurement system is a tool in service of innovation, not an end in itself.

The moment the measurement system becomes the goal—the moment teams optimize for metrics rather than for innovation outcomes—the system has failed.

→ The practitioner's constant vigilance should be: are we measuring to learn, or measuring to look good?

One reading of ROI² has been kept out of this chapter on purpose. Public-sector bodies do not measure return in revenue but in public value created per unit of public money, and the formula bends to match. That policy-level reading—national R&D efficiency, cross-country normalization, the government dashboard—is set out in full in Appendix H, so the method here stays trained on the single firm.

S4IL within a single organization is powerful. But innovation increasingly happens at the boundaries—where organizations meet partners, competitors, regulators, and customers. The next question is whether the compass works when the ship joins a fleet.

The Skipper's Log

Position — Boundaries create freedom. A season with dates, a cost, and a declared horizon split turns innovation from a mood into a portfolio.

Sighted — The boardroom problem of intangibles, and the question that keeps the instrument honest: are we measuring to learn, or measuring to look good?

Charted — The Investment Planning Matrix, and the five-step process that cascades strategy down to the indicators on a single initiative.

Course — Fix the next season's dates and its horizon allocation before selecting a single project. The frame comes first; the cargo after.

Chapter 10: Signals & Open Innovation

A solo sailor can cross an ocean. A fleet can control one. The difference between a single vessel and a coordinated flotilla is not speed—it is coverage. In a fleet, each boat has a role: pathfinder, supply vessel, communications relay, rescue craft. No single boat carries everything. The ecosystem works because each participant contributes a capability that the others lack. Innovation ecosystems operate on precisely the same principle. The organizations that try to do everything internally are solo sailors in a fleet race. They may finish, but they will not win.

The Foresight Compass: Scanning for Tomorrow's Signals

Open innovation extends the organization's knowledge boundary beyond its own walls. Foresight extends the organization's knowledge boundary beyond the present moment. The combination of open innovation and foresight—looking outward and looking forward simultaneously—is the most powerful expression of what the framework calls extended Memory Capital.

The distinction between foresight and forecast is not semantic. A forecast assigns probabilities to a predetermined future. It asks: how likely is this outcome? Foresight constructs a range of plausible futures and asks: what would we do if each of these arrived? Forecasts fail under genuine uncertainty because they require stable patterns that do not exist. Foresight does not fail under uncertainty—it is designed for it. An organization that confuses the two will build dashboards full of confident numbers about an unpredictable future and invest nothing in the preparedness that actually matters. The Foresight Compass is a foresight instrument. It produces scenarios, not probabilities. It prepares, it does not predict.

The Foresight Compass is a structured approach to detecting, evaluating, and acting on weak signals—early indicators of emerging trends, technologies, and market shifts that have not yet reached mainstream awareness. It operates through four stages that mirror the four-stage learning cycle described in Chapter 5:

- **Signal Detection.** Systematic scanning of external sources—academic publications, patent filings, startup activity, regulatory proposals, social media trends—for signals that are relevant to the organization's strategic domains. The key metric is the Signal Detection Rate: how many relevant signals does the organization identify per quarter?
- **Signal Assessment.** Each detected signal is assessed for potential impact, time horizon, and relevance to the organization's innovation portfolio. The assessment is not a prediction—weak signals are inherently uncertain—but a structured evaluation of possibility.
- **Opportunity Mapping.** The Opportunity Radar visualizes assessed signals on a two-dimensional map: proximity (how close is this signal to affecting our market?) and magnitude (how significant could the impact be?). Signals in the high-proximity, high-magnitude quadrant demand immediate investigation. Signals in the low-proximity, high-magnitude quadrant require monitoring.
- **Response Activation.** For signals that pass the assessment threshold, the Foresight Compass triggers an innovation response: a research sprint, a partnership exploration, a pilot

project, or a strategic pivot. The key metric is the average Response Time—the number of days from signal detection to the initiation of an organizational response.

What those four stages produce is not yet a scenario. They produce assessed signals. The scenario is built in a fifth, often neglected step: clustering. Signals that share a common driver—a regulatory shift, a demographic movement, a technology threshold—are grouped together. Each cluster describes a pressure on the environment. When two or three clusters are combined, they generate a plausible future: not the most likely future, but a coherent one that the organization must be prepared to navigate.

A well-constructed scenario answers a precise question: if this combination of pressures materialized within the next three years, which of our current innovation bets would accelerate, which would become irrelevant, and which capabilities would we need that we do not yet have? That question, put to the portfolio at the start of each Season, is the operational link between foresight and investment. It does not tell the organization where the world will go. It tells the organization what it needs to build regardless of where the world goes.

The Foresight Compass is not a crystal ball. It does not predict the future. What it does is ensure that the organization is systematically watching the horizon rather than sailing with its eyes fixed solely on the compass. In the nautical metaphor that runs through this book, the ROI² compass tells you where you are and how fast you are moving. The Foresight Compass tells you what the weather will be.

The Opportunity Pipeline: From Signal to Value

The Foresight Compass generates a continuous flow of signals and opportunities. Managing this flow requires what we call the

Opportunity Pipeline—a structured funnel that tracks opportunities from initial detection through to portfolio integration.

The Pipeline has four stages, each with its own metrics:

- **New Opportunities.** Newly detected signals that have passed initial relevance screening. The target is a minimum of four new opportunities entering the pipeline per quarter—fewer suggests the scanning function is too narrow; more than twenty suggests inadequate filtering.
- **Qualified Opportunities.** Opportunities that have been assessed, validated, and assigned to a team for investigation. The key metric is the conversion rate from new opportunity to qualified opportunity.
- **Ideas in Development.** Qualified opportunities that have progressed to the ideation stage—generating specific project proposals, partnership frameworks, or strategic recommendations. Measured by the number of ideas generated per qualified opportunity.
- **Portfolio Commitments.** Ideas that have been integrated into the innovation portfolio as funded initiatives. The ultimate measure of the effectiveness of foresight is whether detected signals translate into portfolio commitments.

The Opportunity Pipeline operates at the intersection of the organization's internal innovation portfolio (managed through the dashboard) and its external knowledge environment (scanned by the Foresight Compass). When an organization has both systems operating effectively, it achieves what we might call temporal ambidexterity—the ability to optimize current innovation investments while simultaneously preparing for the opportunities and threats that have not yet fully materialized.

The output of the Foresight Compass feeds a third piloting indicator that sits alongside Progression and ROI² in the portfolio review: the Signal Landscape. A project enters the portfolio because its initial signal environment was favourable enough to justify the investment. That decision is made once. What the Signal Landscape tracks is different: it monitors how that environment continues to evolve while the project is being built. A regulation that was neutral when the project launched may have become hostile. A technology that was emerging when the first prototype was designed may have since been commoditised by a competitor. A market behaviour that was assumed may have shifted.

The Signal Landscape asks, at every review cycle, the same question: is the world still moving toward this project, or has it started moving away? Progression and ROI² tell you how well you are executing. The Signal Landscape tells you whether what you are executing still matters.

It is deliberately qualitative, read in four states.

> **Favourable**: incoming signals confirm and strengthen the original hypothesis. Regulatory momentum is building in your direction, early adopters are appearing in adjacent markets, and the technology dependencies your project relies on are maturing faster than planned. The project deserves acceleration.
>
> **Mixed**: signals are contradictory. Some confirm the original hypothesis; others challenge a specific assumption. A key technology is evolving in an unexpected direction. A competitor has entered the space with a different approach. The original adoption timeline may need revisiting. The correct response is not to stop—it is to monitor closely and protect optionality.

Turbulent: the environment is in active disruption. The regulatory framework the project was designed around is being challenged. A platform shift is underway that changes the adoption pathway. The customer behaviour the project was built for is fragmenting. Turbulence does not mean termination—it means the project's assumptions require an explicit review before the next Season investment is committed.

Critical: the environment has closed. The signals no longer describe a difficult path to adoption—they describe the absence of one. This is what Kodak's teams would have been reading in the early 2000s, had they been watching: not a challenging market, but a market that was structurally replacing itself. A Critical Signal Landscape is not a signal to work harder. It is a signal to send the project to Purgatory, extract what was learned, and redirect the investment. The organizations that survived those transitions were not the ones that ignored the signals. They were the ones whose memory systems allowed them to act on them before the window closed.

In 2019, a European automotive supplier discovered that its battery thermal management challenge had already been solved—not by its own engineers, but by a university research team in South Korea that had published the solution two years earlier. The solution sat in an open-access journal that no one in the company had read. The company spent 14 months and 900,000 euros arriving at essentially the same answer. This is not a failure of engineering. It is a failure of ecosystem memory.

Signal Intelligence looks forward. It scans the horizon, detects weak signals, and prepares the organization for futures it cannot predict. But it has a structural limitation: it can only see what is visible from the organization's own vantage point. A ship with the most powerful radar in the fleet still has a limited arc. To see what lies beyond that arc—the opportunities being developed by partners, the threats being incubated in adjacent markets, the solutions already discovered by organizations working on adjacent problems—requires something more than looking outward alone. It requires collaboration.

Open Innovation extends Signal Intelligence from a unilateral scan to a networked intelligence. It adds range. It adds resolution. And it introduces a new set of challenges—appropriation risk, coordination cost, ecosystem trust—that the internal compass was never designed to handle.

The sections that follow trace the evolution of Open Innovation from a simple outside-in pipeline to a full ecosystem architecture, and show how the system adapts its measurement framework when the ship joins a fleet.

Where this sits on the compass. Open Innovation lives mostly in the first phase, Where to Play, and reaches into the third, How to Deliver. In Where to Play it widens the aperture of scanning: instead of seeing only the opportunities your own people surface, you draw signals from partners, suppliers, universities, and customers—the same exploration-completeness question Chao1 asks, now answered across a network rather than a single organization. In How to Deliver it changes the build decision, turning a binary make-or-not into the fuller calculus of build, buy, or partner. What it does not do is tell you how to win between those two moments, nor how to get the result adopted; prioritization and gamification own those. Used alone it floods you with external signal and appropriation risk; combined with a disciplined scan and a shared-memory layer, it turns that flood into sourced opportunity. Its returns land on both needles: relational reach feeds Growth, while the knowledge absorbed from outside feeds Readiness.

It doesn't begin with a lab. A brilliant idea slips out of a silo, bumps into an outsider, and becomes something no internal team could have built alone. Think of ASML, the Dutch company whose extreme-ultraviolet lithography machines print the circuitry of the most advanced chips on Earth. ASML does not build them alone, and could not. The optics come from Zeiss—mirrors ground to a smoothness measured in fractions of an atom—and the precision mechanics from partners like VDL. The machine exists only because those companies co-develop it over years, each feeding the others' design choices, so that a problem in the optics reshapes the rest of the system before it becomes anyone's crisis. No single firm holds the whole picture, and none could have built it alone. That is the promise—and the provocation—of Open Innovation.

By the early 2000s, the closed R&D model was faltering. Product cycles were shorter, knowledge was diffusing globally, and the costs of doing everything in-house spiralled. In 2003, Henry Chesbrough gave this shift a name in *Open Innovation: The New Imperative for Creating and Profiting from Technology*. His thesis was simple and radical: valuable ideas can and should move both into and out of the firm. Companies could no longer rely only on internal labs; they had to build bridges to universities, startups, suppliers, and competitors.

Open Innovation 1.0 (OI 1.0) crystallized as a set of practices:

- **Outside-in sourcing** technology scouting, licensing-in, corporate venture capital
- **Inside-out commercialization** licensing-out, spinouts, patent pools
- **Boundary-spanning partnerships** joint ventures, university alliances, user communities.

It answered a key question of the dot-com and post-dot-com era: how to accelerate time-to-market and reduce R&D risk without owning every asset.

However, it also treats knowledge as tradable inventory. It struggled with adoption at scale, underestimated the power of digital platforms, and assumed IP would remain the central moat.

By the 2010s, three forces made an update necessary:

1. **Platformization** (mobile, cloud, AI) shifted value from products to ecosystems.
2. **Globalization of R&D** made cross-border collaboration the rule rather than the exception.
3. **Public-private missions** (energy transition, health, digital sovereignty) demanded multi-stakeholder cooperation.

Open Innovation 2.0 (OI 2.0) emerged as a **quadruple-helix** model—industry, academia, government, and citizens—co-creating shared value through rapid prototyping and **living labs**. The EU adopted this language to drive systemic missions.

It shifted the focus:

- From transactions to ecosystem orchestration
- From IP bargaining to data-enabled collaboration
- From outputs to adoption and diffusion
- From **firm ROI** to **societal impact**

OI 1.0 had optimized the pipeline; OI 2.0 acknowledged that innovation unfolds across networks. Yet scholars warned that OI 2.0 often romanticized collaboration while underestimating conflict, antitrust risks, and the political economy of platforms. Practitioners, meanwhile, began to share lessons from real projects where OI 2.0 had been applied, raising equally tough questions:

- **Appropriation risk**: Sharing can leak advantage.
- **Coordination costs**: Ecosystems bring overhead and misaligned incentives.
- **Value capture**: Platforms reward orchestrators more than contributors.
- **Measurement fog**: ROI and even ROI^2 stumble with ecosystem effects.

While experts debated the relevance of OI 2.0, innovation management continued to unfold. For instance, the quadruple-helix model became the **quintuple-helix** model. This refinement, introduced by Carayannis and Campbell, added the natural environment as a fifth helix alongside industry, academia, government, and civil society. The move reflected the growing realization that sustainable innovation could not be understood apart from ecological systems. In practice, the quintuple helix positioned sustainability and environmental responsibility not as peripheral concerns but as central drivers of innovation policy and practice, anticipating today's emphasis on climate, biodiversity, and energy transition.

Even for organizations that kept pace with the revisions to Open Innovation, the connection between sustainability and innovation often remained unclear—or seemed difficult to apply in practice. ESG became a trend that required organizations, especially publicly traded ones, to ask themselves questions that investors and stakeholders will soon ask under public pressure.

What Open Innovation Fills—and What It Doesn't

Open Innovation is another legacy tool we still use to navigate today's innovation landscape. It has proven helpful in filling critical needs for collaboration and acceleration. Yet it was forged in an earlier era, and its blind spots show.

What worked well in 2010—breaking silos, opening pipelines, accelerating access—no longer fully matches the dynamics of a world driven by data, platforms, and global ecosystems.

What OI fills	What OI misses
Breaks the "not invented here" trap	Weak on **data strategy**
Increases option value through scouting and partnering	Silent on **algorithmic advantage**
Encourages recombination across domains	Struggles with **scaling adoption**
Links R&D to public missions through living labs	Ambiguous on **value capture**

From IP Moats to Data Moats

OI 2.0 remains tethered to IP logic in an era when data is the true differentiator. IP is no longer the moat. Code can be copied, patents skirted, and enforcement delayed. The moat is now unique data, and the models are trained on it. With privileged, high-signal datasets, firms can ship features without signalling their roadmap.

The organizations that moved fastest in the AI era were not those with the most sophisticated models—those became commodities within months. They were the ones with the most proprietary, highest-signal datasets. Firms that had spent years accumulating unique data on customer behaviour, biological systems, or operational processes found themselves able to launch, iterate, and relaunch before competitors could respond. The model was the same for everyone. The data was not.

Why Data Uniqueness matters

- It enables **quiet innovation**—surprising markets before rivals know what to copy.
- It powers **learning effects**—each use makes the product smarter.
- It supports **ecosystem lock-in**—switching becomes costly because the data context is unique.

Consider Tesla. Each kilometre or mile driven trains the Autopilot, compounding an advantage that rivals without data scale cannot replicate. Or Apple: the Watch integrates health data, hardware, and apps into a closed loop. WearOS lags not for lack of code, but for lack of data richness.

OI 2.0 hints at this shift but doesn't codify it. The next frontier is Open Innovation with Data Discipline: partnering widely while building non-replicable data assets and learning loops.

For most of the twentieth century, a company's competitive moat had a name and a legal registration number. It was the patent. The formula, the process, the invention—locked away in a vault of exclusive rights, protected for twenty years, enforced by courts. Innovation strategy was, in large part, an IP strategy.

Elon Musk broke with that orthodoxy in 2014 when he announced that Tesla would not initiate patent lawsuits against anyone using its technology in good faith. Many observers interpreted this as idealism. It was a strategy. Tesla had calculated that growing the entire electric vehicle ecosystem—more manufacturers, more charging infrastructure, more consumer familiarity—would benefit Tesla more than excluding competitors from its patents. The moat was no longer the patent. The moat was adopted.

That shift—from protection to adoption as the primary competitive instrument—is what this chapter examines. IP is not dying. But the organizations that will lead the next decade are not the ones with the largest patent portfolios. They are the ones who understand how ideas spread, why some innovations get adopted and others don't, and how to engineer the conditions for uptake. The science of adoption—growth hacking, gamification, referral dynamics, the psychology of engagement—is the new IP strategy. It is also, as we will see, deeply connected to organizational memory.

Before we celebrate the end of intellectual property, we need to unpack what is really changing. IP is not dying, but its role is evolving. The focus is shifting from owning ideas to orchestrating ecosystems and driving adoption.

Re-examining Intellectual Property in the Age of AI and Data

Traditional IP systems were designed in a world where inventions were discrete, physical and scarce. A patent granted the inventor exclusive rights to exploit a novel device or process for a limited period. Copyright protects the authorship of books, music, and software. Trade secrets shielded recipes and formulas. The assumption was that exclusive rights incentivized investment by guaranteeing a return. For many industries—pharmaceuticals, hardware, manufacturing—this remains true. However, the nature of innovation is changing:

Innovation is increasingly digital and data-driven. Software, algorithms and machine learning models evolve rapidly. Their iterative nature makes the notion of a static patent questionable. AI models are often trained on vast amounts of public data; their novelty lies in how they are fine-tuned and applied. Industry analysis highlights that the real competitive advantage in AI comes from proprietary data and context. Patent protection for algorithms matters less when everyone has access to similar models; what matters is the uniqueness of the training data.

Innovation happens in ecosystems. A single firm cannot solve complex problems such as energy transition and climate adaptation. They require coordinated action among government, industry, academia and citizens. This is the premise of Open Innovation 2.0. The Innovation Value Institute describes OI2 as a new paradigm built on five principles: integrated collaboration, co-created shared value, cultivated innovation ecosystems, unleashed exponential technologies and extraordinarily rapid adoption. Under OI2, intellectual property is not abandoned but reimagined as a tool for ecosystem orchestration.

Data is the new monopoly. As generative AI commoditizes models, the scarcity shifts to data. Organizations with unique datasets derived from customer interactions, sensors or domain expertise can train AI models that no competitor can replicate. This proprietary data constitutes a new form of IP—one that is not covered by traditional patents but by data governance, contracts and trust.

Speed of adoption trumps exclusivity. In fast-moving markets, holding on to exclusive rights can delay adoption and allow competitors to outpace you. In some cases, openly releasing technology accelerates market formation, benefiting the originator in the long run. This is the logic behind Tesla's approach.

The Ecosystem Frontier

Everything in this book works at the scale of a single organization—its four capitals, its seasons, its memory, its compass. But knowledge does not respect the firm's edge, and neither does innovation. It increasingly lives in the spaces between organizations: consortia, university-industry partnerships, public-private missions where no single actor holds the whole picture. The Four Capitals and the ROI² index extend, in principle, to that level. The knowledge that matters most in such a network is precisely the knowledge generated between its members rather than inside any one of them—and it is the knowledge most easily lost when a joint venture dissolves and its lessons walk out the door with the people who learned them.

Government innovation is the sharpest case. A ministry almost never innovates alone; it convenes universities, firms, agencies, and citizens around a shared mission, which makes public-sector innovation ecosystemic by nature. Measuring the return on that kind of effort is the same problem S4IL was built to solve, scaled up one level—and it is a problem I have spent a good part of my career inside. But the ecosystem extension is a book of its own, and this one is already long enough. Whether I set that experience down on paper is a decision the reception of this one will help me make. For now, the compass stays aboard a single ship.

AI-Augmented Leadership and the Innovation Compass

The convergence of AI-enabled organizational memory, foresight capability, and open innovation infrastructure creates a new leadership challenge: how does the Chief Innovation Officer operate when the volume of available information exceeds any individual's capacity to process it?

A four-stage maturity model captures how this capability matures inside an organization:

- **Stage 1: AI-Assisted.** AI tools handle data aggregation and visualization. Human leaders make all decisions. The AI reduces the time required to prepare for decision-making but does not influence the decisions themselves.
- **Stage 2: AI-Advised.** AI tools provide recommendations alongside the data. Human leaders review recommendations and exercise judgment. The AI begins to influence the framing of decisions but not the decisions themselves.
- **Stage 3: AI-Delegated.** AI systems manage routine decisions within predefined parameters (e.g., portfolio rebalancing within approved Horizon targets). Human leaders intervene for strategic, novel, or high-stakes decisions. The AI handles the volume; the human provides the judgment.
- **Stage 4: AI-Partnered.** AI and human leaders operate as genuine partners, each contributing their distinctive capabilities. The AI provides pattern recognition, memory retrieval, and scenario modelling. The human provides strategic vision, stakeholder judgment, and ethical reasoning. Neither operates effectively without the other.

Most organizations are at Stage 1 or early Stage 2. The framework is designed to support progression through all four stages by providing the governance architecture, measurement system, and trust infrastructure that enables increasingly sophisticated human-AI collaboration. The four-agent AI-OM Orchestrator described in Chapter 6 is the technical architecture. The four-stage maturity model described here is the human architecture.

The compass metaphor holds even at this level of sophistication. The most advanced GPS in the world does not remove the need for a captain who understands the sea. It changes what the captain spends their time on—less time calculating position, more time making strategic decisions about where to sail next.

The compass works. The instruments are calibrated. The ecosystem is connected. Now the question is: how do you actually start? Not in six months. Not after the next reorganization. In ninety days.

The ecosystem is mapped. The partnerships are forming. But a partnership measured only by the press release that announced it is no better than an innovation measured only by the workshops that filled the calendar. What an organization gains at its boundaries—the knowledge that crosses them, the capability it absorbs, the readiness it builds—has to be read on the same two needles as everything else, or it is not being managed at all. The walls come down for a reason, and the reason has to show up in the measurement.

The Skipper's Log

Position — The compass holds at the boundary. What crosses an organization's walls must read on the same two needles as everything inside them.

Sighted — Partnership theatre — alliances measured by the press release that announced them — and the signals a foresight discipline catches before competitors do.

Charted — What open innovation fills, what it misses, and how ecosystem gains register as capital built rather than activity performed.

Course — For each active partnership, name the capital it builds and the needle it should move. If you cannot name either, you have found this quarter's hardest conversation.

Chapter 11: A 90-Day Journey

The Plant Engineer

Maria Torres had been at the facility for eleven years. She knew the machines the way a musician knows an instrument: not from the manual but from the thousands of hours of listening to what they sounded like when they were running correctly, and the specific, slightly different sounds they made when something was beginning to go wrong.

She was not, by formal title, an innovation professional. Her title was Senior Process Engineer. She had never attended an innovation workshop. She had never put a Post-it note on a whiteboard in a facilitated session. But she was, in the most functional sense, one of the most innovative people in the organization, because she had spent eleven years accumulating exactly the kind of knowledge that innovation depends on: the precise understanding of what the process could do, what had been tried to improve it, what the failures had looked like, and what the constraints were that no simulation had ever managed to capture.

When the organization's innovation program arrived—with its innovation coaches, its horizon framework, its indicator dashboards—it arrived as a system designed for people who did not yet know what they were doing, built to help them learn faster. For someone who already knew, it was a different challenge: how do you take eleven years of knowledge that lives in your hands and your ears and your accumulated memory, and convert it into something that the measurement system can see?

This chapter is her chapter. It is the chapter for the people who already know—who have deep domain expertise, who understand their organization's innovation potential from the inside—and who need a practical framework for connecting what they know to what the organization can measure, and for building the memory infrastructure that will make their knowledge organizational rather than merely personal.

The 90-Day Kick-off

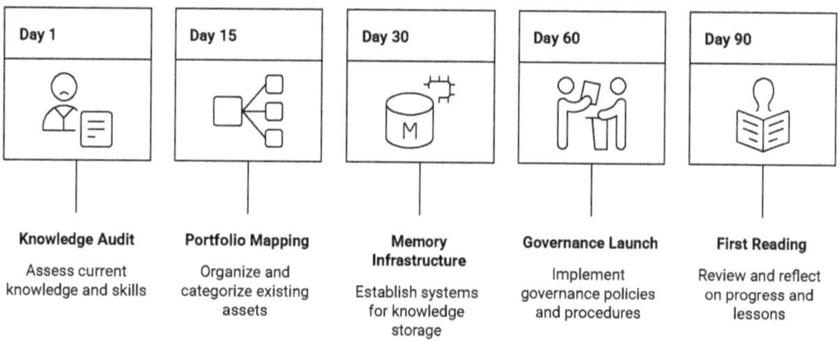

A question that practitioners in smaller organizations often raise: is S4IL only for large enterprises with dedicated innovation teams, mature portfolios, and enterprise-level AI infrastructure? The answer is no, and the reason is structural. S4IL scales down by reducing the number of initiatives in the portfolio, not by removing the framework. An organization with two active innovation projects in each season still benefits from thinking in seasons rather than in isolated projects, still benefits from capturing what each project learns before the knowledge walks out the door, and still benefits from the discipline of asking: are these two projects pollinating each other, or are they running in parallel silos? The paradox that this book returns to throughout—that more structure enables more creativity, not less—applies at every scale. The 90-day plan that follows is calibrated for an organization with five to fifteen active initiatives. For organizations with fewer, compress the audit and simplify the portfolio mapping. The governance logic remains identical.

The 90-Day Kick-off is designed for a specific situation: an organization that has decided to implement the Compass framework and needs to move from intention to operational reality without a multi-year transformation program. It is deliberately designed to be achievable by a single motivated team without requiring enterprise-wide buy-in at the outset, significant IT investment, or disruption to ongoing operations.

It is also designed to produce real measurement data—not proof-of-concept outputs or pilot results that require extrapolation, but actual portfolio data the organization can use for management decisions—within 90 days. This is not a transformation program. It is an instrumentation program. The goal is to get the compass working. The navigation comes after.

Before the ninety days begin, understand what they are for. This book has asked you to believe very little. Chapter 7 argued that the honest ledger is insurmountable by hand—and a claim like that deserves a test, not a nod. The ninety days are the test. Everything that follows runs on a spreadsheet and an AI assistant: no platform purchase, no transformation program, no army of consultants. And it ends in a number—your duplication, your stalled connections, your forgotten lessons, priced in your own currency. If the number is small, congratulations, your memory is healthy. If it is large—and in three decades I have never once seen it small—you will know precisely what the theatre has been costing you, and the case for what comes next will have written itself.

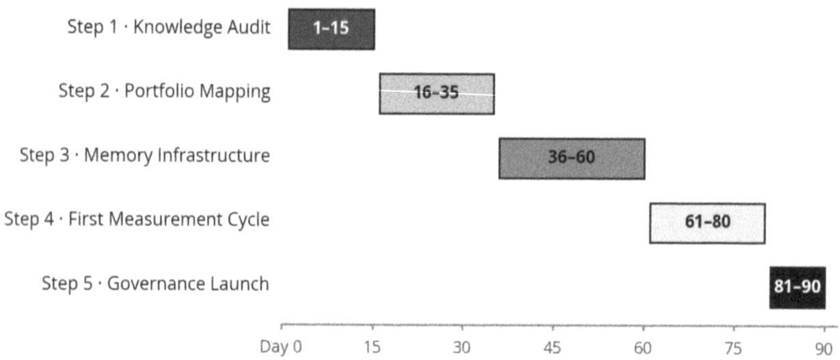

Figure: The 90-Day Journey—five steps from knowledge audit to governance launch.

Step 1: Knowledge Audit (Days 1–15)

The first phase is the knowledge audit—a structured inventory of what the organization already knows about its innovation activity, where that knowledge lives, and what is currently inaccessible.

The audit begins with a simple question asked of ten to fifteen people across the organization: "What innovation-related knowledge do you wish you had easier access to, and where do you think it actually exists?" The answers to this question consistently reveal the same pattern: the knowledge people want is usually present in the organization, in some form, somewhere—but the path from question to answer is not obvious, and in many cases the person asking the question does not know that the answer exists.

The audit also inventories existing knowledge repositories: project management systems, technical documentation, lessons-learned archives, exit interview records, and any structured effort the organization has made over the past decade to capture institutional knowledge. Most organizations find that they have more documented knowledge than they thought—but that it is organized for storage rather than for retrieval, and that the metadata (tags, cross-references, links to related projects) is either absent or inconsistent.

The output of the knowledge audit is a gap map: a visual representation of where knowledge exists, where it is effectively inaccessible, and where it does not exist. This gap map becomes the design specification for the memory infrastructure built in Phase 3.

Workshop 1: The Knowledge Archaeology Session (Day 3)

Assemble a cross-functional team of eight to twelve people. Include at least two individuals who have been with the organization for more than five years, two who joined within the last eighteen months, and at least one person from a support function (finance, HR, legal) who interacts with innovation tangentially. The diversity of tenure is critical: long-tenured members know where the bodies are buried; recent joiners can identify what is invisible to insiders.

The session runs for three hours. Begin with a single prompt: "What is the most valuable thing this organization learned from an innovation project in the last five years—and where is that learning now?"

The answers will reveal the state of your organizational memory more accurately than any audit tool. If participants struggle to name specific learning, the diagnosis is clear. If they can name it but cannot locate it, the problem is retrieval. If they can locate it, but nobody has accessed it, the problem is integration.

Diagnostic Questions for the Knowledge Audit:

- Can any team member locate the outcomes of innovation projects completed more than two years ago?
- When a new initiative is launched, is there a systematic check against previous experiments in the same domain?
- Are failure analyses documented with the same rigour as success stories?
- If the three most experienced innovation staff left tomorrow, what organizational knowledge would leave with them?
- Does the organization have a shared vocabulary for describing innovation outcomes beyond "success" and "failure"?

Political Strategy for Step 1:

The Knowledge Audit will encounter resistance. Three sources of resistance are predictable and should be anticipated:

- **The Vulnerability Objection.** Innovation team members may fear that surfacing past failures will reflect poorly on their competence. Frame the audit as capability mapping rather than performance evaluation. The question is not "who failed?" but "what did the organization learn, and where is that learning now?"
- **The Territorial Objection.** Middle managers whose authority derives from controlling access to information will perceive the audit as a threat. Engage them early as knowledge stewards, not knowledge subjects. Give them a role in the process, not a role as its target.
- **The Sunk Cost Objection.** Leaders who have invested in expensive knowledge management systems may feel that a new audit implies their investment was wasted. Explicitly acknowledge the existing infrastructure and position the audit as an integration exercise rather than a replacement.

Navigating Resistance: The Political Dimension of Measurement

The knowledge audit will reveal uncomfortable truths. It will surface knowledge gaps for which particular leaders are responsible. It will identify knowledge-hiding behaviours that specific teams engage in. It will quantify the cost of amnesia in terms that make someone accountable. This is precisely why the audit is valuable—and precisely why it will generate political resistance.

Experienced practitioners navigate this resistance through four deliberate strategies:

- **Depersonalize the findings.** Never present audit findings as blame. Frame every finding as a systemic issue, not a personal failure. The organization forgot this knowledge because the system was not designed to remember it, not because a specific individual failed to document it.
- **Lead with opportunity, not blame.** For every gap identified, present the future benefit of closing that gap. The board does not want to hear that the organization wasted $3 million on duplicate research. The board wants to hear that implementing a knowledge reuse system could save $3 million per year through avoided duplication.
- **Build a coalition before going public.** Identify the three to five most senior leaders whose support is essential for implementation. Before presenting audit findings to a wider audience, brief these leaders privately, incorporate their feedback, and secure their endorsement. Innovation measurement is too politically sensitive to be launched without executive air cover.

- **Start with a quick win that proves the concept.** The first measurement cycle should demonstrate value quickly—ideally within thirty days. Choose a pilot initiative in which the framework can surface an actionable insight that existing measurement systems have missed. One compelling example is worth more than a hundred slides of methodology.

The political dimension is not a distraction from the measurement work—it is an essential part of it. A technically excellent measurement system that is politically dead on arrival produces no value. A technically adequate system with strong political support transforms the organization.

The Memory Baseline: Establishing Your Starting Point

Before the 90-day journey can measure progress, it must establish a baseline. The Memory Baseline is a structured snapshot of the organization's current state across the four capitals, taken during the knowledge audit phase. It serves as the reference point against which all future measurements are compared.

The baseline assessment covers four dimensions, each scored on a four-point maturity scale (Initial, Developing, Established, Optimizing):

- **Knowledge Maturity.** How well does the organization capture, store, and organize its innovation knowledge? Initial: no systematic capture. Developing: ad hoc documentation. Established: structured knowledge management with regular updates. Optimizing: AI-enabled capture with intelligent retrieval.
- **Relationship Maturity.** How effectively do people collaborate across boundaries and share knowledge honestly? Initial: siloed teams with low trust. Developing: some cross-functional

collaboration. Established: systematic knowledge sharing with psychological safety. Optimizing: ecosystem-level collaboration with shared memory infrastructure.

- **Process Maturity.** How mature are the organization's innovation governance and decision processes? Initial: no formal innovation process. Developing: stage-gate with basic metrics. Established: evidence-based governance with the Four Compass Readings. Optimizing: AI-augmented decision-making with real-time portfolio optimization.
- **Memory Maturity.** How well does the organization learn from its own experience? Initial: no institutional learning—each project starts from scratch. Developing: post-mortems are conducted but rarely referenced. Established: active knowledge reuse with a measurable Reuse Rate. Optimizing: predictive learning—the organization anticipates needs before they arise based on accumulated patterns.

The baseline assessment typically takes two to three days and involves interviews with fifteen to twenty key stakeholders across the innovation ecosystem. The results are plotted on a four-quadrant radar chart that provides an immediate visual of the organization's innovation memory posture. This chart becomes the first page of the dashboard and is updated quarterly to track progress.

Step 2: Portfolio Mapping (Days 16–35)

Before mapping the portfolio, the Head of Innovation must complete the Season Design process by selecting a shortlist of strategic indicators from the full ROI² Indicator Catalogue (Appendix A) to define the success criteria for this investment season. This selection translates the organization's current strategic priorities into concrete, measurable ROI² indicators. Template E.1 in the Appendix provides a structured worksheet for this process. Only once the season's shortlist is established should the portfolio mapping proceed, because the shortlist determines what you are mapping against.

The second phase maps the organization's current innovation portfolio against the Compass framework: identifying all active innovation investments, assigning each to a horizon, estimating its contribution to each of the Four Capitals, and establishing baseline measurements for the core indicator set.

This phase typically reveals surprises. Most organizations discover that their actual innovation portfolio is considerably more extensive than their formal innovation programs suggest. Process improvement projects that were never labelled as innovation, technology explorations funded from operational budgets, and informal knowledge-building activities that practitioners conduct without organizational sanction—all of these are innovation investments. All of them belong in the portfolio map.

You Are Not Starting from Zero: Refitting the Existing Rigging

A confession from the field, because I have charged for the opposite advice and regretted it. Most readers of this chapter are not standing on an empty slipway. They already run an idea platform, a champions network, internal challenges, a Design Thinking curriculum, a stage-gate. The temptation—mine included, in younger engagements—is to treat the new instrument as a replacement and the old rigging as ballast. Wrong on both counts. The mapping is keep, rewire, or retire, and most of it is rewire.

The idea platform is rewired, not retired: it becomes an intake channel of the memory, the source of half your Throughput indicators, and—

Chapter 12—the substrate on which the dark-matter estimator runs the day you export it. The champions become the named owners the cascade has been asking for: evidence owners on initiatives, memory stewards on portfolios; their network is Relational Capital you have already paid for. Internal challenges stop being calendar events and become precision instruments, aimed—as Chapter 9 prescribed—at the specific indicator the portfolio is failing to cover. The Design Thinking curriculum keeps its place in the empathy stage of How to Win, with one new obligation: its outputs enter the experiment log, or they evaporate the way they always have. The stage-gate is kept for Horizon 1, where predictability is the value, and deliberately duplicated into a looser twin for Horizon 3, per the ambidexterity diagnostic of Chapter 7. And the lessons-learned repository is neither kept nor retired: it is the archive your memory system will feed on, once a retrieval layer teaches it to answer.

Retire, then, almost nothing—except the metrics. The activity counts your current dashboard leans on go under the Vanity cap, and the cap does the pruning without a funeral. The crew keeps its rigging. The rigging finally serves a course.

The portfolio map also typically reveals a concentration problem: most organizations have concentrated their measurable innovation investment in Horizon 1 (near-term commercialization) and have little or no formal investment in Horizon 3 (exploratory research). This is partly a measurement artifact—Horizon 3 investment is harder to identify and value—but it is also a real strategic pattern, reflecting the pressure to demonstrate near-term returns that characterizes most innovation governance systems.

Establishing baseline measurements requires collecting data that the organization may not currently track consistently: time from idea to pilot, abandonment rate with documented learning, and knowledge transfer rate between projects. For many of these indicators, the first cycle of measurement will produce imperfect data because the measurement process itself will reveal inconsistencies in how data has been collected. This is normal and expected. Imperfect baseline data is significantly more useful than no baseline data.

Discovering the Dark Matter: Ideas You Don't Know You're Missing

During the portfolio mapping phase, an important question emerges that most innovation leaders never think to ask: how many ideas are out there that we have not yet captured?

This question belongs specifically to the first phase: **Where to Play**. It is here—when the organization must decide which domains to explore before any resource is committed—that the cost of not knowing what you are missing is highest. A portfolio manager who moves directly into the How to Win phase without first asking "have we already explored something like this?" or "what knowledge do we hold that we have not yet connected?" is navigating without a chart. The Chao1 estimator is the instrument designed for this moment. It does not tell you where to go. It tells you how much of the territory you have not yet seen—and where the unseen territory is statistically most likely to be found.

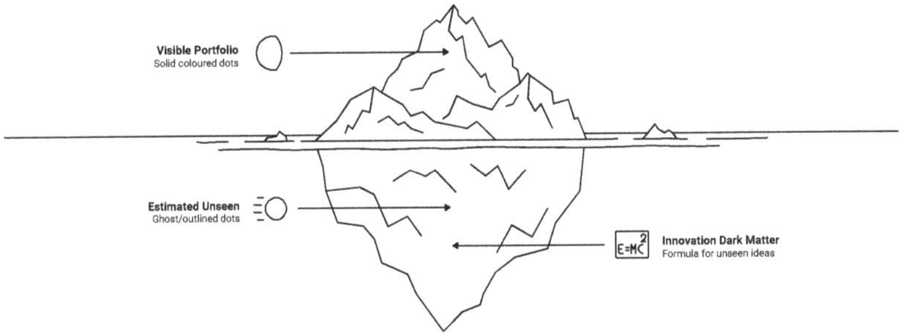

The name this book gives to that unseen pool is the Dark Matter of innovation: the ideation potential the organization holds but has never captured. The mechanics of estimating it—how the frequency of single-contributor ideas reveals the size of the pool you cannot see—are developed in Chapter 12. Here it is enough to know that the estimate runs on data the portfolio map has already gathered.

→ The Dark Matter Insight is a diagnostic metric: the estimated number of uncaptured ideas relative to the captured pipeline.

A high Dark Matter ratio (the organization is capturing only a small fraction of its ideation potential) demands intervention—lowering submission barriers, broadening the contributor base, and actively soliciting ideas from underrepresented teams and roles.

A low Dark Matter ratio (the organization is capturing most of its ideation potential) may indicate either a healthy innovation culture or an exhausted one.

From Raw Ideas to Launched Products

The Dark Matter metric tells you how much potential exists outside the pipeline. The Innovation Funnel Health metric tells you what is happening inside it. A healthy innovation funnel has four measurable stages:

- **Raw Ideas.** The total number of ideas entering the pipeline per quarter. Healthy organizations maintain a ratio of at least ten raw ideas for every idea that progresses to the next stage.
- **Validated Ideas.** Ideas that have been assessed for desirability, feasibility, and viability and have met the minimum threshold for continued investment. The validation rate should be between ten and twenty-five percent of raw ideas—higher suggests insufficient ambition; lower suggests insufficient quality at the intake stage.
- **Funded Projects.** Validated ideas that have received budget, team allocation, and governance oversight. The conversion from validated idea to funded project is where most innovation funnels leak—often because governance processes are too slow or too risk-averse.
- **Launched Products.** Funded projects that have reached market or operational deployment. The ultimate measure of funnel health is the ratio of launched products to raw ideas—the end-to-end conversion rate.

The funnel health metrics should be reviewed quarterly as part of the portfolio mapping exercise and compared against the Horizon balance targets. An organization that launches many Horizon 1 improvements but no Horizon 3 experiments has a funnel that prioritizes safety over ambition.

Step 3: Memory Infrastructure (Days 36–60)

The third phase builds the memory infrastructure: the systems and processes that will allow the organization to capture knowledge from ongoing innovation activity and make it retrievable for future use.

The memory infrastructure has four components. The first is a knowledge capture protocol—a lightweight, standardized process for recording key decisions, insights, and lessons from innovation projects at the point of occurrence. The protocol should be simple enough that practitioners will actually use it under real working conditions: no more than five minutes of effort per significant decision, no specialized training required, integrated into existing project management workflows rather than requiring a separate system.

The second component is a metadata standard: a consistent tagging system that allows knowledge artifacts to be connected across projects, time periods, and organizational functions. The standard should include, at a minimum: a project identifier, date, innovation domain, horizon, knowledge type (decision rationale, experimental result, adoption learning, failure analysis), and links to related projects. This metadata is the connective tissue that allows the retrieval system to find relevant knowledge in response to new questions.

The third component is an indexing review process: a regular (ideally monthly) process in which someone with cross-functional visibility reviews recently captured knowledge, confirms that it is correctly tagged, and identifies connections to prior work that should be explicitly documented. This review process is the most consistently underinvested component of knowledge infrastructure, and it is the one that most determines whether the system improves over time or accumulates data without compounding learning.

The fourth component is a retrieval interface: the mechanism by which practitioners can ask questions of the organization's knowledge base. In 2025, this increasingly means an AI-assisted search capability—but the AI is only as useful as the quality of the underlying indexed knowledge. Organizations that build AI retrieval on top of poorly structured knowledge bases get sophisticated retrieval of disorganized information. Organizations that build AI retrieval on top of well-structured, consistently tagged knowledge bases get genuinely intelligent organizational memory.

Step 4: First Measurement Cycle (Days 61–80)

The fourth step runs the first complete measurement cycle using the Compass framework: collecting portfolio data, calculating the indicators across all four dimensions, and producing the first edition of the Innovation Compass report.

The first measurement cycle will be imperfect in several ways, and that is expected. Some indicators will produce results that seem implausible on first review—usually because a measurement definition is ambiguous or a data collection process is inconsistent. Some aspects of the portfolio map produced in Phase 2 will need to be revised based on the measurement exercise.

The value of the first cycle is not in the perfection of the numbers. It is in the creation of a measurement baseline from which improvement can be tracked, and in the organizational learning that the measurement exercise produces. Every anomaly in the data is a diagnostic signal about how the organization actually operates. Every data gap is a map of where the memory infrastructure needs to be built out. The imperfect first cycle is the most informative document the organization will produce in the entire 90-day process.

Building Your First S4IL Dashboard

By Day 80, the organization should have enough data to build its first dashboard. This is a pivotal moment—the first time the innovation leadership team can see its portfolio through the lens of the four capitals and the Four Compass Readings.

Which hull you build it in is your call, and Appendix J holds the yard drawings: the same seven stations render as tabs in a spreadsheet, tables behind a small program, panels on an internal page, or modules of the platform you already license. Build the smallest hull that floats. You can always change boats; you cannot change a season you failed to measure.

The first dashboard should be simple. Resist the temptation to build the full measurement architecture immediately. The initial dashboard should contain four sections:

- **Section 1: Innovation Memory Posture.** A four-quadrant radar chart showing the Memory Baseline assessment from Step 1 (Knowledge Maturity, Relationship Maturity, Process Maturity, Memory Maturity). This provides the qualitative foundation.
- **Section 2: Portfolio Health Overview.** A simple table showing, for each active innovation initiative, the four compass readings (Input, Throughput, Output, Outcome) with traffic-light colour coding (green = on track, amber = needs attention, red = at risk). This provides the initiative-level view.

- **Section 3: Leading Indicators.** The four key risk indicators are: Memory Fracture Risk score, Horizon balance (percentage of the portfolio in H1, H2, and H3), Reuse Rate, and ambidexterity balance (explore-versus-exploit ratio). These provide early warning.
- **Section 4: Recommended Actions.** The top three actions are recommended by the innovation leadership team based on the data. Actions should be specific, time-bound, and linked to a metric that confirms whether the action was effective.

The first dashboard will be imperfect. Some data will be missing. Some indicators will be estimates rather than precise measurements. This is expected and acceptable. The value of the first dashboard is not precision—it is visibility. For the first time, the innovation leadership team can see the shape of their portfolio across all four capitals and all four compass readings. That visibility, even when imperfect, is transformative.

Reading the Signals: What Your First Dashboard Will Tell You

The most common patterns observed in first-time dashboards are:

- **Pattern 1: High Output, Low Outcome.** Strong outputs (prototypes, patents, products) but weak outcomes (revenue, adoption, strategic impact). This pattern indicates that the organization is producing innovative deliverables but failing to convert them into value, often due to weak adoption processes or misaligned market timing.
- **Pattern 2: Knowledge Rich, Memory Poor.** Knowledge Capital is strong, but Memory Capital is weak. The organization generates a wealth of knowledge but cannot reuse it effectively. This pattern indicates a retrieval problem—the knowledge

exists but is not findable or not accessible at the moment of decision.

- **Pattern 3: Strong Silos.** Relational Capital is high within teams but low across teams. People collaborate well within their immediate group but do not share knowledge across organizational boundaries. This is the signature for Scenario 2 (Strategic Ambiguity) from the knowledge-hiding framework in Chapter 3.
- **Pattern 4: Uniform Mediocrity.** All four capitals show moderate scores with no distinctive strengths or weaknesses. This pattern is deceptive—it appears healthy but often signals an organization that invests equally in everything and excels at nothing. The North Star Metric exercise described in Chapter 4 is the remedy: choose the capital that matters most and concentrate improvement efforts there.

Each pattern suggests a different intervention strategy. The first dashboard does not provide answers—it provides the right questions. And the right questions, in innovation management, are worth more than premature answers.

Step 5: Governance Launch (Days 81–90)

The fifth and final phase establishes the governance structures that will maintain and improve the Compass system over time: the review cadence, the responsibility assignments, and the escalation paths that connect portfolio measurement to strategic decision-making.

The governance launch requires securing three commitments from organizational leadership. The first is a commitment to data consistency: the measurement definitions established in Phase 4 will be maintained unchanged for at least three annual cycles, even if the numbers are inconvenient, to allow genuine trend analysis. The second is a commitment to memory investment: the knowledge capture and indexing processes established in Phase 3 will be resourced as ongoing operational activities rather than time-limited project work. The third is a commitment to portfolio transparency: the Innovation Compass report will be shared with the leadership team regularly, with the explicit expectation that it will surface problems and that the appropriate response to them is to address them rather than adjust the measurement system.

The plant engineer who began this chapter did not need a Compass to know what her process could do. She carried her compass in her head, built from eleven years of accumulated experience. The 90-Day Start builds the organizational equivalent of that compass—not in one person's head, but in the institution itself. The goal is an organization that learns the way she learns: continuously, from everything it does, without forgetting.

Measuring Adoption: The Final Mile of Innovation

The 90-day journey described in this chapter builds the foundation: knowledge audit, portfolio mapping, memory infrastructure, measurement cycle, and governance. But there is a sixth dimension that determines whether all of this work produces lasting change: adoption.

Adoption is the final mile of innovation—the distance between a launched product or process and its actual integration into the organization or market. Many innovation initiatives that succeed technically fail commercially because adoption was treated as an afterthought rather than as a measured, managed process.

The Adoption Compass: Four Metrics That Matter

The framework measures adoption through four metrics inspired by the startup world's AARRR framework (Acquisition, Activation, Retention, Revenue, Referral) but adapted for corporate innovation contexts:

- **Awareness Rate.** The percentage of target users (internal or external) who have been exposed to the innovation. An innovation that solves a real problem but reaches only ten percent of its target audience is an adoption failure, not a product failure.
- **Activation Rate.** The percentage of aware users who have actually tried the innovation. The gap between awareness and activation reveals friction in the onboarding process—too many steps, unclear value proposition, or insufficient training.
- **Retention Rate.** The percentage of activated users who continue using the innovation after the initial trial period. Retention is the truest measure of product-market fit for internal innovations. A low retention rate signals that the innovation does not solve a sufficiently important problem, or that it creates more friction than it removes.
- **Viral Coefficient.** The rate at which adopted innovations spread organically through word of mouth or peer influence. A viral coefficient above 1.0 means the innovation is growing through user advocacy; below 1.0, adoption requires a continuous push from the innovation team.

The Adoption Compass should be deployed for every innovation initiative that reaches the launch stage. It provides the feedback loop that tells the innovation team whether the market (internal or external) is actually receiving the value that the development process intended to deliver.

Before designing any motivational architecture for innovation, one distinction must be made explicit. An engagement platform and an adoption campaign serve different purposes, operate on different timescales, and require different mechanics. Confusing them produces interventions that are well-designed for the wrong problem.

An engagement platform motivates an internal audience to participate continuously in the innovation system itself—contributing knowledge, documenting experiments, reviewing signals, and updating the portfolio. The audience is the innovation community. The behaviour being rewarded is habitual. The timeframe is the full duration of the Season and beyond. This is what the InnoPoints system described below addresses.

An adoption campaign, by contrast, motivates a specific audience—internal or external—to adopt a specific innovation that the organization is trying to diffuse. The audience is the target user of that innovation. The behaviour being sought is a one-time transition: from non-user to user. The timeframe is bounded by the adoption window of that specific initiative.

The tools overlap—both use recognition, progression, and social proof—but their design logic is reversed. An engagement platform is always on. An adoption campaign has a beginning, a peak, and an end. Running a campaign logic on a platform produces burnout.

Running a platform logic on a campaign produces diffusion without urgency. The framework uses both, but never interchangeably.

Gamification and the InnoPoints System

One of the most persistent challenges in innovation management is sustaining engagement beyond the initial enthusiasm of a new program launch. The knowledge audit generates excitement. The first measurement cycle feels novel. By the third quarter, participation often declines as the innovation program competes with operational priorities for people's attention and energy.

Gamification—the application of game-design elements to non-game contexts—offers a structured approach to sustaining engagement over time. When applied thoughtfully, gamification does not trivialize innovation. It provides the same feedback loops that make well-designed games compelling: clear goals, immediate feedback, progressive challenge, and social recognition.

The InnoPoints system is a gamification framework designed specifically for this implementation. It awards points for four categories of contribution, each mapped to one of the four capitals:

- **Knowledge Contributions.** Points awarded for documenting knowledge—writing up project retrospectives, filing lessons learned, and contributing to the organizational memory system. The points reward the act of knowledge creation, which is otherwise invisible in most performance systems.
- **Collaboration Actions.** Points awarded for cross-team collaboration—sharing knowledge with teams outside your own, participating in innovation challenges, and mentoring colleagues in other departments. The points make Relational Capital building visible.

- **Reuse Events.** Points awarded for applying documented knowledge to current projects—citing prior work, building on existing research, and adapting lessons learned from other teams. The points reward reuse, which is the behaviour that makes organizational memory functional.
- **Governance Participation.** Points awarded for completing innovation governance activities—submitting measurement data, participating in portfolio reviews, and conducting phase-gate evaluations. The points ensure that governance is treated as a valuable contribution rather than a bureaucratic burden.

InnoPoints are tracked on the dashboard and can be displayed at both the individual and team levels. The system should include a clear reward structure—not necessarily monetary, but always meaningful: recognition in leadership forums, priority access to innovation resources, invitations to strategic planning sessions, or the authority to sponsor small innovation experiments.

The most important design principle for innovation gamification is alignment with the four capitals. Every point category should reinforce the behaviours that build Knowledge, Relational, Process, and Memory Capital.

→ If the gamification system rewards activities that do not build one of the four capitals, it is generating noise rather than a signal.

The compass does not sail the ship. The crew sails the ship. But a crew with a compass reaches the destination. A crew without one merely has an adventure. But Maria Torres, staring at her newly built dashboard on Day 91, asked the question that every navigator must eventually face: "This dashboard shows me what I can see. But what about what I cannot see? How do I know what my organization is hiding from itself?" The answer to that question comes from an unexpected source—a Taiwanese statistician who spent her career counting butterflies.

The Skipper's Log

Position — The system starts in ninety days. Not after the reorganization, not next fiscal year. Ninety days.

Sighted — Maria's route — knowledge audit, portfolio mapping, memory infrastructure, first measurement cycle, governance launch — and adoption, the final mile most programs never walk.

Charted — Five steps with day ranges, and the InnoPoints mechanics that reward only what builds one of the four capitals.

Course — Put Days 1–15 in the calendar today, and name the auditor. A start date is a commitment; everything else is intention.

Chapter 12: The Unseen Metric

Every innovation portfolio has a shape its managers can see: the projects funded, the ideas logged, the bets on the board. It also has a shadow—the opportunities the organization could be pursuing but has never even noticed—and the shadow is almost always larger than the shape. Most innovation leaders have never measured it, for the same reason no one counts what they cannot see. Ecology can. It counts, routinely, the species in a forest that a survey missed, and its method transfers with unsettling precision to the projects a portfolio never imagined. S4IL gives that gap a name and a fixed place in the model. The name is Innovation Dark Matter (IDM). The place is the first phase, Where to Play—the one phase whose whole job is to decide what to explore before a dollar is committed. Anne Chao's estimator—built from the ratio of singletons to doubletons in a species survey—is the engine that measures it, describing the dark matter of an idea portfolio with the same precision it describes the dark matter of a tropical forest.

Where this sits on the compass. Innovation Dark Matter is the measure the system runs in the first phase, Where to Play; Chao1 is the estimator beneath it. The measure answers one question and only one: of the opportunities your organization could be exploring, how large is the share you have not yet seen? It says nothing about which of those opportunities is worth pursuing, nothing about how to build them, nothing about whether a market will adopt them—a foresight scan, a prioritization matrix, and an adoption model each pick up where it stops. Its worth is that it refuses to let you mistake the catalogue you hold for the territory that exists. Fragment it down to a single portfolio and it estimates that portfolio's dark matter; combine its output with your scanning and you have a defensible measure of exploration completeness. That measure feeds the Knowledge Capital behind the Readiness needle: a landscape you have explored exhaustively is one you are readier to invest in than one you merely catalogued.

One dependency must be named before the mathematics, because the estimator inherits it. Chao1 counts species from an inventory of sightings; Innovation Dark Matter counts opportunities from an inventory of ideas. The inventory is the organizational memory. An organization that never captured its ideas—the ones proposed, the ones abandoned, the ones that surfaced twice in different buildings—has no f1 and no f2 to feed the formula, and its dark matter is not merely unmeasured but unestimable. This chapter, like every calculating chapter before it, runs on the same fuel: no memory, no number.

The collision was useful for naming the problem. This chapter is about solving it.

Innovation as an Ecosystem

Every organization's innovation portfolio is an ecosystem. The "species" are the domains of innovation—the technical areas, market segments, customer needs, and capability families in which ideas emerge. Some domains are well explored: the organization has generated dozens of ideas there, run multiple experiments, and accumulated deep knowledge. Other domains are barely touched—a single idea submitted during a hackathon, a lone pilot that was never repeated, a concept that appeared once in a brainstorming session and was never revisited.

The critical question for any innovation leader is not "how many ideas do we have?" but "how much of our innovation landscape have we actually explored?" The Chao1 estimator provides a rigorous, statistically grounded answer.

The Formula: From Forests to Portfolios

The Chao1 estimator, adapted for innovation management to estimate the Innovation Dark Matter (IDM), works as follows:

$$IDM = S\_obs + (f1^2 / (2f2))$$

Where:

- **S_obs** is the number of observed innovation domains—the distinct technical areas, market segments, or capability families in which your organization has generated at least one idea.
- **f1 (Singletons)** is the number of innovation domains represented by exactly one idea. These are the barely-touched territories—domains where a single concept emerged but was never followed up, never replicated, never deepened.
- **f2 (Doubletons)** is the number of innovation domains represented by exactly two ideas. These are the domains that have attracted just enough attention to suggest viability, but not enough to constitute genuine exploration.
- **IDM** is the estimated true number of innovation domains—including those that your organization has not yet discovered or explored.

The mathematical intuition is powerful: if your portfolio contains many singletons—domains explored only once—the formula tells you that your observed landscape is likely a small fraction of the total available landscape. Conversely, if most of your domains have been explored multiple times with few singletons remaining, you are approaching saturation.

One honesty about resolution. The estimator is only as sharp as the inventory beneath it. An export from the idea platform you already run—every submission, tagged by domain—is enough to compute it this quarter, at quarter-level resolution. High-frequency memory traces, once the fourth rung of the maturity ladder is reached, sharpen the same estimate the way a depth sounder sharpens a lead line: same seabed, finer soundings. Start with the lead line.

Three Derived Metrics

The Chao1 estimator produces three derived metrics that are immediately actionable for innovation governance:

The Unseen Gap. The difference between the estimated total domains (IDM) and the observed domains (S_obs). This number represents the innovation white space—the domains that exist in your competitive environment but have not yet appeared in your portfolio. A large unseen gap signals untapped potential. A small unseen gap suggests either market saturation or insufficient imagination, and the distinction matters enormously.

The Saturation Index. The ratio of observed to estimated domains, expressed as a percentage: (S_obs / IDM) × 100. A saturation index of 40% means the organization has explored less than half of its estimated innovation landscape. A saturation index approaching 90% suggests the portfolio is mature and may need deliberate disruption—such as exploring adjacent markets, new technologies, or unfamiliar customer segments—to reignite growth.

Latent Asset Value. The monetized estimate of the unseen gap is calculated by multiplying the number of unseen domains by the average value of an explored domain. This converts an abstract statistical estimate into a financial figure that boards and executives can understand. When the Head of Innovation tells the board, "Our Chao1 analysis estimates that we have explored sixty percent of our innovation landscape, and the unexplored forty percent represents an estimated latent asset value of two hundred million dollars," the conversation about innovation investment changes fundamentally.

Innovation Dark Matter in Practice: A Pharmaceutical Case

Consider a mid-sized pharmaceutical company that has accumulated thirteen thousand ideas across its innovation portfolio over the past decade. When categorized by therapeutic domain, these ideas span 85 distinct domains. Of those 85 domains, 22 are singletons (represented by exactly one idea), and 14 are doubletons (represented by exactly two ideas). Applying the Chao1 estimator:

$$IDM = 85 + (22^2 / (2 \times 14)) = 85 + (484 / 28) \approx 102$$

The estimator suggests that approximately 102 innovation domains exist in the company's therapeutic landscape, of which only 85 have been observed. The unseen gap is 17 domains. The saturation index is approximately 83%. The company has explored most of its landscape, but still has significant unexplored territory.

The 22 singletons are the most strategically interesting data points. Each represents a domain where the organization generated exactly one idea and then moved on. Were these domains abandoned because they lacked merit, or because the organization lacked the patience, resources, or memory to pursue them? The Chao1 analysis does not answer this question directly, but it places it on the strategic agenda in a way that no traditional innovation metric does.

The Bias-Corrected Form

When the number of doubletons (f2) equals zero—meaning no domain has exactly two ideas—the standard formula produces a division by zero. In such cases, the bias-corrected form of Chao1 is used:

$$IDM = S\_obs + f1(f1 - 1) / 2$$

This correction ensures that the estimator remains well-defined even when the data is sparse. For organizations at the beginning of their innovation journey—those with fewer than fifty ideas in their portfolio—the bias-corrected form is the default. As the portfolio grows and doubletons appear, the standard form becomes more appropriate.

Innovation Dark Matter

The Chao1 estimator integrates naturally into the measurement framework as a Knowledge Capital indicator—I call it the Innovation Dark Matter (IDM). It answers the question that no traditional innovation metric addresses: "How much of our innovation landscape remains undiscovered?"

Consider BioNTech. Rather than build general-purpose models, the company acquired the AI firm InstaDeep to embed decision models directly into its research on personalized cancer vaccines. Inside its clinical databases sit thousands of modelled RNA sequences that were tested or studied only once—singletons—or twice—doubletons—

before being set aside for lack of budget or priority at the time. Its AI platforms now read that internal history the way the Chao1 estimator reads a portfolio: by analyzing those orphan leads statistically, they point to where the unexplored regions of the biological landscape lie—the Innovation Dark Matter. BioNTech uses the weight of its rare data to wake dormant molecules and accelerate discovery, turning what was sleeping in the archive into active Knowledge Capital.

In the dashboard, the Innovation Dark Matter metrics should be displayed alongside the existing portfolio indicators. The Saturation Index provides a single number that the board can track over time. A declining saturation index means the organization is exploring new territory faster than it is saturating existing domains—a sign of healthy portfolio diversification. A steadily rising saturation index may signal that the portfolio is maturing and that deliberate diversification is needed.

The Innovation Dark Matter estimator does not tell you which domains to explore next. It tells you how much you have not yet seen.

That distinction—between prescription and awareness—is what makes it a compass instrument rather than a navigation order.

> **→The skipper who knows the river has unexplored channels makes different decisions than one who believes the chart is complete.**

Innovation Dark Matter as an Antidote to Knowledge Hiding

In Chapter 3, we confronted one of the most corrosive forces in organizational life: knowledge hiding. Catherine Connelly and her colleagues demonstrated that in survey after survey, a clear majority of employees admit to some form of knowledge withholding—evasive hiding, playing dumb, or rationalized hiding. The framework addresses knowledge hiding through measurement, governance, and incentives. But the Innovation Dark Matter estimator adds a uniquely powerful weapon to this arsenal: it makes knowledge hiding statistically visible.

Consider how knowledge hiding distorts the innovation landscape. When individuals or teams withhold insights, the organization's observed innovation portfolio (S_obs) shrinks—not because ideas do not exist, but because they are deliberately kept invisible. The Innovation Dark Matter, based on the Chao1 estimator, detects this distortion through its singleton and doubleton counts. In an organization with active knowledge hiding, the number of singletons (f1) rises disproportionately: ideas that should have been shared, built upon, and documented remain trapped in individual silos, appearing only once, if at all. The Unseen Gap widens—the Saturation Index drops. The numbers tell a story that surveys and interviews cannot: somewhere in this organization, knowledge is being actively withheld.

This is the strategic power of Innovation Dark Matter within the framework. Traditional approaches to knowledge hiding rely on self-reported surveys, which are notoriously unreliable—people who hide knowledge rarely admit to it. The Innovation Dark Matter bypasses self-reporting entirely. It analyzes the statistical footprint of the innovation portfolio and reveals the gap between what is visible and what should be visible. A persistently high Unseen Gap, especially when combined with a low Saturation Index, is a quantitative signal of obstructed knowledge flows.

The practical application is straightforward. When the dashboard shows an Innovation Dark Matter estimate significantly higher than the observed portfolio, the innovation governance team should investigate not only which domains remain unexplored (the exploration question), but also whether known domains are being underrepresented due to knowledge hiding (the transparency question). The Innovation Dark Matter metric thus serves a dual diagnostic function: it measures both the breadth of the innovation frontier and the health of the knowledge-sharing culture.

The Innovation Dark Matter does not merely count what is missing. In the context of the framework, it exposes the shadow cast by knowledge hiding—transforming a behavioural problem notoriously difficult to measure into a statistical signal that governance teams can act on.

- → **When the Unseen Gap narrows over successive measurement cycles, it is evidence that the organization's knowledge-sharing culture is improving.**
- → **When it widens, it is an early warning that knowledge hiding may be taking root.**

THE SKIPPER'S LOG

Position — Chao1 turns what the portfolio has not yet surfaced — Innovation Dark Matter — into a number governance can watch.

Sighted — The Unseen Gap doubles as a culture gauge: narrowing, knowledge is flowing; widening, hiding is taking root.

Charted — The estimator, its bias-corrected form, and three derived metrics built from nothing more exotic than singletons and doubletons.

Course — Count this cycle's singletons and doubletons and log the gap. Watch its direction across seasons, not its absolute value. The direction is the signal; the snapshot is only a curiosity.

Chapter 13: The Wind in the Sails

In 2011, Duolingo launched with a simple premise: make language learning feel like a game. No classrooms, no tuition fees, no rigid curricula. Just short lessons, immediate feedback, and a green owl that appeared to guilt-trip you if you missed a day.

Within three years, Duolingo had more active language learners than the entire US public school system. By 2023, it had more than 500 million registered users. The lessons themselves are not exceptional. The pedagogical content is competent, not revolutionary. What made Duolingo extraordinary was not what it taught. It was the mechanism that kept people coming back.

Streaks. Points. Leaderboards. The satisfaction of a perfect lesson. The mild anxiety of a broken streak. The social nudge of watching a friend overtake you in the weekly rankings. None of these is a learning tool. They are motivational tools. And they turned a learning platform into one of the most widely used applications in human history.

The answer to what a language-learning app has to do with innovation management is: everything.

It would be easy to draw the wrong lesson here. Gamification is not a guarantee; the graveyard of consumer software is full of apps that had streaks, points, and leaderboards and died unmourned. Mechanics bolted onto a product nobody wanted only make the abandonment faster. What separated Duolingo from those failures is that the motivation sat on top of something people genuinely valued—a free, low-friction way to learn a language. The mechanics did not create the value; they made an existing value impossible to put down. Hold on to that distinction, because it decides where, in the innovation lifecycle, gamification earns its place—and the answer, as we will see, is at the very end of it, where an addressable market becomes an addressed one.

The hardest problem in innovation is not generating ideas. It is sustaining the behaviours—the documenting, the sharing, the filing of failure narratives, the honest post-mortems, the cross-team brokering—that turn ideas into institutional knowledge. S4IL provides the measurement architecture. The four capitals provide the diagnostic framework. The ROI^2 formula provides the language for the boardroom.

But none of it works if the people inside the organization do not engage with it. And engagement is not a cultural aspiration. It is a design problem.

Innovation management has borrowed extensively from product design, agile methodology, finance, and strategy. It has borrowed almost nothing from the science of human motivation—the field that Duolingo, Strava, Peloton, and a thousand other companies have used to change human behaviour at scale. That field has a name: gamification. And it has a rigorous architecture that goes far beyond points and badges.

Gamification is not new to business. Sales leaderboards, employee recognition programs, loyalty schemes—these are all crude applications of motivational mechanics. What has changed is our understanding of why they work, when they stop working, and how to design them so that the motivation they create is durable rather than manipulative.

Used internally, these mechanisms are what allow an innovation culture to take root and persist through leadership changes, budget cycles, and the quarterly entropy that kills most organizational initiatives. Used externally, they are equally powerful: crowdsourcing platforms succeed because they embed Ownership Mechanics that make contributors feel that what they are creating is genuinely theirs. Open-source communities thrive because they activate both Social Influence and Epic Meaning simultaneously. The most successful corporate innovation challenges—the ones that generate thousands of submissions from employees who had no formal obligation to participate—are not successful because of the prize. They are successful because of the motivational architecture.

After years of implementing S4IL across organizations in multiple industries, I tested several motivational frameworks. Some were too simple—points and badges that created engagement for six weeks and then became invisible. Others were too complex to maintain without dedicated resources. Over time, I converged on one framework that was both comprehensive and practical. It had already mapped the full motivational architecture of human engagement. Its integration into S4IL was not a design decision—it was a discovery. The framework already described exactly what S4IL needed.

It is called **Octalysis.** It was developed by Yu-kai Chou, a gamification pioneer who spent years systematically cataloguing why people engage with systems—and why they stop. The name comes from the octagonal structure of its eight core motivational drives. Understanding those drives is not an academic exercise. It is the missing piece that transforms a measurement system into a movement.

Where this sits on the compass. Octalysis is an instrument of the last phase, How to Get Adopted. It measures one thing: whether the motivation built around an innovation is strong enough to convert an addressable market into an addressed one—internally, the adoption of a new practice; externally, the adoption of a new product. It has nothing to say about whether the territory was worth entering, whether the idea was the right one, or whether the thing actually works; Chao1, prioritization, and validation settled those upstream. Used alone it produces engagement without substance—the streaks-on-a-dead-app failure from the start of this chapter. Fragmented across the eight core drives and combined with a value proposition people already want, it turns latent demand into measured behaviour. Its readings feed the Relational Capital behind the Growth needle: an innovation that is adopted is one that has finally begun to pay.

The Eight Core Drives

When applied to innovation management and S4IL adoption, the eight Core Drives operate as follows:

- **Core Drive 1: Epic Meaning and Calling.** People engage when they believe they are part of something greater than themselves. In innovation management, this means connecting individual contributions to the organization's larger mission. When a researcher understands that documenting a failed experiment contributes to the organization's collective intelligence, the act of documentation transforms from an administrative burden into a meaningful contribution. S4IL activates this drive by making the cumulative impact of individual contributions visible on the innovation dashboard.
- **Core Drive 2: Development and Accomplishment.** The internal drive to make progress, develop skills, and achieve mastery. Innovation programs that provide clear milestones, skill progression paths, and visible markers of achievement sustain engagement far longer than those that treat every contribution identically. InnoPoints tiers—from Innovation

Scout to Innovation Master—activate this drive by providing a sense of growth and progression.

- **Core Drive 3: Empowerment of Creativity and Feedback.** People are most engaged when they can express creativity and receive immediate feedback on their choices. Innovation challenges that allow participants to shape the problem space—not just respond to a pre-defined brief—activate this drive. The framework supports empowerment by giving innovation teams real-time visibility into how their work affects the four capitals, creating a feedback loop between action and impact.
- **Core Drive 4: Ownership and Possession.** People value things more when they feel a sense of ownership. In innovation, this means that contributors who can see their ideas tracked through the pipeline—from submission to evaluation to pilot to outcome—remain engaged far longer than those whose ideas disappear into a black box. The S4IL memory system activates this drive by preserving the provenance of every contribution and making that history accessible.
- **Core Drive 5: Social Influence and Relatedness.** People are motivated by social dynamics—mentorship, competition, companionship, and the desire for social acceptance. Innovation leaderboards, team challenges, and cross-departmental collaboration events activate this drive. The S4IL collaboration density metric provides the data needed to design social interactions that build Relational Capital.
- **Core Drive 6: Scarcity and Impatience.** People want what they cannot easily have. Time-limited innovation challenges, exclusive access to innovation resources for top contributors, and limited-slot pilot programs all activate this drive. When used ethically, scarcity creates urgency and focus. When overused, it creates anxiety and shortcuts.

- **Core Drive 7: Unpredictability and Curiosity.** People are drawn to the unknown. Innovation, by its nature, involves uncertainty, but most innovation programs try to minimize it. The Octalysis perspective suggests the opposite: designing moments of productive surprise—unexpected connections between projects, serendipitous cross-team matches, or random innovation prompts—that keep participants curious and engaged.
- **Core Drive 8: Loss and Avoidance.** People are motivated to avoid negative outcomes. In innovation, this means making the cost of inaction visible. The S4IL Innovation Tax calculation—showing the annual cost of duplication, coordination failure, decision delay, and amnesia—activates this drive by framing non-participation as a measurable loss rather than a passive choice.

White Hat and Black Hat Motivation

The eight Core Drives are divided into two categories that determine the quality of engagement:

White Hat Core Drives (Epic Meaning, Accomplishment, and Empowerment) create positive, intrinsic motivation. People engaged through White Hat drives feel good about their participation. They experience purpose, mastery, and autonomy. White Hat engagement is sustainable over long periods because it aligns with people's deeper psychological needs.

Black Hat Core Drives (Scarcity, Unpredictability, and Avoidance) create urgent, extrinsic motivation. People engaged through Black Hat drives act quickly but may feel manipulated or anxious over time. Black

Hat engagement is powerful for short-term activation but unsustainable as a primary strategy.

The remaining drives—Ownership and Social Influence—sit between the two categories and can be deployed in either direction depending on implementation.

For S4IL adoption, the design principle is clear: build the foundation on White Hat drives and use Black Hat drives sparingly for activation moments. An innovation program that relies primarily on scarcity and loss avoidance will generate compliance but not commitment. An innovation program built on epic meaning, accomplishment, and creative empowerment will generate the sustained engagement that organizational memory requires.

The Innovation Motivation Radar

Each of the eight Core Drives can be scored from 0 to 10 for any innovation program, producing an octagonal radar chart that reveals the program's motivational profile. A well-designed innovation system should score at least 5 on each White Hat drive and no more than 7 on any Black Hat drive. The total White Hat score should always exceed the total Black Hat score.

The radar chart becomes a diagnostic tool. When innovation participation declines in the third quarter—as it often does—the Octalysis radar can identify which motivational drives have weakened. Has the sense of epic meaning faded because leadership stopped communicating the innovation vision? Has the accomplishment drive stalled because the progression system offers no new milestones? Has social influence declined because cross-team events were cancelled?

The Octalysis radar should be assessed quarterly as part of the S4IL governance rhythm. It provides the motivational counterpart to the operational and value metrics described in earlier chapters. Innovation measurement without motivational measurement is like measuring wind speed without measuring crew morale—technically accurate but practically incomplete.

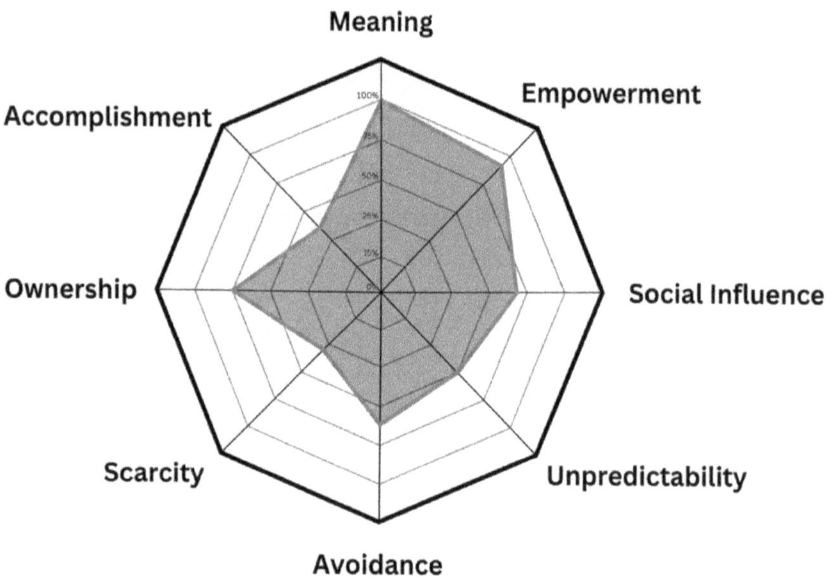

Figure: The Innovation Motivation Radar—the eight Core Drives read on one instrument.

Connecting the Octalysis to the Four Capitals

Each Core Drive maps naturally to one or more of the four capitals that form the backbone of the framework:

- **Knowledge Capital** is built through Epic Meaning (connecting contributions to purpose), Accomplishment (rewarding knowledge creation), and Ownership (preserving provenance of insights).
- **Relational Capital** is built through Social Influence (collaboration events, mentorship, team challenges) and Empowerment (giving teams autonomy to define innovation problems).
- **Process Capital** is built through Accomplishment (governance milestones), Scarcity (time-bounded innovation sprints), and Loss Avoidance (making the Innovation Tax visible).
- **Memory Capital** is built through Ownership (preserving contribution history), Unpredictability (surfacing forgotten insights), and Epic Meaning (framing memory as institutional legacy).

Octalysis and the Four Phases

The four phases present different motivational challenges—and require different Octalysis profiles.

In the **Where to Play** phase, the challenge is activation: getting people to contribute ideas, signals, and knowledge before any initiative is formally launched. The dominant drives are Epic Meaning and Calling—people contribute when they believe the mission matters—and Unpredictability and Curiosity, because open-ended exploration is inherently engaging. Loss Avoidance is supported by making the Dark Matter gap visible: the cost of not scanning, quantified by Chao1, becomes a motivational signal in its own right.

In the **How to Win** phase, the challenge is sustained engagement through failure. Most experiments fail, most prototypes are abandoned, and most teams lose momentum before reaching validated concepts.

The dominant drives are Development and Accomplishment—visible progress markers that sustain effort through the trough of experimentation—and Empowerment of Creativity and Feedback, which gives teams real-time visibility into how each experiment moves the ROI² needle. Scarcity drives focused sprints; Social Influence sustains team cohesion when individual results disappoint.

In the **How to Deliver** phase, the challenge shifts from motivation to discipline. The excitement of discovery is behind; the reward of adoption is not yet visible. Teams are building and iterating in a space that offers fewer intrinsic rewards. Ownership and possession keep contributors engaged by allowing them to track their work from prototype to product. Accomplishment sustains momentum through the delivery grind with clear milestones. Loss Avoidance—the visible cost of a delayed launch in a competitive market window—provides urgency without requiring artificial pressure.

In the **How to Get Adopted** phase, Octalysis reaches its full expression. This is where innovation becomes culture—where the behaviours that S4IL requires (documenting, sharing, filing failure narratives, honest post-mortems, cross-team brokering) must become habits rather than mandates. No governance framework, no measurement system, and no technology platform can produce this transformation through compliance alone. It requires motivation. Social Influence drives communities of practice and peer recognition. Epic Meaning sustains long-term engagement by connecting individual contributions to collective intelligence. Ownership ensures contributors can see the downstream impact of what they shared. Unpredictability surfaces the unexpected connection—the old project that saves the new one—that makes the memory system feel alive rather than archival. This is why How to Get Adopted is where Octalysis is most critical: it is the cycle that determines whether S4IL becomes a living system or another abandoned dashboard.

The practical implication is direct: when designing the motivational architecture for a specific initiative, identify its current phase first. The Octalysis drives to activate, and the InnoPoints mechanics to deploy, differ depending on whether the initiative is in exploration, experimentation, delivery, or adoption. A single motivational design applied uniformly across all four cycles will underperform. A cycle-sensitive Octalysis design will compound.

- → **A ship with a compass, a chart, and a capable crew still needs wind.**
- → **The Octalysis Framework is the wind in S4IL's sails—the motivational energy that keeps the crew engaged when the sea is calm, and the destination feels distant.**

Without it, even the most sophisticated measurement system risks becoming another abandoned dashboard.

The Skipper's Log

Position — A measured ship still needs wind. Motivation is the energy that keeps the crew working the instrument when the destination feels distant.

Sighted — White Hat drives that sustain, Black Hat drives that burn — and the failure of any single motivational design applied uniformly across all four cycles.

Charted — The eight Core Drives mapped to the four capitals, the Motivation Radar, and cycle-sensitive InnoPoints design.

Course — Audit your reward mechanics against one rule: every point, badge, and leaderboard must build one of the four capitals. What rewards nothing measures nothing — retire it.

Afterword: Get ready to sail through the uncertainty

The argument of this book can be stated in a single sentence: innovation becomes measurable when organizations learn to value what they remember, not just what they produce.

That sentence took eleven chapters to unpack, three frameworks to formalize, and a lifetime of navigating—both literal and professional—to believe. But the core conviction has not changed from the moment it first crystallized on a sailboat in the St. Lawrence, wrestling with a paper chart and a compass while the river moved faster than my pencil.

Part I diagnosed the disease. Organizations measure innovation with instruments designed for a different purpose: financial ROI, built for assembly lines and predictable cash flows, applied to a domain that is neither predictable nor linear. The result is not merely inaccuracy—it is systematic blindness. The things that matter most to long-term innovation capability—knowledge accumulated, relationships forged, processes refined, memory preserved—remain invisible to the dashboard. The corollary is equally true: what remains unmeasured remains unmanaged; what gets ignored gets forgotten.

Part II introduced the compass. The Four Capitals—Knowledge, Relational, Process, and Memory—provide the coordinate system. The Four Readings—Input, Throughput, Output, and Outcome—provide the measurement logic. Together, they create a navigation instrument that does not predict the weather but tells you, with honesty, where you are and what your vessel is capable of. That is more than most innovation dashboards have ever offered.

One needle points to growth—the value innovation creates today. The other points to readiness—the capability it builds for tomorrow. The organizations that read both needles navigate. The ones that read only one eventually run aground.

Part III built the instruments. S4IL—the methodology whose name encodes its own sailing metaphor—provides the implementation architecture: a scorecard, a governance model, an indicator catalogue, a formula, a portfolio aggregation logic, an extension to open innovation ecosystems, and a ninety-day journey that turns theory into practice without requiring anyone's permission to begin.

That architecture rests on four disciplines, each of which stands alone and each of which is diminished without the others. Innovation Seasons give the portfolio a boundary: a defined budget, a defined period, and a defined accountability. Signal Intelligence keeps the portfolio honest about the world outside: not predicting where it will go, but tracking whether it is still moving toward what the organization is building.

Organizational Memory ensures that nothing learned is lost: that every experiment, every failure, every near-miss feeds the next cycle rather than disappearing with the team that lived it. And ROI²—measured across financial, intangible, strategic, and learning dimensions—ensures that the whole enterprise remains legible to the governance bodies that fund it. Four disciplines. One compass.

The question is never whether you need them. The question is whether you build them before the storm arrives or after.

One honest caveat, of exactly the kind this book has spent its length telling you to demand. The Compass was built and proven in a particular kind of organization: research-heavy, knowledge-dense, with enough of its own history already written down to give the instrument something to read. It transfers most cleanly to organizations that look like that. In a small firm whose memory still lives entirely in people's heads, or a culture where nothing is recorded until it is safe to record, the framework is a hypothesis you are testing, not a guarantee you are cashing. That is not a flaw in the method. It is the method being honest about its own edge—which, after everything, is the whole point of carrying a compass instead of a map.

The biological parallel that runs through this book is deliberate. Organizations that build Memory Capital are doing something analogous to what resilient species do in nature: they are encoding survival knowledge into structures that outlast any individual. The DNA of organizational innovation is not a product or a patent. It is the accumulated, structured, retrievable record of what was tried, what was learned, and what the organization is genuinely capable of doing next.

Generative AI changes the economics of this enterprise. For the first time, the cost of retrieving, synthesizing, and contextualizing organizational knowledge has dropped to near zero. An AI copilot trained on twenty years of project archives can surface relevant precedents in seconds—not because the technology is magical, but because the underlying knowledge was preserved in a form that machines can read. The organizations that invested in Memory Capital before AI arrived are now discovering that their investment compounds. Those that did not are discovering that there is nothing for the AI to retrieve.

The compass does not eliminate uncertainty. It does not guarantee that the next innovation initiative will succeed. What it guarantees is that the organization will know where it stands—and that it will carry forward everything it learned from the last voyage into the next one. In a field that has spent decades confusing activity with progress and output with value, that is a transformation worth making.

The River, Again

It is October again. The river is the same—the St. Lawrence, two kilometres wide at this crossing, the Laurentian escarpment rust-orange in the afternoon light, the cargo ships moving in their deliberate, oceanic way. The beluga pods are less visible than they were a decade ago. Climate scientists who study this estuary can tell you exactly why, in the same way that the river pilots can tell you exactly where the ice forms first. Both kinds of knowledge are irreplaceable. Both are the product of years of patient attention to something vast and complex that will not simplify itself to accommodate impatience.

I have stood at this railing many times in the years it has taken to write this book. I have stood here thinking about pharmaceutical compounds that sat unrecognized in archives. About an engineer who found what she needed in a notebook that had been digitized four years earlier and never indexed. About fourteen CEOs on a racing sailboat in the Atlantic, discovering that what made the difference between a good crossing and a difficult one was not individual skill but the quality of collective memory—who remembered what, and whether that remembering was available when the wind shifted in the night.

The Compass, as I have described it throughout these pages, is not a new invention. Navigators have been using compasses for centuries, not because the compass tells them where to go—it does not—but because it tells them where they are. The instrument does not replace judgment. It provides the orientation that makes judgment possible.

What is new is the recognition—emerging slowly, unevenly, in organizations that are paying attention—that innovation management requires the same orientation. Not a guarantee of where you will end up. Not a formula that converts investment into output. But an honest, continuously updated picture of where you are: what you know, what you have tried, what you have learned, what your organization is genuinely capable of doing next.

The biological parallel that I have returned to throughout this book is not accidental. Organisms that survive in complex, changing environments do so not primarily through strength or speed but through the quality of their learning. The immune system remembers every pathogen it has encountered; the next encounter triggers not a blind response but an informed one, calibrated by experience. The nervous system builds models of its environment from accumulated sensory data; prediction precedes response. Evolution itself is a form of memory—the encoded history of what worked and what didn't, transmitted across generations without conscious intention.

Organizations are not organisms, and the analogy has limits. But the principle—that the capacity to remember and build on experience is the foundation of adaptive capability—applies with striking precision to the challenge of sustainable innovation. The organizations that will navigate the next decade most effectively are not necessarily the ones with the largest R&D budgets, the most sophisticated AI tools, or the most visionary leaders. They are the organizations that have built the memory infrastructure that allows their learning to compound.

The compass is clear. What comes next is harder: the organizational commitment to value memory as intensely as you value money, to measure learning as rigorously as you measure revenue, and to treat the knowledge your people carry as the strategic asset it has always been—but that no one thought to put on the balance sheet. The river is still there. The pilots are waiting. The question is whether you are ready to navigate by what your organization already knows—and to measure what that knowledge is worth.

The Promise of Measured Innovation

The journey from Chapter 1's diagnosis of the innovation measurement crisis to Chapter 13's motivational architecture covers substantial ground. It asks you to rethink what innovation is (a multi-capital investment, not a single-return gamble), to rethink how it is measured (four compass readings across four capitals, not a single ROI number), and to rethink who is responsible for it (everyone who creates, shares, or applies knowledge, not just the innovation team).

The framework is ambitious in scope but pragmatic in implementation. It does not require a massive technology deployment or a multi-year transformation program. It requires four things: a knowledge audit that reveals the current state, a curated set of indicators that make innovation health visible, a governance rhythm that connects measurement to decisions, and an organizational memory system—increasingly AI-enabled—that turns accumulated experience into compounding advantage.

The organizations that will thrive in the coming decade are not those with the biggest R&D budgets or the most sophisticated AI tools. They are the organizations that learn from their own experience—that remember what worked and why, what failed and why, and that use that accumulated wisdom to make better decisions faster, with less waste and more impact.

If you keep one line from these pages, keep the chain: generative AI made organizational memory possible at scale, and organizational memory makes ROI^2 possible at all. Every instrument in this book—the capitals, the readings, the tax, the dark matter, the season—is that sentence, unpacked. The theatre ran for decades because the audit was impossible. It no longer is.

APPENDICES

Appendix A: The ROI² Indicator Catalogue

The Complete Compass Indicator Set

This catalogue represents the most comprehensive set of innovation measurement indicators the author has been able to assemble from thirty years of practice. It is a living document. Innovation practitioners are encouraged to suggest additional indicators for inclusion in future editions. Indicators are measured at the cadence of each initiative's investment cycle—not on a fixed calendar frequency—as described in Chapter 9.

The following tables present the full Compass indicator set, organized by the four measurement categories: Inputs, Throughputs, Outputs, and Memory. Each indicator is defined with its measurement unit, data source, applicable horizons, and benchmark guidance. The indicator set is designed to be adoptable in modules: organizations beginning a Compass implementation should start with the Input and Output indicators, which require the least new data collection, and progressively add Throughput and Memory indicators as the measurement infrastructure matures.

Legend of the table:

Reading: I: Input, TP: Throughput, OC: Outcome, OT: Output. ST: Strategic, OM: Organizational Memory, PT: Portfolio

Type: VA: Value Metric, VY: Vanity Metric (shaded background for Vanity Metric that can become Value Metric depending on the context)

Reading	Capital	Indicator Name	Description	Formula / Metric	Focus	Orientation	H1	H2	H3	Type	Book Ref
I	Process	**R&D Investment Intensity**	Total R&D spend as proportion of revenue	R&D Expenditure / Total Revenue	R&D	READ Y	●	●	○	VY	Ch2, Ch7
I	Process	**Innovation Budget Allocation**	Dedicated innovation budget beyond BAU R&D	Innovation Budget / Total Operating Budget	INNO	READ Y	●	●	●	VY	Ch7
I	Knowledge	**TAM Utilization Rate**	Proportion of total addressable market being targeted	Targeted Market / Total Addressable Market	INNO	GROW	○	●	●	VA	Ch7
I	Process	**Cost of Opportunity Pursued**	Investment committed per innovation opportunity	Total Investment / Number of Opportunities	INNO	READ Y	●	●	○	VA	Ch7
I	Relational	**External Partnership Investment**	Spend on open innovation partnerships and collaborations	Partnership Spend / Innovation Budget	INNO	GROW	○	●	●	VA	Ch8
I	Knowledge	**Talent Acquisition for Innovation**	Proportion of new hires with innovation-relevant skills	Innovation Hires / Total New Hires	R&D	READ Y	●	●	○	VY	Ch4
I	Process	**Innovation Infrastructure Spend**	Investment in innovation labs, tools, and platforms	Infrastructure Spend / Innovation Budget	R&D	READ Y	●	○	—	VY	Ch7
I	Knowledge	**Training Investment per Innovator**	Learning & development spend allocated to innovation practitioners	Innovation Training Spend / Number of Practitioners	R&D	READ Y	●	●	○	VY	Ch4, Ch11
I	Relational	**Customer Co-creation Investment**	Resources allocated to customer involvement in innovation	Co-creation Spend / Innovation Budget	INNO	GROW	○	●	●	VA	Ch8
I	Memory	**Knowledge Management Investment**	Spend on systems to capture and retrieve institutional knowledge	KM System Spend / Innovation Budget	R&D	READ Y	●	●	●	VA	Ch3, Ch5
I	Process	**Exploration vs Exploitation Ratio**	Balance of spending between new exploration and existing optimization	Exploration Spend / Exploitation Spend	INNO	GROW	●	●	●	VA	Ch7
I	Process	**Time Allocated to Innovation**	Proportion of employee time formally allocated to innovation activities	Innovation Time / Total Working Time	R&D	READ Y	●	●	○	VY	Ch7
I	Relational	**Ecosystem Access Investment**	Investment in accelerators, incubators, and ecosystem participation	Ecosystem Spend / Innovation Budget	INNO	GROW	○	●	●	VY	Ch8

Reading	Capital	Indicator Name	Description	Formula / Metric	Focus	Orientation	H1	H2	H3	Type	Book Ref
I	Knowledge	**Data & Insight Acquisition Cost**	Spend on market intelligence, research, and data for innovation decisions	Data Acquisition Spend / Innovation Budget	R&D	READ Y	•	•	○	VY	Ch7
I	Process	**Portfolio Diversity Investment**	Distribution of investment across Horizon 1, 2, and 3 initiatives	H3 Spend / Total Innovation Spend	INNO	GROW	•	•	•	VA	Ch7, Ch10
I	Memory	**Legacy System Remediation Spend**	Investment to modernize systems that impede innovation	Remediation Spend / IT Budget	R&D	READ Y	•	○	—	VA	Ch5
I	Relational	**Supplier Innovation Fund**	Budget allocated for supplier-driven innovation initiatives	Supplier Innovation Fund / Procurement Budget	INNO	GROW	○	•	•	VY	Ch8
I	Knowledge	**Intellectual Property Filing Budget**	Resources dedicated to protecting innovation outputs	IP Filing Spend / Innovation Budget	R&D	GROW	•	•	○	VY	Ch7
I	Process	**Rapid Prototyping Capacity**	Number of prototyping resources (labs, 3D printers, dev sprints) available	Prototyping Resources / Active Projects	R&D	READ Y	•	•	○	VA	Ch7
I	Relational	**Cross-functional Team Investment**	Resources dedicated to multidisciplinar y innovation teams	Cross-functional Team Budget / Innovation Budget	INNO	READ Y	•	•	○	VY	Ch4, Ch8
I	Process	**Innovation Governance Overhead**	Cost of managing the innovation funnel (stage gates, reviews)	Governance Cost / Innovation Budget	R&D	READ Y	•	•	○	VA	Ch7
I	Knowledge	**Horizon 3 Scouting Budget**	Dedicated investment in breakthrough/d isruptive opportunity identification	H3 Scouting Spend / Innovation Budget	INNO	GROW	—	○	•	VA	Ch7, Ch10
I	Memory	**Innovation Onboarding Investment**	Resources to bring new team members up to speed on innovation history	Onboarding Investment / New Innovator Count	R&D	READ Y	•	•	○	VA	Ch3, Ch5
I	Process	**Fail-Fast Budget Allocation**	Dedicated budget for experiments expected to have high failure rates	Fail-Fast Budget / Total Innovation Budget	INNO	GROW	○	•	•	VA	Ch7
I	Relational	**Academic Research Partnerships**	Investment in university/rese arch institution collaborations	Academic Partnership Spend / R&D Budget	R&D	GROW	○	•	•	VY	Ch8
TP	Process	**Idea Conversion Rate**	Proportion of submitted ideas progressing beyond initial screening	Ideas Advancing / Total Ideas Submitted	INNO	GROW	•	•	○	VA	Ch7

Reading	Capital	Indicator Name	Description	Formula / Metric	Focus	Orientation	H1	H2	H3	Type	Book Ref
TP	Relational	**Collaboration Index**	Intensity of cross-functional interaction during innovation process	Cross-team Interactions / Total Project Interactions	INNO	GROW	•	•	•	VY	Ch4, Ch8
TP	Process	**Experiment Success Ratio**	Proportion of experiments yielding actionable results	Successful Experiments / Total Experiments	R&D	READY	•	•	○	VA	Ch7
TP	Process	**Process Efficiency Index**	Ratio of value-adding activities to total innovation activities	Value-Add Activities / Total Activities	R&D	READY	•	○	—	VY	Ch7
TP	Process	**Stage-Gate Velocity**	Average time for an initiative to pass through each stage gate	Total Stage Time / Number of Stage Gates Passed	R&D	READY	•	•	○	VA	Ch7
TP	Process	**Pivot Rate**	Frequency of strategic direction changes within active projects	Number of Pivots / Active Projects	INNO	GROW	○	•	•	VA	Ch7
TP	Knowledge	**Insight Generation Rate**	Number of validated customer/market insights produced per period	Validated Insights / Time Period	INNO	GROW	•	•	•	VA	Ch7
TP	Process	**Prototype Cycle Time**	Average time from concept to testable prototype	Days from Concept to Prototype	R&D	READY	•	•	○	VA	Ch7
TP	Relational	**Stakeholder Engagement Score**	Level of active participation from key stakeholders in innovation	Engaged Stakeholders / Total Required Stakeholders	INNO	READY	•	•	○	VY	Ch4, Ch8
TP	Process	**Innovation Pipeline Throughput**	Number of initiatives moving through pipeline stages per period	Initiatives Advanced / Time Period	INNO	GROW	•	•	○	VY	Ch7
TP	Knowledge	**Knowledge Hiding Incidence Rate**	Measured frequency of evasive hiding, playing dumb, or rationalized hiding	Hiding Incidents Detected / Total Knowledge Requests	R&D	READY	•	•	•	VA	Ch3
TP	Knowledge	**Knowledge Accessibility Score**	Ease of retrieving institutional knowledge when needed	Successful Retrievals / Total Knowledge Requests	R&D	READY	•	•	•	VA	Ch3, Ch5
TP	Process	**Coordination Tax Rate**	Overhead cost of aligning cross-team innovation efforts	Coordination Overhead / Total Project Cost	R&D	READY	•	•	○	VA	Ch5
TP	Memory	**Duplication Tax Rate**	Cost of redundant parallel efforts due to poor organizational memory	Duplicated Effort Cost / Total Innovation Spend	R&D	READY	•	•	•	VA	Ch5
TP	Process	**Decision Tax Rate**	Delay cost from slow or unclear innovation governance decisions	Decision Delay Cost / Total Project Value	R&D	READY	•	•	○	VA	Ch5

Reading	Capital	Indicator Name	Description	Formula / Metric	Focus	Orientation	H1	H2	H3	Type	Book Ref
TP	Memory	**Amnesia Tax Rate**	Cost of relearning what the organization previously knew	Relearning Cost / Total Innovation Spend	R&D	READ Y	●	●	●	VA	Ch5
TP	Relational	**Open Innovation Contribution Rate**	Volume and quality of contributions from external innovation partners	External Contributions / Total Contributions	INNO	GROW	○	●	●	VA	Ch8
TP	Process	**Resource Utilization Efficiency**	Productive use of allocated innovation resources	Productive Hours / Allocated Hours	R&D	READ Y	●	○	—	VY	Ch7
TP	Knowledge	**Experiment Learning Velocity**	Speed at which validated learnings are produced from experiments	Validated Learnings / Experiment Duration	R&D	GROW	●	●	●	VA	Ch7
TP	Process	**Kill Rate**	Proportion of initiatives terminated at stage gates (healthy portfolio pruning)	Killed Initiatives / Total Reviewed	INNO	READ Y	●	●	○	VA	Ch7
TP	Relational	**Innovation Champion Activation**	Proportion of designated champions actively leading initiatives	Active Champions / Designated Champions	INNO	READ Y	●	●	○	VA	Ch4, Ch9
TP	Process	**Hypothesis Validation Rate**	Proportion of hypotheses tested per innovation cycle	Hypotheses Tested / Hypotheses Defined	R&D	GROW	●	●	●	VA	Ch7
TP	Memory	**Knowledge Reuse in Process**	Frequency of leveraging prior innovation learnings in current projects	Reuse Instances / Total Design Decisions	R&D	READ Y	●	●	●	VA	Ch3, Ch5
TP	Relational	**Cross-pollination Rate**	Transfer of ideas and methods between business units or teams	Cross-unit Transfers / Total Innovation Activities	INNO	GROW	●	●	○	VA	Ch4, Ch8
TP	Process	**Innovation Backlog Health**	Ratio of ready-to-execute items to total backlog	Ready Items / Total Backlog Items	R&D	READ Y	●	●	○	VY	Ch7
TP	Knowledge	**Technical Feasibility Validation Speed**	Time to determine technical viability of a concept	Days to Feasibility Assessment	R&D	READ Y	●	●	○	VA	Ch7
TP	Relational	**Mentorship Engagement Rate**	Proportion of innovation practitioners receiving active mentorship	Mentored Practitioners / Total Practitioners	INNO	READ Y	●	●	○	VY	Ch4, Ch11
TP	Process	**Gamification Engagement Rate**	Participation rate in gamified innovation activities (Octalysis-driven)	Engaged Participants / Total Eligible Participants	INNO	READ Y	●	●	●	VA	Ch11
OT	Knowledge	**Product Innovation Rate**	Proportion of revenue from products launched within defined period	New Product Revenue / Total Revenue	R&D	GROW	●	●	○	VA	Ch7

Reading	Capital	Indicator Name	Description	Formula / Metric	Focus	Orientation	H1	H2	H3	Type	Book Ref
OT	**Knowledge**	**Patent Utilization Ratio**	Proportion of patents actively used in products or licensing	Active Patents / Total Patents	R&D	GROW	•	•	○	VA	Ch7
OT	**Process**	**IP Licensing Revenue**	Income from licensing intellectual property to third parties	Licensing Revenue / Total Revenue	R&D	GROW	○	•	•	VA	Ch7
OT	**Process**	**Cost Reduction from Innovation**	Savings achieved through process or product innovations	Cost Savings / Pre-innovation Cost	R&D	READ Y	•	○	—	VA	Ch7
OT	**Process**	**Process Automation Impact**	Efficiency gains from automating previously manual innovation processes	Automated Processes / Total Processes	R&D	READ Y	•	○	—	VA	Ch7
OT	**Knowledge**	**Knowledge Reuse Rate**	Frequency of leveraging existing knowledge assets in new outputs	Reused Assets / Total Assets Used	R&D	READ Y	•	•	•	VA	Ch3, Ch5
OT	**Knowledge**	**New-to-Market Innovations**	Count of innovations representing genuine market firsts	Market-first Launches / Total Launches	INNO	GROW	—	•	•	VA	Ch7
OT	**Knowledge**	**New-to-Firm Innovations**	Count of innovations new to the organization but not to market	Firm-first Launches / Total Launches	INNO	GROW	•	•	○	VA	Ch7
OT	**Process**	**Time-to-Market**	Average duration from concept approval to market launch	Days from Approval to Launch	R&D	READ Y	•	•	○	VA	Ch7
OT	**Relational**	**Co-created Outputs**	Proportion of outputs developed with external partners	Co-created Outputs / Total Outputs	INNO	GROW	○	•	•	VA	Ch8
OT	**Process**	**Minimum Viable Product Delivery Rate**	Proportion of projects delivering an MVP within target timeline	On-time MVPs / Total MVPs Planned	R&D	READ Y	•	•	○	VA	Ch7
OT	**Knowledge**	**Innovation Revenue Contribution**	Total revenue attributable to innovations within defined period	Innovation Revenue / Total Revenue	INNO	GROW	•	•	•	VA	Ch7
OT	**Process**	**Spin-off Creation Rate**	Number of new ventures or business units created from innovation	Spin-offs Created / Active H3 Initiatives	INNO	GROW	—	○	•	VA	Ch7
OT	**Knowledge**	**Publications & Thought Leadership**	Innovation-related publications, conference papers, or public contributions	Publications / Innovation Practitioners	R&D	GROW	○	•	•	VY	Ch4

Reading	Capital	Indicator Name	Description	Formula / Metric	Focus	Orientation	H1	H2	H3	Type	Book Ref
OT	Relational	**Platform Adoption Rate**	Uptake of innovation platforms or tools by target users	Active Users / Target User Base	INNO	GROW	•	•	○	VA	Ch7, Ch11
OT	Process	**Regulatory Approval Success Rate**	Proportion of innovations clearing regulatory hurdles	Approved Innovations / Submitted for Approval	R&D	READY	•	•	○	VA	Ch7
OT	Knowledge	**Technical Debt Reduction**	Innovation outputs that reduce accumulated technical debt	Tech Debt Retired / Total Tech Debt	R&D	READY	•	○	—	VA	Ch5
OT	Memory	**Documented Innovation Outputs**	Proportion of completed innovations with full documentation captured	Documented Outputs / Total Outputs	R&D	READY	•	•	•	VA	Ch3, Ch5
OT	Process	**Service Innovation Index**	Non-product innovations: new services, business models, or delivery methods	Service Innovations / Total Innovations	INNO	GROW	•	•	•	VA	Ch7
OT	Relational	**Customer-Validated Outputs**	Proportion of outputs validated through customer testing before launch	Customer-Validated / Total Outputs	INNO	GROW	•	•	○	VA	Ch7, Ch8
OT	Process	**Innovation Yield**	Revenue generated per unit of innovation investment	Innovation Revenue / Innovation Spend	INNO	GROW	•	•	•	VA	Ch2, Ch7
OT	Knowledge	**IP Portfolio Growth Rate**	Net increase in intellectual property assets over period	(New IP - Expired IP) / Starting IP Portfolio	R&D	GROW	•	•	•	VY	Ch7
OT	Process	**Innovation Failure Recovery Rate**	Speed and effectiveness of pivoting or salvaging failed initiatives	Recovered Value / Total Failed Initiative Investment	INNO	READY	•	•	•	VA	Ch7
OT	Relational	**Ecosystem Output Multiplier**	Additional value created by ecosystem partners from shared innovation	Ecosystem-derived Value / Direct Innovation Value	INNO	GROW	○	•	•	VA	Ch8
OT	Memory	**Lessons Learned Capture Rate**	Proportion of completed projects with formal lessons documented	Projects with Lessons / Total Completed Projects	R&D	READY	•	•	•	VA	Ch3, Ch5
OT	Process	**Standard-Setting Contributions**	Organization's role in defining industry standards from innovation	Standards Influenced / Industry Standards Set	INNO	GROW	—	○	•	VA	Ch8
OT	Knowledge	**Breakthrough Innovation Count**	Innovations that create new market categories or redefine existing ones	Breakthrough Launches / Total Launches	INNO	GROW	—	○	•	VY	Ch7, Ch10

Reading	Capital	Indicator Name	Description	Formula / Metric	Focus	Orientation	H1	H2	H3	Type	Book Ref
OT	Process	**Internal Innovation Adoption Rate**	Uptake of internally developed innovations across business units	Adopting Units / Total Business Units	INNO	READY	●	●	○	VA	Ch7
OC	Knowledge	**Market Share Growth from Innovation**	Incremental market share attributable to innovation outputs	(New Market Share - Previous) / Previous Market Share	INNO	GROW	●	●	○	VA	Ch7
OC	Relational	**Customer Adoption Rate**	Speed and depth of customer uptake of innovation outputs	Adopting Customers / Target Customer Base	INNO	GROW	●	●	○	VA	Ch7
OC	Relational	**Ecosystem Leverage Index**	Value multiplier from ecosystem partnerships	Ecosystem-derived Revenue / Partnership Investment	INNO	GROW	○	●	●	VA	Ch8
OC	Process	**Environmental Efficiency Gain**	Sustainability improvements from innovation	Resource Reduction / Pre-innovation Resource Use	R&D	GROW	●	●	●	VA	Ch7
OC	Knowledge	**Failed Experiment Insight Index**	Value of insights extracted from unsuccessful experiments	Actionable Insights from Failures / Total Failed Experiments	R&D	READY	●	●	●	VA	Ch7
OC	Knowledge	**Revenue per Innovation Dollar**	Revenue return on each dollar invested in innovation	Innovation-attributed Revenue / Innovation Spend	INNO	GROW	●	●	●	VA	Ch2, Ch7
OC	Process	**Operational Excellence Uplift**	Efficiency improvements in operations resulting from innovation	Post-innovation Efficiency / Pre-innovation Efficiency	R&D	READY	●	○	—	VA	Ch7
OC	Relational	**Net Promoter Score Lift from Innovation**	NPS improvement attributable to innovation outputs	Post-launch NPS - Pre-launch NPS	INNO	GROW	●	●	○	VY	Ch7
OC	Relational	**Brand Perception Shift**	Change in brand perception due to innovation reputation	Post-innovation Brand Score - Pre-innovation Score	INNO	GROW	○	●	●	VY	Ch7
OC	Knowledge	**Competitive Moat Depth**	Sustained competitive advantage from accumulated innovation capital	Innovation-based Advantages / Total Competitive Factors	INNO	GROW	○	●	●	VA	Ch7, Ch10
OC	Process	**Innovation ROI (ROI³)**	Comprehensive return on innovation investment across all capitals	Total Innovation Value Created / Total Innovation Investment	INNO	GROW	●	●	●	VA	Ch2, Ch7, Ch9
OC	Memory	**Organizational Learning Velocity**	Speed at which the organization improves innovation performance over time	Performance Improvement Rate / Time Period	R&D	GROW	●	●	●	VA	Ch3, Ch5

Reading	Capital	Indicator Name	Description	Formula / Metric	Focus	Orientation	H1	H2	H3	Type	Book Ref
OC	Relational	**Talent Attraction from Innovation**	Ability to attract top talent due to innovation reputation	Innovation-motivated Hires / Total Hires	INNO	GROW	○	•	•	VY	Ch4
OC	Process	**Innovation Portfolio Balance Score**	Health of H1/H2/H3 balance relative to strategic intent	Actual H1:H2:H3 Ratio vs Target Ratio	INNO	READ Y	•	•	•	VA	Ch7, Ch9
OC	Knowledge	**New Market Creation**	Revenue from markets that did not exist before the innovation	New Market Revenue / Total Innovation Revenue	INNO	GROW	—	○	•	VA	Ch7
OC	Process	**Regulatory Advantage Gained**	First-mover advantages in regulatory or compliance domains	Regulatory Advantages / Innovation Outputs in Regulated Domains	INNO	GROW	○	•	•	VA	Ch7
OC	Relational	**Customer Lifetime Value Uplift**	Increase in CLV attributable to innovation	(New CLV - Previous CLV) / Previous CLV	INNO	GROW	•	•	○	VA	Ch7
OC	Process	**Speed-to-Scale**	Time from successful pilot to full-scale deployment	Days from Pilot Success to Scale	INNO	GROW	•	•	○	VA	Ch7
OC	Knowledge	**Innovation Premium in Valuation**	Market valuation premium attributable to innovation capabilities	Innovation Premium / Total Market Cap	INNO	GROW	○	•	•	VY	Ch7
OC	Memory	**Institutional Knowledge Compound Return**	Value growth from accumulated innovation learnings over multiple cycles	Current Cycle Value / First Cycle Value (compounded)	R&D	GROW	•	•	•	VA	Ch3, Ch5
OC	Relational	**Strategic Partner Value Creation**	Value generated through strategic innovation partnerships	Partnership Value / Partnership Investment	INNO	GROW	○	•	•	VA	Ch8
OC	Process	**Innovation Culture Score**	Measured innovation culture health across the organization	Culture Survey Innovation Dimensions / Total Possible Score	INNO	READ Y	•	•	•	VY	Ch4, Ch11
OC	Knowledge	**Adjacent Market Penetration**	Success in entering markets adjacent to core business through innovation	Adjacent Market Revenue / Total Revenue	INNO	GROW	○	•	•	VA	Ch7
OC	Process	**Cost of Innovation Failure**	Average cost when an initiative fails (lower is healthier)	Total Failed Initiative Costs / Number of Failures	R&D	READ Y	•	•	○	VA	Ch7
OC	Relational	**Social Impact from Innovation**	Measurable social/environ mental impact from innovation outputs	Impact Metrics Achieved / Impact Metrics Targeted	INNO	GROW	○	•	•	VA	Ch7
OC	Memory	**Innovation Maturity Progression**	Movement along an innovation capability maturity model	Current Maturity Level - Previous Level	R&D	READ Y	•	•	•	VA	Ch9

Reading	Capital	Indicator Name	Description	Formula / Metric	Focus	Orientation	H1	H2	H3	Type	Book Ref
OC	Knowledge	**Technology Readiness Advancement**	Progression of technologies along TRL scale due to innovation investment	Average TRL Improvement / Innovation Cycle	R&D	GROW	○	●	●	VA	Ch7
OC	Process	**Portfolio Optionality Value**	Strategic option value embedded in the innovation portfolio	NPV of Options / Current Investment	INNO	GROW	○	●	●	VA	Ch7, Ch10
ST	Knowledge	**Competitive Resilience Index**	Ability to withstand competitive disruption through innovation	Innovation-protected Revenue / Total Revenue	INNO	GROW	○	●	●	VA	Ch7
ST	Relational	**Ecosystem Position Strength**	Centrality and influence within innovation ecosystem	Ecosystem Influence Score / Max Possible Score	INNO	GROW	○	●	●	VY	Ch8
ST	Process	**Strategic Alignment Index**	Degree to which innovation portfolio aligns with corporate strategy	Strategically Aligned Initiatives / Total Initiatives	INNO	READ Y	●	●	●	VA	Ch7, Ch9
ST	Process	**Transformatio n Impact Score**	Contribution of innovation to organizational transformation	Transformation Milestones Achieved / Planned	INNO	GROW	○	●	●	VA	Ch7
ST	Knowledge	**IP Portfolio Strength**	Strategic value and defensibility of IP assets	Strategically Critical Patents / Total Patents	R&D	GROW	●	●	●	VY	Ch7
ST	Process	**Innovation Governance Effectiveness**	Quality and speed of innovation governance decisions	Decisions Within SLA / Total Decisions	R&D	READ Y	●	●	○	VA	Ch7, Ch9
ST	Knowledge	**Disruptive Potential Score**	Portfolio's potential to disrupt existing markets or create new ones	Disruptive Initiatives / Total Portfolio	INNO	GROW	—	○	●	VY	Ch7, Ch10
ST	Process	**Innovation Strategy Coherence**	Internal consistency of innovation strategy across business units	Coherence Score from Assessment / Max Score	INNO	READ Y	●	●	●	VA	Ch9
ST	Relational	**Board Innovation Engagement**	Level of board-level attention and support for innovation	Board Agenda Innovation Time / Total Board Time	INNO	READ Y	●	●	●	VY	Ch9
ST	Process	**Ambidexterity Index**	Organization's ability to simultaneously exploit and explore	Explore Investment / Exploit Investment (vs Target Ratio)	INNO	GROW	●	●	●	VA	Ch7
ST	Knowledge	**Future-readiness Score**	Assessment of preparedness for anticipated industry shifts	Capabilities vs Identified Future Needs	INNO	GROW	○	●	●	VY	Ch7, Ch10
ST	Process	**Innovation Risk-Return Profile**	Risk-adjusted return across the innovation portfolio	Weighted Portfolio Return / Portfolio Risk Score	INNO	GROW	●	●	●	VA	Ch7, Ch9

Reading	Capital	Indicator Name	Description	Formula / Metric	Focus	Orientation	H1	H2	H3	Type	Book Ref
ST	Relational	**Stakeholder Confidence in Innovation**	C-suite and board confidence in innovation function delivery	Confidence Survey Score / Max Score	INNO	READY	●	●	●	VY	Ch9
ST	Memory	**Strategic Memory Utilization**	Extent to which strategic innovation decisions draw on institutional memory	Memory-informed Decisions / Total Strategic Decisions	R&D	READY	●	●	●	VA	Ch3, Ch5, Ch9
ST	Process	**Investment Season Completeness**	Collective coverage of ROI^2 indicators across portfolio in each investment season	Indicators Covered / Indicators Selected for Season	INNO	READY	●	●	●	VA	Ch7, Ch9
OM	Knowledge	**Experiment Learning Ratio**	Learnings generated per experiment regardless of outcome	Validated Learnings / Total Experiments	R&D	GROW	●	●	●	VA	Ch7
OM	Knowledge	**Knowledge Diffusion Index**	Speed and breadth of innovation knowledge spreading across organization	Informed Stakeholders / Total Stakeholders	R&D	READY	●	●	●	VA	Ch3, Ch4
OM	Process	**Innovation Capability Maturity**	Assessed maturity level of innovation management capabilities	Capability Assessment Score / Max Score	R&D	READY	●	●	●	VA	Ch9
OM	Knowledge	**Learning Transfer Efficiency**	Effectiveness of transferring learnings from one project to another	Applied Learnings / Available Learnings	R&D	READY	●	●	●	VA	Ch3, Ch5
OM	Memory	**Memory Retention Rate**	Institutional knowledge retained after employee turnover	Knowledge Retained / Knowledge at Risk from Departures	R&D	READY	●	●	●	VA	Ch3, Ch5
OM	Memory	**Knowledge Retrieval Speed**	Time to locate and apply prior innovation insights	Average Retrieval Time (hours or days)	R&D	READY	●	●	●	VA	Ch3, Ch5
OM	Knowledge	**Innovation Literacy Rate**	Proportion of employees who understand innovation frameworks and vocabulary	Literate Employees / Total Employees	INNO	READY	●	●	○	VY	Ch4, Ch11
OM	Relational	**Peer Learning Network Density**	Strength of informal learning connections among innovation practitioners	Active Learning Connections / Possible Connections	INNO	READY	●	●	○	VY	Ch4
OM	Memory	**Post-mortem Completion Rate**	Proportion of completed/killed initiatives with formal post-mortem	Post-mortems Completed / Initiatives Ended	R&D	READY	●	●	●	VA	Ch3, Ch5
OM	Knowledge	**Absorptive Capacity Index**	Organization's ability to recognize, assimilate, and apply external knowledge	External Knowledge Applied / External Knowledge Accessed	INNO	GROW	○	●	●	VA	Ch4, Ch8

Reading	Capital	Indicator Name	Description	Formula / Metric	Focus	Orientation	H1	H2	H3	Type	Book Ref
OM	**Memory**	**Innovation Playbook Utilization**	Extent to which documented playbooks guide innovation practice	Playbook-guided Activities / Total Activities	R&D	READY	•	•	•	VA	Ch9
OM	**Process**	**Continuous Improvement Rate**	Frequency of process improvements within innovation function	Improvements Implemented / Time Period	R&D	READY	•	•	○	VA	Ch7
OM	**Knowledge**	**Knowledge Capital Growth Rate**	Net growth in the organization's knowledge assets	(New Knowledge Created - Knowledge Lost) / Starting Knowledge Base	R&D	GROW	•	•	•	VA	Ch4
OM	**Relational**	**Community of Practice Activity**	Engagement levels in innovation communities of practice	Active Participants / Total Community Members	INNO	READY	•	•	○	VY	Ch4, Ch8
OM	**Memory**	**Organizational Agility Index**	Speed of adapting innovation approach based on new learnings	Adaptation Implementations / Needed Adaptations	INNO	GROW	•	•	•	VA	Ch7
OM	**Process**	**Core Drive Activation Coverage**	Proportion of Octalysis core drives activated in innovation programs	Activated Core Drives / 8 Core Drives	INNO	READY	•	•	•	VA	Ch11
OM	**Knowledge**	**White Hat vs Black Hat Balance**	Ratio of intrinsic (White Hat) to extrinsic (Black Hat) motivation in programs	White Hat Drive Score / Black Hat Drive Score	INNO	READY	•	•	•	VA	Ch11
OM	**Memory**	**Innovation Story Repository Health**	Richness and accessibility of documented innovation narratives	Documented Stories / Total Significant Innovation Events	R&D	READY	•	•	•	VA	Ch3, Ch5
PT	**Knowledge**	**Unseen Innovation Gap**	Estimated undiscovered innovations using Chao1 biodiversity estimator	IDM - S_observed	INNO	GROW	○	•	•	VA	Ch10
PT	**Knowledge**	**Portfolio Saturation Index**	Observed innovation diversity as proportion of estimated total	S_observed / IDM	INNO	READY	○	•	•	VA	Ch10
PT	**Knowledge**	**Latent Asset Value**	Estimated value of undiscovered innovation potential	Unseen Gap × Average Innovation Value	INNO	GROW	—	○	•	VA	Ch10
PT	**Knowledge**	**Singleton Rate (f1)**	Proportion of innovation types observed only once — signals untapped diversity	Single-occurrence Types / Total Types Observed	R&D	GROW	○	•	•	VA	Ch10
PT	**Knowledge**	**Doubleton Rate (f2)**	Proportion of innovation types observed exactly twice — Chao1	Double-occurrence Types / Total Types Observed	R&D	READY	○	•	•	VA	Ch10

Reading	Capital	Indicator Name	Description	Formula / Metric	Focus	Orientation	H1	H2	H3	Type	Book Ref
			stability indicator								
PT	Process	**Portfolio Coverage Completeness**	Extent to which all selected ROI² indicators are covered across the portfolio	Covered Indicators / Selected Season Indicators	INNO	READY	•	•	•	VA	Ch7, Ch9, Ch10
PT	Process	**Innovation Type Diversity (Shannon)**	Shannon entropy of innovation types in portfolio — measures balance	-Σ(pi × ln(pi)) for each innovation type	INNO	GROW	•	•	•	VA	Ch10
PT	Process	**Portfolio Concentration Risk**	Gini coefficient of investment distribution across innovation types	Gini Coefficient of Investment Allocation	INNO	READY	•	•	•	VA	Ch10
PT	Process	**Horizon Migration Rate**	Movement of initiatives between horizons (H1→H2→H3 or reverse)	Migrated Initiatives / Total Active Initiatives	INNO	GROW	•	•	•	VA	Ch7, Ch10
PT	Knowledge	**Chao1 Confidence Interval Width**	Precision of the Chao1 estimate — narrower means better portfolio visibility	Upper Bound - Lower Bound of Chao1 Estimate	R&D	READY	○	•	•	VA	Ch10

Detailed indicators

Input Indicators

Innovation Intensity (II): Total innovation expenditure divided by total revenue, expressed as a percentage. Measure at the cadence of each initiative's investment cycle. Applicable to all horizons. Data source: finance/accounting. Benchmark: OECD surveys for comparable industry and firm size. Note: 'Innovation expenditure' should be defined broadly to include R&D, design, experimentation, knowledge acquisition, and training with a clear innovation purpose—not limited to formal R&D line items.

Innovation Headcount (IH): Full-time equivalents (FTEs) dedicated primarily to innovation activities, expressed as a percentage of the total workforce. Measure at the cadence of each initiative's investment cycle. Applicable to all horizons. Data source: HR. Note: Partial allocations should be aggregated—for example, a researcher spending 40% of their time on innovation counts as 0.4 FTE. The Frascati Manual provides guidance on allocation methodology.

External Knowledge Investment (EKI): Expenditure on externally sourced knowledge—licences, partnerships, university collaborations, technology acquisitions—as a percentage of total innovation expenditure. Measure at the cadence of each initiative's investment cycle. Applicable to all horizons. Data source: finance, business development. This indicator tracks the openness of the organization's innovation model; low EKI combined with low II typically indicates an underinvesting posture.

Leadership Time on Innovation (LTI): Hours per quarter spent by C-suite and senior leadership on innovation governance activities—portfolio reviews, innovation committee participation, external scouting—as a percentage of total working hours. Measure at the cadence of each initiative's investment cycle. Data source: calendar analysis or self-reported. This indicator has strong predictive value for innovation culture; it is also the most commonly gamed indicator in the set and should be cross-validated against other culture measures.

Throughput Indicators

Idea-to-Pilot Velocity (IPV): Average time, in weeks, from formal idea submission to pilot launch, measured across all ideas that advance to pilot in a given period. Measure at the cadence of each initiative's investment cycle. Data source: innovation management system. Note: This metric is meaningless without also tracking selectivity (what percentage of ideas advance to pilot), since a very fast IPV driven by low selectivity represents not speed but insufficient filtering.

Pilot Selectivity Rate (PSR): Percentage of submitted ideas that advance to pilot stage. Measure at the cadence of each initiative's investment cycle. Target range: 5–15% depending on the innovation domain; very high or very low rates are both problematic—high rates indicate insufficient filtering, while low rates may indicate overly conservative gates that prevent useful learning.

Documented Abandonment Rate (DAR): Percentage of abandoned projects (at any stage) that produce a formal knowledge artifact—a decision memo, lessons-learned document, or equivalent—within thirty days of abandonment. Measure at the cadence of each initiative's investment cycle. This is the single most diagnostic indicator of memory quality in the innovation process. Organizations with high DAR are turning their failures into organizational learning; those with low DAR are simply destroying the capital invested in abandoned projects—target: above 80%.

Cross-Project Knowledge Transfer (CPKT): Percentage of active projects that cite at least one prior project's documented learning in their project documentation. Measure at the cadence of each initiative's investment cycle. This indicator measures whether the memory infrastructure is actually being used—whether practitioners are drawing on institutional knowledge rather than reinventing—target: above 50% for organizations with more than three years of documented project history.

Output Indicators

New-to-Market Revenue Share (NTMRS): Revenue from products and services introduced in the past thirty-six months as a percentage of total revenue. Measure at the cadence of each initiative's investment cycle. Applicable to all horizons. This is the most widely used output indicator and the most subject to definitional gaming—'new' can mean anything from a genuine discontinuous innovation to a minor packaging change. Organizations should define 'new' consistently and conservatively.

Process Efficiency Delta (PED): Quantified efficiency improvement (cost reduction, throughput improvement, error rate reduction) attributable to process innovations in the measurement period, expressed as a percentage of baseline. Measure at the cadence of each initiative's investment cycle. Applicable to all horizons. Data source: operations management. This indicator captures a category of innovation value—process improvement—that is systematically undervalued in product-focused measurement systems.

Patent Quality Index (PQI): Forward citation rate of patents filed in the period, measured after a five-year lag. Measure as a lagged annual indicator. This is a better measure of patent value than raw patent count, which is easily inflated. The five-year lag requirement means the indicator reflects decisions made five years earlier—a useful discipline for governance reviews.

Adoption Rate at Six Months (AR6): Percentage of target users or customers actively using a deployed innovation six months after launch. Measure for each deployment. This indicator addresses the adoption gap—the difference between deployment and actual use—that is the most common site of innovation value destruction.

Memory Indicators

Knowledge Artefact Production Rate (KAPR): Number of structured knowledge artifacts (decision memos, experimental logs, lessons-learned documents, knowledge capsules) produced per FTE per quarter in the innovation function. Measure at the cadence of each initiative's investment cycle. This indicator measures the throughput of the knowledge capture process; very low KAPR indicates that capture is not happening; very high KAPR may indicate that capture is happening without retrieval (documenting rather than remembering).

Retrievability Score (RS): Percentage of standard test questions about past projects (selected from a regularly updated question bank) that can be answered accurately from existing documentation within a specified time limit. Measure semi-annually. This is the most direct test of whether the memory infrastructure is functional. Organizations should build their retrievability question banks from actual questions that arose in practice—'what was tried and why was it abandoned,' 'what were the key constraints that shaped this design decision,' 'what did we learn about this customer segment that informed this product choice.'

Knowledge Age Index (KAI): Average age, in months, of the knowledge artifacts being actively retrieved and cited in current projects. A very high KAI indicates that the organization is drawing primarily on old knowledge and may not be capturing new learning effectively; a very low KAI may indicate excessive recency bias and failure to draw on relevant historical experience. Target range: 18–48 months for most organizations.

Expert Knowledge Succession Rate (EKSR): Percentage of identified 'critical knowledge holders'—individuals whose departure would create a knowledge gap—for whom a documented succession knowledge transfer has been completed. Measure at the cadence of each initiative's investment cycle. Applicable to all horizons. This indicator addresses the single most acute risk to organizational memory: the departure of key individuals without knowledge transfer. Organizations should proactively identify their critical knowledge holders (not only when a departure is anticipated) and maintain a succession-readiness inventory.

Appendix B: The ROI² Executive Dashboard Blueprint

One caution before the templates: every figure in this appendix is sample data, shown to make the blueprints concrete. Replace it with your own. For how to interpret the composite itself—typical first-season bands, and why the pair matters more than the level—see "Reading the Number" in Chapter 8.

This appendix turns the Compass measurement system into four instruments the leadership team fills in directly: a one-page scorecard, a quarterly review, an annual report, and a horizon investment plan. Each is a working template, not a description of one. Copy them into a spreadsheet and adapt the row counts to your portfolio.

The Innovation Compass Scorecard

The scorecard is the one-page instrument leadership reads each cycle. Enter the strategic indicator shortlist selected for the season (Appendix E), grouped by the four readings, and track each against its target. The two needles at the foot carry the ROI² ordered pair: Readiness and Growth are read together, never collapsed into one number.

Indicator	Cap.	Current	Target	Status
Input — what we put in				
Throughput — how it moves				

Output — what it produces				
Outcome — what changed				

ROI² this cycle

Readiness: __________ **Growth**: __________

read as the pair [__________ , __________]

Quarterly Portfolio Review Worksheet

Completed by the Innovation Director in three to four hours, then reviewed by the Innovation Committee. Flag any project 'on track' for more than four consecutive quarters without reaching a milestone—the signature of a project consuming resources without generating learning.

Section 1—Portfolio Status

Project	Hor.	Stage	Spend (act / plan)	Status

Section 2—Throughput Indicators (vs prior quarter / prior year)

Idea-to-Pilot Velocity:

__________ (prior: __________ / __________)

Pilot Selectivity Rate:
__________ (prior: __________ / __________)

Documented Abandonment Rate:
__________ (prior: __________ / __________)

Significant movements and likely causes:
____

Section 3—Memory Capture

Abandoned projects this quarter with knowledge artifacts produced:
__________ / __________

Knowledge Artefact Production Rate: __________

Domains with CPKT below 30% (retrieval problem—needs attention):
____

Section 4—Decisions Required

Decision required	Memory context (what we tried, learned, what is different)	Owner

Annual Innovation Compass Report

The primary longitudinal document. Produce it consistently year over year, using the same indicator definitions, so the trend is genuine. Year one sets the baseline; later years measure progress. Open each year's report with progress against the prior year's committed actions.

Indicator	This year	Last year	2-yr trend	Commentary
Input indicators				
Throughput indicators				

Indicator	This year	Last year	2-yr trend	Commentary
Output indicators				
Memory indicators				

Memory Capital Assessment

Rate the health of the innovation memory infrastructure on each criterion (1–5), with a note.

Completeness—are all relevant projects documented? Score: ____
Note: ______________________________

Retrievability—can documentation be accessed efficiently? Score: ____
Note: ______________________

Quality—is it rich enough to answer practical questions? Score: ____
Note: ____________________

Succession—is tacit knowledge captured before it walks out the door?
Score: ____ Note: _____________

Actions for the Coming Year (three to five; lowest-performing indicators first)

Action	Owner	Timeline

Horizon-Linked Investment Planning Worksheet

Ensures the portfolio's allocation across horizons reflects both the current weight configuration and the strategic intent for capability development.

Hor.	Budget / FTE	# Proj.	% of total	Capitals to build
H1				
H2				
H3				

H1 : H3 investment ratio: __________ (balanced range 3:1 to 5:1; above 8:1 starves exploration; below 2:1 is premature exploration before translation capability exists).

As a guide for the last column: H1 typically builds Process Capital and generates financial return; H2 builds Knowledge and Relational Capital; H3 should build Memory Capital above all—the primary output of exploratory work is organizational learning about which questions are worth asking, not the research result itself.

Appendix C: Standards and Frameworks Reference

Three international standards frameworks are directly relevant to the Compass measurement system. The following one-page summaries describe what each standard covers, why it matters for innovation management, and how it connects to the Compass indicator set.

ISO 56002—Innovation Management System

ISO 56002 (2019, revised 2023) is the international standard for innovation management systems. It provides a systematic approach to managing innovation activities within an organization, covering the full innovation cycle from context analysis through strategy, operations, performance evaluation, and improvement. The standard is not prescriptive about specific methods or tools; it describes what a well-functioning innovation management system should achieve rather than exactly how to achieve it.

For Compass implementation, ISO 56002 is relevant primarily as a governance framework. Its requirements for performance evaluation—systematic monitoring, measurement, analysis, and evaluation of innovation activities—align directly with the Compass indicator set. Organizations implementing the Compass as part of an ISO 56002 conformance program will find that most Compass indicators satisfy the ISO 56002 performance evaluation requirements. At the same time, the Memory Indicators provide capabilities beyond the standard's explicit requirements.

ISO 56002 certification is optional and not required for Compass implementation. However, organizations working toward ISO 56002 conformance will find the Compass framework a practical implementation vehicle for performance evaluation requirements.

OECD Oslo Manual (2018, 4th Edition)

The Oslo Manual is the primary international reference for innovation statistics, developed jointly by the OECD and Eurostat. The fourth edition (2018) significantly expanded its scope from product and process innovation to include business process, marketing, and organizational innovation, reflecting the contemporary reality that innovation value is generated across a much broader range of activities than earlier frameworks captured.

The Oslo Manual is the authoritative source for the definitions used in the Compass Input and Output indicator set. Innovation intensity, R&D expenditure classification, and new-to-market revenue measurement all follow Oslo Manual definitions to ensure comparability with industry benchmarks and national statistical databases. Organizations that want to benchmark their Compass results against industry norms should use the Oslo Manual definitions as the measurement standard rather than national adaptations.

The Oslo Manual does not cover Memory Indicators, which are a Compass innovation. However, its treatment of knowledge-based capital—intangible investments including training, design, databases, and organizational capital—provides useful conceptual grounding for the Memory Capital dimension of the Compass framework.

Frascati Manual (2015, 7th Edition)

The Frascati Manual is the international standard for measuring research and development. It defines the core concepts—basic research, applied research, experimental development—that underlie the classification of R&D investment globally. The seventh edition (2015) updated the definitions to reflect contemporary research practice, including software development, digital infrastructure, and knowledge-intensive services.

For the Compass implementation, the Frascati Manual is directly relevant to classifying innovation expenditure in the Input indicators. The line between R&D (as defined by Frascati) and innovation (as defined by Oslo) is the most common source of inconsistency in measuring organizational innovation. Clear application of both frameworks prevents the double-counting and definitional inflation that undermine comparability.

My personal introduction to the Frascati Manual came in 1999, when I was advising technology companies on R&D tax credits under Canada's SR&ED program. The program uses a modified Frascati framework to determine what qualifies as scientific research or experimental development for tax purposes. The experience of applying these definitions to hundreds of real projects convinced me that the underlying conceptual framework is sound—the challenge for most organizations is not the framework itself but the discipline of applying it consistently.

S4IL and the Balanced Scorecard

Practitioners familiar with Kaplan and Norton's Balanced Scorecard (1992) will recognize structural similarities: both frameworks organize performance measurement across multiple dimensions, connect strategy to operational indicators, and resist the reduction of organizational health to a single financial number. The comparison is legitimate and worth naming explicitly.

The distinction lies in scope and object of measurement. The Balanced Scorecard measures overall organizational performance across four perspectives—financial, customer, internal processes, and learning & growth. S4IL measures a specific organizational capability: the capacity to innovate systematically, learn from that innovation, and compound that learning across investment seasons. Where the Balanced Scorecard asks "how is the organization performing?", S4IL asks "how is the organization's innovation system improving over time?"

A second distinction is the role of memory. The Balanced Scorecard captures a state at a point in time. S4IL is explicitly longitudinal—its diagnostic value increases with each measurement cycle, because the Factorless Income Residual and the Memory Capital indicators only become meaningful when compared across seasons. The compass requires time to calibrate.

Organizations already using a Balanced Scorecard will find that S4IL is complementary rather than competing: the Balanced Scorecard provides the business context; S4IL provides the innovation measurement layer within it.

Appendix D: Innovation Memory Self-Assessment

The following twenty-question diagnostic allows organizations to assess the current maturity of their innovation memory infrastructure. Each question should be scored on a five-point scale: 1 (not in place), 2 (partially in place), 3 (in place but inconsistently applied), 4 (consistently in place), 5 (in place and continuously improving). The total score out of 100 maps to a memory maturity level described at the end of the assessment.

Self-Assessment Questions

Section 1: Knowledge Capture (Questions 1–5)

1. Does your organization have a standard protocol for documenting key decisions in innovation projects at the time they are made, including the rationale and alternatives considered? Score your current practice on the 1–5 scale.

2. When an innovation project is abandoned at any stage, is a knowledge artifact (lessons-learned document, decision memo, or equivalent) routinely produced within 30 days of abandonment? Score your current practice.

3. Are the insights generated in innovation pilots and experiments captured in a form that is accessible to future project teams in the same domain? Score your current practice.

4. Is tacit knowledge from departing key personnel (practitioners with significant domain expertise) systematically captured before departure? Score your current practice.

5. Does your organization have a defined standard for what constitutes a 'knowledge artifact' and what minimum information each artifact should contain? Score your current practice.

Section 2: Knowledge Organization (Questions 6–10)

6. Is your organization's innovation knowledge base organized with consistent metadata (tags, cross-references, domain classifications) that allows systematic search? Score your current practice.

7. Can a practitioner unfamiliar with your organization's history find relevant prior project learning in under thirty minutes using your current knowledge systems? Score your current practice.

8. Are knowledge artifacts linked to related artifacts from other projects, time periods, or domains, allowing navigational browsing across the knowledge base? Score your current practice.

9. Is your knowledge base maintained and indexed by a designated person or team responsible for its quality and accessibility? Score your current practice.

10. Are knowledge artifacts reviewed and updated when organizational context changes—when a market assumption is invalidated, a technology is superseded, or an organizational capability changes? Score your current practice.

Section 3: Knowledge Retrieval (Questions 11–15)

11. When innovation projects begin, is a systematic search of prior project learning in the same domain a standard part of the project initiation process? Score your current practice.

12. Is your organization's knowledge base searchable by natural-language questions, not just keyword search or document browsing? Score your current practice.

13. Can you retrieve, within one business day, the documented rationale for a significant innovation decision made three or more years ago? Score your current practice.

14. Is there a mechanism for surfacing relevant prior learning proactively—without waiting for practitioners to know what to search for? Score your current practice.

15. Does your organization track and measure the rate at which knowledge artifacts are retrieved and cited in new projects (the CPKT indicator described in Appendix A)? Score your current practice.

Section 4: Memory Governance (Questions 16–20)

16. Is there explicit organizational accountability for the health of the innovation memory infrastructure—a named owner with responsibility for its quality and completeness? Score your current practice.

17. Does your organization's innovation governance process include a regular review of memory infrastructure quality, distinct from portfolio performance review? Score your current practice.

18. Are 'critical knowledge holders'—individuals whose departure would create a significant knowledge gap—identified proactively, and is

their succession knowledge transfer status tracked? Score your current practice.

19. Is the innovation memory infrastructure resourced as an ongoing operational capability, with dedicated budget and personnel, rather than funded as a time-limited project? Score your current practice.

20. Does your organization have a target for memory infrastructure quality—a specific Retrievability Score or equivalent—that is tracked over time and tied to improvement commitments? Score your current practice.

Scoring Guide

Scores of 80–100 (Memory Leader): Your organization has a mature, well-maintained innovation memory infrastructure. Focus on continuous improvement and on extending ecosystem memory. Consider contributing to industry knowledge standards.

Scores of 60–79 (Memory Capable): Your infrastructure is in place in most dimensions, but inconsistently applied. Priority actions: establish the knowledge-capture protocol for abandoned projects (the highest-impact single intervention); designate a named memory-infrastructure owner; set a Retrievability Score target.

Scores of 40–59 (Memory Emerging): You have the awareness and partial mechanisms, but lack consistency and integration. Priority actions: complete the 90-Day Start process (Chapter 11); focus Step 3 specifically on closing the largest gaps revealed by this assessment.

Scores below 40 (Memory Deficit): Your organization is at significant risk of repeating past mistakes and failing to compound its innovation learning. The good news is that this is a solvable problem. Start with the knowledge audit (Phase 1 of the 90-Day Start) and build from there. The most important first step is naming the problem clearly, which this assessment has helped you do.

Appendix E: Innovation Season Design Templates

The following two templates operationalize the strategic indicator selection process described in Chapter 9. Template E.1 is used by the Head of Innovation (or Chief Innovation Officer) at the beginning of each investment season to translate the organizational strategy into a shortlist of measurable ROI² indicators. Template E.2 is used by Innovation Managers who support individual initiative owners in selecting their project-level subset from the season shortlist.

Innovation Season Design Worksheet (Template E.1)

Purpose: To design the innovation investment season by selecting the strategic ROI² *indicator shortlist that will govern the entire portfolio. Complete this template before the portfolio planning cycle begins.*

Section A: Strategic Context

Investment Season: _______________ (e.g., FY2026 H1, Q3 2026)

Organization's Top 3 Strategic Priorities for This Period:

1. ____

2. ____

3. ____

Innovation North Star Metric for This Season: ____________________

Current North Star Baseline Value: __________ Target End-of-Season Value: __________

Section B: Indicator Shortlist Selection (from Appendix A Catalogue)

Instructions: Review the full ROI² *Indicator Catalogue (Appendix A). For each of the Four Capitals, select the indicators that best translate this season's strategic priorities into measurable criteria. Aim for 3–5 indicators per capital. These become the* ROI² *criteria against which every initiative in the portfolio will be evaluated.*

Knowledge Capital Indicators Selected:

1. ____________________________ Rationale: ____________________

2. ____________________________ Rationale: ____________________

3. ____________________________ Rationale: ____________________

4. ____________________________ Rationale: ____________________

5. ____________________________ Rationale: ____________________

Relational Capital Indicators Selected:

1. ____________________________ Rationale: ____________________

2. ____________________________ Rationale: ____________________

3. ____________________________ Rationale: ____________________

4. ____________________________ Rationale:
____

5. ______________________ Rationale: ________________

Process Capital Indicators Selected:

1. ______________________ Rationale: ________________

2. ______________________ Rationale: ________________

3. ______________________ Rationale: ________________

4. ______________________ Rationale: ________________

5. ______________________ Rationale: ________________

Memory Capital Indicators Selected:

1. ______________________ Rationale: ________________

2. ______________________ Rationale: ________________

3. ______________________ Rationale: ________________

4. ______________________ Rationale: ________________

5. ______________________ Rationale: ________________

Total Season Shortlist Count:
__________ (recommended: 12–20 indicators)

Vanity Metrics Cap Check:
__________ % activity-based (must be ≤ 20%)

Section C: Portfolio Coverage Commitment

Instructions: After all initiative owners have completed their Template E.2 selections, aggregate here to verify that every season indicator is covered by at least one initiative. Any uncovered indicator represents a strategic gap requiring executive attention.

Indicator Coverage Matrix: For each shortlisted indicator, list the initiative(s) tracking it.

Indicator: ___________________ Tracked by: ___________________

Indicator: ___________________ Tracked by: ___________________

Indicator: ___________________ Tracked by: ___________________

(Continue for all shortlisted indicators)

Uncovered Indicators (strategic gaps): ____________________________

Action Plan for Gaps:

____

____

Section D: End-of-Season ROI² Reading

Instructions: At the end of the investment season, aggregate results from all initiatives to produce the complete portfolio-level ROI² *reading. Each initiative contributes its subset; the compounded value across all initiatives provides the full picture.*

Season ROI² Composite Score: ___________

North Star Metric End-of-Season Value: ___________

vs. Target: ___________

Key Learnings for Next Season's Shortlist Design: _________________

Initiative Indicator Selection Worksheet (Template E.2)

Purpose: To guide an Innovation Manager in selecting the right ROI² indicators for a specific initiative, ensuring alignment with the season's strategic shortlist. Complete one template per initiative.

Section A: Initiative Profile

Initiative Name: ____

Innovation Champion / Project Manager: ______________________

Innovation Manager (completing this form): ____________________

Investment Season: ___________ Horizon: H1 / H2 / H3 (circle one)

Initiative Category: Opportunity Exploration / Ideation Campaign / POC / MVP (circle one)

Brief Description:

____

____

Section B: Indicator Selection from Season Shortlist

Instructions:

From the season's strategic indicator shortlist (Template E.1, Section B), select the indicators that this specific initiative will track. Choose 2–3 indicators per capital that are relevant to this initiative's scope and horizon. Not every season indicator needs to be tracked by this initiative—but every indicator you select must be measurable within this initiative's timeframe.

Knowledge Capital (select from season shortlist):

1. ____________________ Baseline: __________ Target: __________

2. ____________________ Baseline: __________ Target: __________

3. ____________________ Baseline: __________ Target: __________

Relational Capital (select from season shortlist):

1. ____________________ Baseline: __________ Target: __________

2. ____________________ Baseline: __________ Target: __________

3. ____________________ Baseline: __________ Target: __________

Process Capital (select from season shortlist):

1. ____________________ Baseline: __________ Target: __________

2. ____________________ Baseline: __________ Target: __________

3. ____________________ Baseline: __________ Target: __________

Memory Capital (select from season shortlist):

1. ____________________ Baseline: __________ Target: __________

2. ____________________ Baseline: __________ Target: __________

3. ____________________ Baseline: __________ Target: __________

Section C: Capital Weighting

Instructions: Assign a weight (%) to each capital based on this initiative's horizon and strategic intent. Weights must sum to 100%. Refer to Chapter 9's horizon-weighting guidance.

Knowledge Capital Weight: __________ %

Relational Capital Weight: __________ %

Process Capital Weight: __________ %

Memory Capital Weight: __________ %

Total: __________ % (must equal 100%)

Section D: Portfolio Contribution Statement

Instructions: Identify which season indicators this initiative does NOT track. This is not a deficiency—it is expected. The purpose is to ensure that the portfolio as a whole has no gaps. If this initiative is the only one in the portfolio that could realistically track a particular season indicator, flag it here for discussion with the Head of Innovation.

Season indicators NOT tracked by this initiative:

____

Are any of these indicators at risk of being uncovered across the portfolio? Yes / No

If Yes, flag for Head of Innovation: ___________________________

Section E: Measurement Schedule

Data collection frequency: Weekly / Biweekly / Monthly / Quarterly (circle one)

First measurement date: __________

Mid-season review date: __________

End-of-season aggregation date: __________

Data source(s): ____

Person responsible for data collection: __________________________

Appendix F: Gamification Mechanisms

This appendix documents the eight Core Drives of the Octalysis framework (Yu-kai Chou, Actionable Gamification: Beyond Points, Badges, and Leaderboards, Octalysis Media, 2015) as applied to innovation management and S4IL adoption. Each drive is presented with its motivational role, the concrete mechanics it activates in an innovation context, and the S4IL phase where it is most effective.

The Octalysis framework distinguishes between White Hat drives—which generate sustainable, intrinsic motivation—and Black Hat drives, which produce urgent but short-lived engagement. Innovation programs should be built primarily on White Hat drives, with Black Hat drives deployed sparingly for activation moments only.

The Eight Core Drives: Reference Table

Drive	Name	Type	Motivational Role	How to apply	Most Effective Phase
Core Drive 1	Epic Meaning and Calling	WHITE HAT	People engage when they believe their contribution is part of something larger than themselves.	Connect individual actions (documenting an experiment, filing a failure narrative) to the organization's innovation mission and long-term resilience. Make the cumulative impact of individual contributions visible on the innovation dashboard.	All phases, but especially How to Get Adopted — sustains long-term participation when novelty fades.

Drive	Name	Type	Motivational Role	How to apply	Most Effective Phase
Core Drive 2	Development and Accomplishment	WHITE HAT	The internal drive to make progress, develop skills, and achieve mastery.	Clear progression tiers (Innovation Scout to Innovation Master), milestone badges for knowledge contributions, skill certification for completing experiment registries. Every completed Season becomes a visible marker of capability growth.	How to Win and How to Deliver — sustains effort through experimentation troughs and delivery grind.

Drive	Name	Type	Motivational Role	How to apply	Most Effective Phase
Core Drive 3	Empowerment of Creativity and Feedback	WHITE HAT	People are most engaged when they can express creativity and receive immediate feedback on their choices.	Allow teams to shape the innovation challenge brief, not just respond to it. Real-time ROI[2] dashboard showing how each contribution moves the four capitals. Rapid feedback loops between experiment submission and impact visualization.	Where to Play and How to Win — activates early-stage exploration and ideation.

Drive	Name	Type	Motivational Role	How to apply	Most Effective Phase
Core Drive 4	Ownership and Possession	WHITE HAT	People value things more when they feel genuine ownership over them.	Full provenance tracking: every contributor can see their idea move through the pipeline from submission to outcome. Named authorship of knowledge artifacts in the organizational memory. Personal innovation portfolio visible to the contributor.	How to Deliver and How to Get Adopted — keeps contributors engaged through the long tail of execution.

Drive	Name	Type	Motivational Role	How to apply	Most Effective Phase
Core Drive 5	Social Influence and Relatedness	NEUTRAL	People are motivated by social dynamics: mentorship, peer recognition, competition, and belonging.	Innovation leaderboards at team level (not individual, to prevent hoarding). Cross-departmental collaboration events. Public recognition in leadership forums for knowledge contributions. Collaboration density metric as a visible team indicator.	How to Get Adopted — builds communities of practice that sustain adoption beyond the campaign window.

Drive	Name	Type	Motivational Role	How to apply	Most Effective Phase
Core Drive 6	Scarcity and Impatience	BLACK HAT	People want what they cannot easily have. Time pressure and exclusivity create urgency.	Time-limited innovation challenges with hard deadlines. Exclusive access to innovation resources (pilot funding, strategic planning sessions) reserved for top contributors. Limited-slot accelerator cohorts.	Where to Play — for activation moments only. Overuse produces anxiety and shortcuts rather than quality.

Drive	Name	Type	Motivational Role	How to apply	Most Effective Phase
Core Drive 7	Unpredictability and Curiosity	BLACK HAT	People are drawn to the unknown and to unexpected discoveries.	Surprise signal alerts surfacing unexpected connections between projects. Random cross-team knowledge matches ("your current experiment resembles a 2019 project in a different division"). Mystery milestone reveals that unlock hidden organizational memory content.	Where to Play and How to Win — maintains curiosity during long exploration phases.

Drive	Name	Type	Motivational Role	How to apply	Most Effective Phase
Core Drive 8	Loss and Avoidance	BLACK HAT	People are motivated to avoid negative outcomes and the feeling of losing something already held.	Make the Innovation Tax visible: the annual cost of duplication, decision delay, and amnesia as a calculated number. Frame non-participation as a measurable loss, not a passive choice. Streak mechanics for continuous knowledge contributions.	All phases for onboarding. Use sparingly — sustained reliance on loss avoidance produces compliance without commitment.

Source: Chou, Y. (2015). Actionable Gamification: Beyond Points, Badges, and Leaderboards. Octalysis Media. The Octalysis framework and its eight Core Drives are the intellectual property of Yu-kai Chou. Applications to S4IL and innovation management contexts are the author's own.

Appendix G: Network Influence Mechanisms for Adoption

This appendix documents the principal network influence mechanisms relevant to innovation adoption, covering both external diffusion (market adoption) and internal diffusion (organizational change). It draws on three bodies of work: Cialdini's principles of influence, Rogers' Diffusion of Innovations, and Barabási and Albert's network science. Where the Octalysis framework (Appendix F) addresses the motivational architecture of the innovation platform itself, this appendix addresses the mechanics by which innovations spread through human networks—and how those mechanics can be deliberately activated in an adoption campaign.

Where this sits on the compass. These three bodies of work are all instruments of the last phase, How to Get Adopted, and they operate at three different scales of the same problem. Cialdini works at the level of the individual decision—why one person says yes. Rogers works at the level of the population—which segment adopts when, and what each one needs.

Barabási works at the level of the network—which few nodes, activated, pull everyone else along. None of the three is enough alone: persuade an individual with no sense of the adopter curve and you misjudge timing; map the curve with no sense of the network and you push on the wrong people. Combined—and fragmented to the segment and the hub—they turn an addressable market into an addressed one, the same conversion Octalysis drives from the motivational side. Their yield is adoption itself, which is where Growth finally registers on the compass.

Part 1—Cialdini's Principles of Influence

Robert Cialdini identified six universal principles of influence through decades of field research. A seventh principle, Unity, was added in Pre-Suasion.

Each principle describes a cognitive shortcut that people use when deciding whether to adopt a new behaviour, product, or idea. In innovation adoption, these principles operate at the individual decision level—they explain why a specific person says yes or no to an innovation.

Principle	Mechanism	Application in Innovation Adoption	Internal / External / Both
Reciprocity	People feel obligated to return favours and concessions.	Offer genuine value before asking for adoption: a free pilot, a training session, early access to results. Internal: share knowledge freely with the teams whose adoption you need; they will feel a natural obligation to engage.	Both internal and external. Most effective at the first contact stage of the adoption campaign.

Principle	Mechanism	Application in Innovation Adoption	Internal / External / Both
Commitment and Consistency	Once people commit to a position or action, they feel compelled to behave consistently with that commitment.	Secure a small public commitment early (a sign-up, a pilot participation agreement, a stated interest). Internal: ask teams to publicly declare an innovation objective at the Season opening; they are more likely to follow through.	Internal adoption campaigns. Especially powerful in organizational change contexts.
Social Proof	People look to the behaviour of others, especially similar others, to determine the correct course of action.	Make early adopters visible. Publish adoption metrics by team or unit. Internal: show which departments have already integrated the new process; others follow. External: customer testimonials from peers in the same industry.	Both. Most effective in the Mixed to Turbulent Signal Landscape window, when hesitation is highest.
Authority	People follow the guidance of credible experts and recognized leaders.	Secure endorsement from respected technical or strategic leaders before launching the adoption campaign. Internal: the CIO or CTO visibly using the new system carries more weight than any training program. External: third-party validation, certifications, publications.	Both. Critical at campaign launch to establish legitimacy.

Principle	Mechanism	Application in Innovation Adoption	Internal / External / Both
Liking	People are more easily influenced by those they know, like, and trust.	Use peer champions rather than central communicators. Internal: identify respected informal leaders in each unit and invest in their adoption first. External: draw on existing customer relationships and communities of practice.	Both. The most effective mechanism for overcoming resistance in mature organizations.
Scarcity	People assign more value to things that are rare or becoming unavailable.	Time-limited access windows, early-adopter benefits, limited pilot cohort slots. Internal: the first Season's indicator catalogue is the reference; teams that define their indicators late will work with a sub-optimal shortlist.	External campaigns and initial internal rollouts. Use sparingly — overuse erodes trust.
Unity	People are influenced by shared identity and a sense of belonging to the same group.	Frame the innovation program as an expression of the organization's shared identity and purpose. Internal: 'we are the kind of organization that learns from failure' is more durable than any incentive scheme. External: build user communities around shared missions, not product features.	Internal adoption. Especially powerful for long-term culture change beyond the campaign window.

Source: Cialdini, R.B. *(2001). Influence: The Psychology of Persuasion (rev. ed.). Harper Business. Cialdini,* R.B. *(2016). Pre-Suasion: A Revolutionary Way to Influence and Persuade. Simon & Schuster. Applications to innovation adoption contexts are the author's own.*

Part 2—Rogers' Diffusion of Innovations: Adopter Categories and Adoption Actions

Everett Rogers' Diffusion of Innovations established that innovations spread through social systems in a predictable S-curve pattern, driven by five adopter categories. The key practical insight for innovation managers is that each category requires a different adoption action: the approach that converts an Innovator will not convert an Early Majority member, and the approach that works on the Early Majority will alienate a Laggard. An adoption campaign that treats all targets identically will underperform on every segment.

Adopter Category	Characteristic Behaviour	Required Adoption Action	Internal / External
Innovators (2.5%)	Technology enthusiasts and risk-takers. They adopt for the act of adoption itself.	Give unfinished, imperfect access. They want to be first. Provide technical depth, raw data, direct access to the development team. Internal: invite them to co-design the pilot. External: private beta programs.	Both. They create the proof of concept that the Early Adopters will observe.

Adopter Category	Characteristic Behaviour	Required Adoption Action	Internal / External
Early Adopters (13.5%)	Opinion leaders who adopt strategically, seeking competitive or social advantage.	Provide clear articulation of the relative advantage. They need to understand why this innovation makes them more effective or more credible. Internal: show ROI[2] impact projections. External: case studies from peer organizations.	Both. The most critical segment — their visible adoption triggers the Early Majority.
Early Majority (34%)	Pragmatists who wait for proof before adopting. They follow, they do not lead.	Reduce perceived risk. Provide evidence from the Early Adopters, compatibility with existing systems, and clear implementation support. Internal: peer testimonials from respected colleagues. External: ROI data, reference customers in the same sector.	Both. Converting this segment is the tipping point of any adoption campaign.
Late Majority (34%)	Skeptics who adopt only when the innovation has become the norm or when their current tools stop working.	Remove friction and make adoption the path of least resistance. Internal: deprecate the old system, provide mandatory transition support. External: pricing pressure, ecosystem lock-in, regulatory requirements.	Primarily internal. External campaigns rarely convert this segment; network effects and market structure do.

Adopter Category	Characteristic Behaviour	Required Adoption Action	Internal / External
Laggards (16%)	Traditionalists who resist change and may never adopt voluntarily.	Do not invest campaign resources in converting Laggards. In internal contexts, structural change (policy, tooling mandates) is more effective than persuasion. Measure their resistance as an indicator of organizational friction, not as a campaign target.	Internal only. Laggard resistance is a governance and culture signal, not an adoption campaign problem.

Source: Rogers, E.M. (2003). Diffusion of Innovations (5th ed.). Free Press. Applications to corporate innovation adoption contexts are the author's own.

Part 3—Barabási's Network Science: Small World and Scale-Free Networks

Albert-László Barabási and Réka Albert demonstrated in 1999 that most real-world networks—social, technological, biological—are not random. They are scale-free: a small number of highly connected nodes (hubs) carry a disproportionate share of the network's connections, while most nodes have very few. This structure emerges from two simple mechanisms: growth (the network keeps adding nodes) and preferential attachment (new nodes prefer to connect to already well-connected nodes—the rich-get-richer principle). Watts and Strogatz (1998) had earlier shown that even large networks have surprisingly short average path lengths between any two nodes—the Small World property. Together, these two discoveries transform the practical theory of influence in innovation adoption: the network through which your innovation must travel is not flat, and it is not random. It has hubs. Finding them and activating them is the highest-impact action in any adoption campaign.

Concept	Source	Network Mechanism	Innovation Adoption Action
Scale-Free Networks	Barabási & Albert (1999). Emergence of Scaling in Random Networks. Science, 286, 509–512.	Most adoption networks are scale-free: a small number of highly connected individuals (hubs) account for the majority of connections. These hubs are not necessarily the most senior people — they are the most connected.	Identify the hubs in your target adoption network before launching the campaign. Investing in hub activation is 10× more efficient than broad-based messaging. Internal: map informal communication networks, not org charts. External: identify connector individuals in professional communities, not just official spokespeople.
Preferential Attachment	Barabási & Albert (1999); Barabási, A.-L. (2002). Linked: The New Science of Networks. Perseus Publishing.	New participants in a network tend to connect to nodes that are already well-connected. Innovations that achieve early visibility among well-connected individuals gain adoption momentum that is self-reinforcing.	Ensure your innovation's first visible adopters are well-connected. One adoption by a hub node generates more subsequent adoptions than ten adoptions by peripheral nodes. Internal: the first team to publicly adopt the framework should be a team that other teams look to for guidance — not necessarily the most compliant one.

Concept	Source	Network Mechanism	Innovation Adoption Action
Small World Property	Watts, D.J. & Strogatz, S.H. (1998). Collective dynamics of 'small-world' networks. Nature, 393, 440–442.	In most real-world networks, any two individuals are connected through a surprisingly small number of intermediaries — typically three to six steps. Innovation diffusion rides these short paths: once a hub adopts, the innovation is within a few steps of most of the target network.	Do not try to reach every node directly. Activate the hubs and let the Small World property carry the diffusion. Internal: three well-chosen hub activations will reach the majority of an organization faster than a company-wide communication campaign.
Hub Targeting Strategy	Derived from Barabási (1999, 2002) and Gladwell, M. (2000). The Tipping Point. Little, Brown.	Because scale-free networks have hubs, they are highly efficient for diffusion when hubs are targeted, but highly resistant when only peripheral nodes are reached. Gladwell's Connectors, Mavens, and Salespeople map closely to the hub typology in network science.	Run a pre-campaign network mapping exercise to identify three types of hubs: Connectors (broad reach), Mavens (trusted information sources), and Salespeople (persuasive advocates). Build the adoption campaign architecture around these three hub types before investing in broad outreach. Internal and external adoption campaigns both benefit from this sequencing.

Concept	Source	Network Mechanism	Innovation Adoption Action
Weak Ties as Diffusion Bridges	Granovetter, M. (1973). The Strength of Weak Ties. American Journal of Sociology, 78(6), 1360–1380.	Strong ties (close colleagues, trusted friends) provide redundant information. Weak ties (acquaintances, cross-departmental contacts) bridge otherwise disconnected clusters and carry novel information. Most innovation adoptions travel through weak ties, not strong ones.	Do not concentrate the adoption campaign within existing communities of practice — the people who already agree with each other. Identify and activate the weak-tie bridges between clusters. Internal: cross-departmental champions who have relationships in multiple units are more valuable for diffusion than deeply embedded unit advocates.

Sources: Barabási, A.-L. & Albert, R. (1999). Emergence of scaling in random networks. Science, 286, 509–512. Barabási, A.-L. (2002). Linked: The New Science of Networks. Perseus Publishing. Watts, D.J. & Strogatz, S.H. (1998). Collective dynamics of small-world networks. Nature, 393, 440–442. Granovetter, M. (1973). The strength of weak ties. American Journal of Sociology, 78(6), 1360–1380. Gladwell, M. (2000). The Tipping Point. Little, Brown. Applications to innovation adoption contexts are the author's own.

Appendix H: Policy-Level ROI² for Government Entities

This appendix develops the public-sector reading of ROI² referenced at the close of Chapter 9. The mechanics are the firm-level method unchanged; only the unit of return shifts—from revenue to public value created per unit of public money.

Indicator	Formula	Country A	Country B	OECD Avg
R&D Efficiency	Innovation GDP / R&D	4.2	3.1	3.8
Knowledge Capital (% GDP)	Intangibles / GDP	17	22	19
Innovation Adoption Rate	Innovating firms / Total	45	62	55
ROI² Index	Weighted National Indicators	56	64	60

The ROI² framework is not only for companies. Government entities—ministries of economy, national innovation agencies, science and technology councils—also need to measure the return on their innovation investments. They allocate public funds to R&D programs, tax incentives, grants, and innovation ecosystems. They need to know: Is this investment producing results?

Governments use the same ROI^2 methodology as corporations, with one critical addition: they carry an extra layer of responsibility. Like companies, government entities are also responsible for designing, issuing, and enforcing the regulatory frameworks within which innovation occurs. They set patent laws, define R&D tax credits, establish data governance rules, and create the institutional environment that either accelerates or stifles innovation. This regulatory design function is unique to the public sector and must be factored into their ROI^2 assessment.

There is a further complexity: cross-country comparison. When France compares its innovation performance to Germany, South Korea, or the United States, the premises are radically different—different industrial structures, different education systems, different IP regimes, different cultural attitudes toward risk. Policy-level ROI^2 indicators must be normalized to account for these differences, often using the OECD Oslo Manual and Frascati Manual frameworks as common denominators.

The policy-level dashboard, therefore, includes additional dimensions: R&D Efficiency (Innovation GDP / R&D investment), Knowledge Capital as a percentage of GDP, Collaboration Density across the ecosystem, and Adoption Rate of new technologies at the national level. These indicators allow governments to benchmark their innovation ecosystems, identify structural weaknesses, and design evidence-based policy interventions.

Appendix I: The AI-OM Operating Model

Why Memory Needs Input Channels

The body of this book described the retrieval side of the AI-augmented Organizational Memory—the four agents that surface what the organization knows, and the Contextual Recall Sidecar that places that knowledge alongside a team's work at the moment of decision. But retrieval is only the second half of the problem. An agent can surface only what was captured. The most common failure I have watched organizations make is not a weak agent or a poor search—it is an empty channel, a memory that no one fed. A brilliant librarian in an empty library is still standing in an empty library.

Chapter 6 called this the work of domestication: taking knowledge that lives wild—tacit, scattered, undocumented—and capturing it, connecting it, making it answer when called. The seven channels below are the domestication apparatus; the four agents that follow are what makes the domesticated stock answer. Neither half works without the other, and the order is not negotiable: nothing can be activated that was never captured.

Organizational memory serves the investment portfolio only when knowledge flows into it as deliberately as money flows out of it. Every initiative in the portfolio—every H1 refinement, every H2 adjacency, every H3 bet—both draws on the memory and owes something back to it. This appendix maps the input channels that keep the memory fed, and the operating discipline that keeps those channels open. It is written at the level of function and governance, not technology. The tools will change; a channel that captures decisions at the moment they are made will still have to exist whatever surfaces next.

The Seven Input Channels

Each channel captures a different kind of knowledge, at a different moment, and feeds a different capital. Together they are what the four agents read from. Remove a channel and the corresponding capital starves: the agent that serves it has nothing to surface, and the dashboard needle it drives goes flat.

Input channel	What it captures, and when	Feeds	Serves
Decision Log	Significant innovation decisions and the reasoning behind them, recorded as they are made—not reconstructed later	Knowledge	Every initiative; the first thing a new project should query
Abandonment Record	Lessons from every project killed or sent to Purgatory: why it stopped, what was learned, what would change the answer	Memory	H2 / H3: keeps the portfolio from re-buying dead ends
Experiment & Pilot Log	The structured outcome of every pilot—what worked, what did not, and under which conditions	Knowledge	H1 / H2: turns one team's test into everyone's evidence

Input channel	What it captures, and when	Feeds	Serves
Exit Debrief	The tacit knowledge of departing experts, captured before they walk out the door	Knowledge & Relational	Any initiative that depends on scarce expertise
External Signal Intake	Market, regulatory, and technology signals from the Foresight Compass, bound to the projects they bear on	Relational	H2 / H3: whether the world is still moving toward a bet
Cross-Initiative Link	Connections between related projects, domains, and seasons that make the memory navigable rather than a heap	Process	Portfolio coordination across teams and seasons
Reuse Trace	What was actually retrieved and reused, and with what result—closing the loop and driving the Reuse Rate	Memory	Portfolio-level learning about the memory itself

The chain runs in one direction: capture feeds a capital, the capital feeds an agent, the agent serves a decision. The Reuse Trace is the only channel that loops back—it tells you whether the rest of the system is working, the way the Reuse Rate of Chapter 5 tells you whether the Sidecar is earning its place.

Channel Audit Worksheet

The diagnostic that matters is not how sophisticated your memory technology is, but how many of these channels are actually open. Mark each channel's state, name its owner, and the single next step that would open or strengthen it.

Investment portfolio under review: ______________________________ Date: ______________

1. Decision Log — State (Open / Partial / Closed): __________ Owner: ________________ Next step: ____________________________

2. Abandonment Record — State (Open / Partial / Closed): __________ Owner: ________________ Next step: ____________________________

3. Experiment & Pilot Log — State (Open / Partial / Closed): __________ Owner: ________________ Next step: ____________________________

4. Exit Debrief — State (Open / Partial / Closed): __________ Owner: ________________ Next step: ____________________________

5. External Signal Intake — State (Open / Partial / Closed): __________ Owner: ________________ Next step: ____________________________

6. Cross-Initiative Link — State (Open / Partial / Closed): __________ Owner: ________________ Next step: ____________________________

7. Reuse Trace — State (Open / Partial / Closed): __________
Owner: ________________ Next step:
____

Channels Open (count): _____ / 7 A portfolio served by fewer than four open channels is running on intuition, not on memory.

The Four Agents: The Reading Side

The channels are read by the four agents of the AI-OM Orchestrator. Each serves one capital and depends on specific channels for its raw material. This restates the architecture from the body as the consumption side of the input channels, so the two halves can be read together.

Agent	Serves	Reads mainly from	The durable question it answers
Retrieval	Knowledge	Decision Log; Experiment & Pilot Log	What have we already learned about this?
Policy Alignment	Process	Decision Log; Cross-Initiative Link	Are we allowed to, and is it aligned with the strategy in force?
Market Intelligence	Relational	External Signal Intake	Is the world still moving toward this bet?
Risk, Failure & Synthesis	Memory	Abandonment Record; Reuse Trace	Where have we already failed, and what does the pattern say?

The crew metaphor of Chapter 6 holds: the navigator, the quartermaster, the lookout, and the skipper who turns failure into a course correction. None of them sails the boat—and none of them can read a channel that was never opened.

Each agent, properly run, does the two jobs Chapter 6 assigned to activated memory. It measures: retrieval traffic feeds the Reuse Rate, failure patterns feed the Amnesia Tax, and the Readiness half of ROI²—the dark half, the one no P&L reads—finally has a data supply. And it stimulates: the same retrieval that counts duplication is what prevents it, surfacing the Munich answer while the Singapore question is still being framed. An agent that only audits is running at half power. When you review agent performance each season, review both jobs: what it measured, and what it made happen.

The AI-OM Maturity Ladder

The relationship between human judgment and machine memory matures in four stages. This is not a measure of the technology; it is a measure of how much of the decision the organization is willing to share. The stages, in brief: AI-Assisted (the machine prepares, the human decides everything); AI-Advised (the machine recommends, the human judges); AI-Delegated (the machine decides routine cases within set bounds, the human intervenes by exception); AI-Partnered (machine and human each contribute what the other cannot see).

Place your organization for each decision type, and name the stage you intend to reach in the coming year.

Decision type 1: ______________________________________

Current (Assisted / Advised / Delegated / Partnered): ___________
Target: ___________

Decision type 2: ______________________________________

Current (Assisted / Advised / Delegated / Partnered): ____________
Target: ____________

Decision type 3: ______________________________________

Current (Assisted / Advised / Delegated / Partnered): ____________
Target: ____________

One anticipation belongs here, because the worksheet above will outlive its first use. The ladder is climbed per decision type, not per organization—and not only by the innovation function. The same memory that advises a portfolio decision can advise a hiring decision, a pricing decision, a make-or-buy. Chapter 6 argued that every managerial function will eventually lean on the activated layer; when they do, each new function adds capture the innovation team never had to fight for, and the channels fill from angles this appendix does not list. Plan for it: the owner of each channel should expect neighbours. An AI-OM that starts as innovation infrastructure ends as management infrastructure—and the organizations that understand this early will simply have more seasons of compounding behind them when the others arrive.

Governance: Keeping the Channels Open

Input channels close quietly. No one decides to stop capturing decisions; it simply stops happening under deadline pressure, and a year later the memory has a hole no one notices until a project re-buys a dead end. The governance of an AI-OM is mostly the governance of its inputs. None of these principles depends on the technology that implements them.

Capture discipline

[ ] Every significant decision is logged with its rationale, not just its outcome.

[ ] Every abandonment produces a knowledge artifact before the team disbands.

[ ] Failure is captured as readily as success—the Abandonment Record is a source, not a graveyard.

Human-in-the-loop boundaries

[ ] The decisions that may never be delegated to the machine are named in writing: ____________________________

[ ] Every machine-surfaced recommendation carries an audit trail a human can follow.

[ ] A human retains authority to accept, reject, or modify any surfaced knowledge.

Provenance and hygiene

[ ] Each artifact records its source, its date, and the context in which it was true.

[ ] Artefacts are revisited when their context changes—an invalidated assumption is marked, not left to mislead in silence.

Ownership

[ ] Each of the seven channels has a named owner accountable for keeping it open.

[ ] The Reuse Rate is reviewed each season; a falling rate is read as a channel problem, not a user problem.

A Note on Durability

This appendix names no product, no model, and no prompt. That is deliberate. The channels, the agents understood as roles, and the governance of capture will outlast whatever technology is currently fashionable for implementing them. When the tools change—and they will change faster than this book can be revised—the operating model does not. A memory still needs feeding. The portfolio still needs serving. The discipline is the durable part.

Appendix J: Building Your Own ROI² Tool

Every chapter of this book has insisted that ROI² is computable with tools you already own. This appendix is where the insistence becomes a drawing. It is a specification, not a product: the instrument described here can be built as a spreadsheet, as a small program, as an internal web page, or as a configuration of the innovation-management platform you already license. The stations are invariant. The material is yours. One principle governs the whole yard, and it is worth bolting to the wall before the first plank: the instrument must be auditable by a stranger. Every number traceable to an input, every input to a source, every source to a date. An instrument that only its builder can defend is not an instrument; it is a hostage situation.

The Seven Stations

Station 1—Parameters. One place, and only one, holds the season's identity and its dials: the season name and dates; the total cost C; the four capital weights, which must sum to one and none of which may be zero; the horizon profile of each capital—what share of its value arrives in the current cycle, the adjacent horizon, the transformational one—with a time-to-monetization for each; the discount rate, your cost of capital or a declared proxy; and the sector and market-phase settings that calibrate the conversion coefficients. The rule of this station is absolute: parameters live here, are referenced everywhere, and are hardcoded nowhere. A weight typed directly into a formula is a parameter that has escaped governance.

Station 2—The catalogue. The registry of indicators, seeded from Appendix A and alive thereafter. Every indicator—stock or custom—carries the same fields: an identifier; its capital; its compass reading; its horizon; its type, value or vanity; its one or two required inputs, each with a unit; its conversion shape—one of the four of Chapter 8; its coefficient, with the default value, the source citation, and the provenance flag (peer-reviewed, industry benchmark, or internal estimate); its method tag—income, cost, or market—if it belongs to Memory; and one line each for what it measures and why it matters. The catalogue is the single source of truth. Everything downstream looks it up; nothing downstream restates it.

Station 3—Selection. The season shortlist and the per-initiative subsets, with the constraints of Chapters 8 and 9 enforced rather than remembered: at least one indicator per capital per initiative; the Vanity share at or under twenty percent; Memory selected toward all three methods, or a cost-only mode declared openly; and the non-overlap rule applied at the moment of choice—one anchor indicator per conversion shape per capital, overlapping candidates demoted to context. A selection screen that cannot say no is a suggestion box.

Station 4—Conversion. Where readings become currency. For each selected indicator: its raw inputs for the season, the coefficient pulled from the catalogue and calibrated by the sector and phase of Station 1, and the priced value the conversion shape produces. One design rule here was learned at cost and is offered at none: never silently substitute a missing input. An empty cell that halts the calculation is a question someone will answer; a quietly assumed value is a lie with a plausible face, and it will surface in front of exactly the wrong audience.

Station 5—Computation. The arithmetic of Chapter 8, in the order Chapter 8 taught it. Sub-scores first: F, I, and S as sums of non-overlapping priced indicators; L as the triangulated mean of its available methods, with the spread computed and flagged past thirty percent. Then the two needles—Readiness as the weighted Intangible and Learning gains over cost, Growth as the weighted Financial and Strategic gains over cost—displayed first, always, because the pair is the reading and the composite is only its sum. Then the composite. And beside it, when seasons are compared, the horizon-adjusted figure from the tide tables, computed from Station 1's profiles.

Station 6—Trajectory. The season-over-season record: the pair, the composite, the four sub-scores, their deltas, and the targets carried from season design. A simple projection of the next season is permitted if it is labelled an anchor rather than a forecast. This station is small and disproportionately valuable: it is the difference between a number and a course.

Station 7—The logbook. The audit trail that converts a challenge into a citation. A frozen snapshot of every parameter with its source and rationale, taken when the season locks. A deviations log: every coefficient tuned away from its published reference, and why. The method declarations for Memory. The date and owner of every change. When a board member asks where a number came from—and one will—this station answers in writing, in advance, in a tone no meeting can achieve.

Four Hulls, One Instrument

In a spreadsheet, the stations become tabs. Parameters take named cells; the catalogue is a reference tab feeding dropdowns; conversion and computation carry the formulas; checks are coloured so that a failed constraint is visible from across the room. It is the fastest hull to launch and it lives where finance already lives. Its weakness is silent breakage: spreadsheets do not complain when a layout shift strands a reference on the wrong row, so after any structural edit, re-verify every cross-tab reference against a known example. The habit costs a morning. Skipping it costs a board meeting.

In a small program, the stations become tables and one computation script. The gains are versioning and tests: the instrument can refuse to compute when a constraint fails, rather than warning politely and proceeding. If a developer owes you a favour, spend it here.

As an internal web page, the same tables sit behind a form, and the virtue is adoption: the initiative owner enters two numbers in the place where they already work, and Station 4 does the rest. Nothing recruits data like removing the walk to it.

As a configuration of your innovation-management platform, the intake and throughput arrive natively—the platform already counts what moves. What no platform ships is your pricing, your computation, and your logbook: Stations 4, 5, and 7 are always yours to add, as custom fields shaped to the catalogue schema and an export to wherever the computation lives. Configure the platform to feed the instrument. Do not mistake the platform for it.

The Six Questions of a Custom Indicator

The catalogue will not contain every indicator your season needs, and it should not. When you mint one, answer six questions in order, and refuse the mint if any answer is missing. Which capital does it build? What is its name, in plain words a sceptic can repeat? Is it value or vanity—does it price an outcome, or count an activity? In which horizon does it monetize? Which conversion shape does it use, and therefore which one or two inputs, in which units? And what coefficient converts it—from what source, at what provenance? An indicator of Memory answers a seventh: which of the three methods it serves. Write the finished row into Station 2 with every field the stock indicators carry. A custom indicator with fewer fields than the others is not custom; it is exempt—and exemptions are the crack through which theatre re-enters the ship.

Safeguards the Instrument Must Enforce

Whatever the hull, the instrument enforces its own seaworthiness: the weights sum to one; each capital's horizon profile sums to one; the Vanity share stays under its cap; the non-overlap attestation is made at selection; the Memory spread is computed and flagged; no missing input is ever silently replaced; no coefficient exists without a source; and no parameter changes except through the logbook. Build these as checks that fail loudly, not as advice that scrolls past. An instrument that cannot fail a check cannot pass an audit.

Where the AI Assistant Fits

Consistent with Appendix I, this section names roles, not products. The assistant drafts the first catalogue, adapting Appendix A's stock to your sector and proposing coefficients with citations for a human to accept or overrule. It tags the idea-platform export by domain, which is the entire preparation the Chapter 12 estimator requires. It extracts decisions, abandonments, and lessons from the documents where they hide, and files them where Station 2's evidence fields can reach them. It reconciles the logbook before a review, listing every parameter that drifted from its source. And at the fourth rung of the maturity ladder, it feeds Station 4 the longitudinal traces that make the income view of

Memory computable at all. The assistant fills stations. It never owns them.

The yard is open, and the drawings are done. Whatever you build—a workbook, a script, a page, a platform profile—build it so a stranger can read it, an auditor can test it, and a successor can sail it. That is the whole specification. It fits on a bulkhead.

The body of the book allowed itself a few dated names—an industrial model trained on ninety years of proprietary data in 2024, a personal knowledge graph popular in 2025, an activation skill reaching organizations in 2026—precisely because the dates, not the names, are the point: a new name every year is not churn, it is a direction. Expect the division of labour to sharpen along the way. Public models will keep mastering what humanity knows in public; the systems worth governing with this appendix are the ones turned inward, reading the internal information and proprietary data no public model will ever see. Whatever those systems are called the year you run the channel audit, these seven channels are what they will need to read. Feed them accordingly.

A companion page for this book—worked examples, templates, and corrections to this edition—lives at yrp.me/compass.

Bibliography

- Ackerman, M.S., & Halverson, C.A. (2000). Reexamining organizational memory. Communications of the ACM.
- Adams, R., Bessant, J., & Phelps, R. (2006). Innovation management measurement: A review. International Journal of Management Reviews.
- Alavi, M., & Leidner, D.E. (2001). Knowledge management and knowledge management systems: Conceptual foundations and research issues. MIS Quarterly.
- Alexy, O., George, G., & Salter, A. (2013). Cui Bono? The selective revealing of knowledge and its implications for innovative activity. Academy of Management Review.
- Argote, L. & Miron-Spektor, E. (2011). "Organizational Learning: From Experience to Knowledge." Organization Science, 22(5), 1123–1137.
- Argote, L. (2013). Organizational Learning: Creating, Retaining and Transferring Knowledge. Springer.
- Argyris, C. (1990). Overcoming Organizational Defenses: Facilitating Organizational Learning. Allyn and Bacon.
- Arslan, M., Ince, H., & Imamoglu, S.Z. (2025). Effects of standardized innovation management systems on innovation ambidexterity and innovation performance. Sustainability.
- Arundel, A., Bloch, C., & Ferguson, B. (2019). Innovation metrics for a new era. Research Policy.
- Balagtas, J. (2024). Innovation accounting: Measuring the impact of experiments. Strategic Innovation Journal.
- Blomqvist, K., Hurmelinna-Laukkanen, P., & Mention, A.L. (2023). Toward integrating trust in open innovation. In The Oxford Handbook of Open Innovation. Oxford University Press.
- Bogers, M., & West, J. (2023). Open innovation: A theory-based view. Strategic Management Review.
- Boldrin, M., & Levine, D. (2008). Against Intellectual Monopoly. Cambridge University Press.
- Bonvillian, W., & Van Atta, R. (2011). ARPA-E and DARPA: Applying the DARPA model to energy innovation. The Journal of Technology Transfer.
- Brynjolfsson, E., & McAfee, A. (2017). Machine, Platform, Crowd. W. W. Norton.
- Brynjolfsson, E., Li, D., & Raymond, L. (2023). Generative AI at work. NBER Working Paper No. 31161.
- Brynjolfsson, E., Rock, D., & Syverson, C. (2019). Artificial intelligence and the modern productivity paradox. In The Economics of Artificial Intelligence, University of Chicago Press.
- Carayannis, E., & Campbell, D. (2009). 'Mode 3' and the Quadruple Helix. International Journal of Technology Management.
- Chao, A. (1984). Nonparametric estimation of the number of classes in a population. Scandinavian Journal of Statistics, 11(4), 265–270.
- Chen, K., Li, X., & Li, J. (2011). The role of government in China's innovation system. R&D Management.
- Chesbrough, H. (2003). Open Innovation: The New Imperative for Creating and Profiting from Technology. Harvard Business Press.
- Chesbrough, H.W. (2003). The era of open innovation. MIT Sloan Management Review.
- Chou, Y. (2015). Actionable Gamification: Beyond Points, Badges, and Leaderboards. Octalysis Media.
- Christensen, C. (1997). The Innovator's Dilemma. Harvard Business Review Press.

- Cohen, W.M., & Levinthal, D.A. (1990). Absorptive capacity: A new perspective on learning and innovation. Administrative Science Quarterly.
- Conklin, J. (2001). Designing Organizational Memory. CogNexus Institute.
- Connelly, C.E., Zweig, D., Webster, J., & Trougakos, J.P. (2012). Knowledge hiding in organizations. Journal of Organizational Behaviour, 33(1), 64–88.
- Cooper, R.G. (2019). The drivers of success in new-product development. Industrial Marketing Management.
- Corbett, L.M. (2002). How do organizations remember? The influence of organizational structure on organizational memory. The Electronic Journal of Knowledge Management.
- Corrado, C., Haskel, J., Jona-Lasinio, C., & Iommi, M. (2017). Intangible investment in the EU and US before and since the Great Recession. Journal of Infrastructure, Policy and Development.
- Corrado, C., Haskel, J., Miranda, J., & Sichel, D. (Eds.) (2021). Measuring and Accounting for Innovation in the Twenty-First Century. University of Chicago Press.
- Corrado, C., Hulten, C., & Sichel, D. (2009). Intangible capital and U.S. economic growth. Review of Income and Wealth, 55(3), 661–685.
- Crossan, M.M., & Apaydin, M. (2010). A multi-dimensional framework of organizational innovation: A systematic review of the literature. Journal of Management Studies.
- Curley, M., & Salmelin, B. (2017). Open Innovation 2.0. Springer/Palgrave.
- Dahlander, L., & Gann, D. (2010). How open is innovation? Research Policy.
- Danylenko, Yu.A., Yurchyshyn, O.Ya., & Hrinchenko, H.S. (2025). Self-assessment of the company innovation management system. Science and Innovation.
- Davenport, T.H., & Mittal, N. (2022). All-in on AI: How Smart Companies Win Big with Artificial Intelligence. Harvard Business Review Press.
- Dhanaraj, C., & Parkhe, A. (2006). Orchestrating innovation networks. Academy of Management Review.
- Di Vaio, A., et al. (2024). Knowledge management meets artificial intelligence: A systematic review and future research agenda. Journal of Knowledge Management.
- Diehl, M., & Stroebe, W. (1987). Productivity Loss in Brainstorming Groups: Toward the Solution of a Riddle. Journal of Personality and Social Psychology, 53(3), 497–509.
- DiMasi, J. A., Grabowski, H. G., & Hansen, R. W. (2016). Innovation in the pharmaceutical industry: New estimates of R&D costs. Journal of Health Economics.
- Dosi, G. (1982). Technological paradigms and technological trajectories. Research Policy.
- Edmondson, A. (1999). Psychological safety and learning behaviour in work teams. Administrative Science Quarterly, 44(2), 350–383.
- Freeman, C. (1987). Technology Policy and Economic Performance: Lessons from Japan. Pinter.
- Gama, F., & Magistretti, S. (2023). Artificial intelligence in innovation management: A review of innovation capabilities and a taxonomy of AI applications. Journal of Product Innovation Management.
- Gama, F., & Magistretti, S. (2025). From hybrid to AI-first innovation management. IEEE Engineering Management Review.
- Gawer, A. (2021). Platforms, Markets, and Innovation.
- Gawer, A., & Cusumano, M. (2014). Industry platforms and ecosystem innovation. Journal of Product Innovation Management.
- Godet, M. (2006). Creating Futures: Scenario Planning as a Strategic Management Tool. Economica.

- Gompers, P., & Lerner, J. (2001). The Venture Capital Revolution. Journal of Economic Perspectives.
- Government Accountability Office. (2002). NASA: Better mechanisms needed for sharing lessons learned (GAO-02-195). Washington, DC: U.S. General Accounting Office.
- Griffin, A., & Hauser, J.R. (1996). Integrating R&D and marketing: A review and analysis of the literature. Journal of Product Innovation Management.
- Hagiu, A., & Wright, J. (2020). Data-enabled learning in platforms. American Economic Review Papers & Proceedings.
- Irani, L. (2015). Hackathons and the Making of Entrepreneurial Citizenship. Science, Technology, & Human Values, 40(5), 799–824.
- ISO (2019). ISO 56002: Innovation management—Innovation management system—Guidance.
- Iyer, B., & Davenport, T. (2008). Reverse engineering Google's innovation machine. Harvard Business Review.
- Jacobsson, S., & Lauber, V. (2006). The politics and policy of energy system transformation—explaining the German diffusion of renewable energy technology. Energy Policy.
- Jarrahi, M.H. (2018). Artificial intelligence and the future of work: Human-AI symbiosis in organizational decision making. Business Horizons.
- Johansson-Sköldberg, U., Woodilla, J., & Çetinkaya, M. (2013). Design Thinking: Past, Present, and Possible Futures. Creativity and Innovation Management, 22(2), 121–146.
- Kimbell, L. (2011). Rethinking Design Thinking: Part I. Design and Culture, 3(3), 285–306.
- Kosaraju, P., Nolte, A., Porras, J., et al. (2020). 10 Years of Research With and On Hackathons. CHI EA'20 (ACM Extended Abstracts).
- Laursen, K., & Salter, A. (2006). Open for innovation: The role of openness in explaining innovation performance. Strategic Management Journal.
- Laursen, K., Moreira, S., & Reichstein, T. (2023). Complementarities and tensions between appropriability and open innovation. In The Oxford Handbook of Open Innovation. Oxford University Press.
- Lewrick, M., Link, P., & Leifer, L. (2018). The Design Thinking Playbook: Mindful Digital Transformation of Teams, Products, Services, Businesses and Ecosystems. John Wiley & Sons.
- Lundvall, B.-Å. (Ed.) (1992). National Systems of Innovation: Towards a Theory of Innovation and Interactive Learning. Pinter.
- MacNeil, R.T. (2024). Observing Dark Innovation: After Neoliberal Tools and Techniques. Bristol University Press.
- Markham, S.K. (2013). The fuzzy front end of innovation. Research-Technology Management.
- Mayer-Schönberger, V., & Cukier, K. (2013). Big Data. Houghton Mifflin Harcourt.
- Milbergs, E., & Vonortas, N. (2004). Innovation Metrics: Measurement to Insight. National Innovation Initiative.
- Moorman, C., & Miner, A.S. (1997). The impact of organizational memory on new product performance and creativity. Journal of Marketing Research.
- Mullen, B., Johnson, C., & Salas, E. (1991). Productivity Loss in Brainstorming Groups: A Meta-Analytic Integration. Basic and Applied Social Psychology, 12(1), 3–23.
- Nakash, M., & Bolisani, E. (2025). The transformative impact of AI on knowledge management processes. Business Process Management Journal.
- NASA Office of Inspector General. (2012). Review of NASA's lessons learned information system (Report No. IG-12-012). Washington, DC: NASA.
- Nonaka, I. & Takeuchi, H. (1995). The Knowledge-Creating Company. Oxford University Press.

- Nonaka, I. (1994). A dynamic theory of organizational knowledge creation. Organization Science.
- OECD (2015). Frascati Manual 2015. OECD Publishing.
- OECD (2015). Frascati Manual 2015: Guidelines for Collecting and Reporting Data on Research and Experimental Development. OECD Publishing.
- OECD/Eurostat (2018). Oslo Manual 2018: Guidelines for Collecting, Reporting and Using Data on Innovation. OECD Publishing/Eurostat.
- Perng, S.-Y., Kitchin, R., & Mac Donncha, D. (2018). Hackathons, Entrepreneurial Life and the Making of Smart Cities. Geoforum, 97, 189–197.
- Saudi Aramco. (2024, March 4). Aramco unveils Metabrain AI, first industrial generative AI model [Announcement, LEAP, Riyadh].
- Saudi Aramco. (2026). Fourth quarter and full-year 2025 results [Technology Realized Value disclosure]. Dhahran: Saudi Aramco.
- Schumpeter, J. (1942). Capitalism, Socialism and Democracy. Harper & Brothers.
- Schumpeter, J.A. (1911). The Theory of Economic Development. Harvard University Press.
- Shapiro, C., & Varian, H. (1999). Information Rules. Harvard Business School Press.
- Stein, E.W., & Zwass, V. (1995). Actualizing organizational memory with information systems. Information Systems Research.
- Teece, D.J. (2007). Explicating dynamic capabilities: The nature and microfoundations of (sustainable) enterprise performance. Strategic Management Journal.
- Teece, D.J., Pisano, G., & Shuen, A. (1997). Dynamic capabilities and strategic management. Strategic Management Journal.
- Tidd, J., & Bessant, J.R. (2020). Managing Innovation: Integrating Technological, Market and Organizational Change. Wiley.
- Tushman, M.L., & O'Reilly, C.A. (1996). Ambidextrous organizations: Managing evolutionary and revolutionary change. California Management Review.
- von Hippel, E. (1994). Sticky information and the locus of problem solving: Implications for innovation. Management Science.
- Von Hippel, E. (2005). Democratizing Innovation. MIT Press.
- Walsh, J.P. & Ungson, G.R. (1991). Organizational Memory. Academy of Management Review, 16(1), 57–91.
- Webster, J., et al. (2008). Beyond knowledge sharing: Withholding knowledge at work. In Research in Personnel and Human Resources Management, Vol. 27. Emerald.
- Weick, K.E. (1995). Sensemaking in Organizations. SAGE Publications.
- West, J. (2006). Does appropriability enable or retard open innovation? In Open Innovation: Researching a New Paradigm. Oxford University Press.
- West, J., & Bogers, M. (2014). Leveraging external sources of innovation: A review of research on open innovation. Journal of Product Innovation Management.
- Yams, N.B., et al. (2020). Integrated AI and innovation management: The beginning of a beautiful friendship. Technology Innovation Management Review.
- Zahra, S.A., & George, G. (2002). Absorptive capacity: A review, reconceptualization, and extension. Academy of Management Review.

Index

K

L

M

N

O

P

R

S

T

U

V

W

X

Acknowledgement

A book about organizational memory accumulates debts the way a hull accumulates barnacles—quietly, continuously, and well below the waterline. These are mine.

To my mentor, Cécile Arian, who has been correcting my course for longer than any instrument in this book.

To Gilles Barbot, who put me on a racing sailboat in the middle of the Atlantic—fourteen months of preparation, fourteen days of racing, Québec to Saint-Malo—and to the nine entrepreneurs who shared that crossing. Most of what this book believes about navigation, humility, and the difference between a chart and a voyage was learned out there, well beyond the sight of land.

To the dozens of innovation practitioners who, over the decades, tested and improved the S4IL techniques under my direction on hundreds of clients before the framework had a name. You will recognize your scars in these pages; I hope I have honoured them.

To Vimala Sanjeevkumar, my research supervisor at the Universidad Católica de Murcia, who held the academic line while I kept trying to smuggle a practitioner's book through it.

To the organizations, ministries, small and large companies that opened their doors to my research and my practice—in France, Canada, Vietnam, and Saudi Arabia—for trusting an outsider with an honest look at how innovation is really measured.

To the thinkers whose shoulders this book stands on: Clayton Christensen, who taught a generation that good innovation management welcome failures for the right reasons—and whose title family this book is proud to sail beside; Michel Godet, whose school of prospective at the Conservatoire National des Arts et Métiers taught me that the future is a discipline, not a guess; Julian Bleecker, who showed me that the future is something you prototype, not predict; Henry Chesbrough, who taught organizations to innovate with their doors open; Albert-László Barabási, who mapped the networks that carry ideas from one mind to the next; Yu-kai Chou, whose Octalysis puts wind in a crew's sails; Anne Chao, whose butterflies taught me to count what has not yet been seen; and my favourite science-fiction storytellers, from Isaac Asimov to Gene Roddenberry, who convinced a teenager that ideas, properly compounded, outlast empires.

And to my wife, Anne-Sophie Hoffmann—every navigator steers by a North Star, and she is mine.

And to the readers who will take this compass to sea: the errors that remain are mine, and the corrections will live at yrp.me/compass.

About the Author

Yann Rousselot-Pailley has spent twenty-five years turning innovation from a slogan into a discipline—as an entrepreneur who has built companies on three continents, as a consultant to ministries and national research agencies across North America, Asia, Europe, and the Gulf, and as a translator between the people who invent things and the people who fund them. He created S4IL and the ROI^2 measurement system at the heart of this book after too many years of watching organizations celebrate motion and call it progress.

He holds a master's degree in strategic foresight, innovation, and disruption from the Conservatoire National des Arts et Métiers in Paris, France and is completing a doctorate in bridging R&D and innovation management at the Universidad Católica de Murcia, Spain. His previous book, Play Nice (2021), taught competitors how to cooperate. He has crossed the Atlantic under sail, which is where most of the metaphors in these pages were earned. Born in France, forged in Canada, he now lives in Saudi Arabia. He writes at *yrp.me*.

www.ingramcontent.com/pod-product-compliance
Lightning Source LLC
LaVergne TN
LVHW070826220926
848486LV00027B/19
9798996394111